The regional planning process

Edited by

DAVID GILLINGWATER
Department of Town and Country Planning
Trent Polytechnic

D.A. HART
Institute of Local Government Studies
University of Birmingham

SAXON  HOUSE

British Library Cataloguing in Publication Data

The regional planning process.
  1. Regional planning – Addresses, essays, lectures
  I. Gillingwater, David II. Hart, Douglas Allen
  301.2'5'08   HT391

  ISBN 0-566-00130-6

Published by
Saxon House, Teakfield Limited,
Westmead, Farnborough, Hants., England

ISBN 0 566 00130 6

Printed and bound by Ilfadrove Limited,
Barry, Glamorgan, S. Wales.

Contents

Tables

Figures

This book has its roots in a general feeling of unease about the ways in which regional planning has been concieved, and is currently being practiced. We are particularly concerned with the 'ideal—real' gap which has, it seems to us, begun to emerge as a result.

If the book has a theme it is one which turns on the idea that regional planning is an inherently political and politicised activity. It operates in the arena of politics, and is subject to the same problems, pressures and prospects as those which determine and influence the legitimacy associated with the political administration of state-societal relationships. If the gap between theory and practice is to be narrowed the political-administration dimension needs to be more fully explored.

To our knowledge there are few books on regional planning which explicitly and directly concern themselves with these kind of issues. This book is an attempt to play a part in redressing the imbalance. Eleven of some of the most relevant writings on the political administration of regional planning have been brought together in this volume; an attempt has been made to provide a context for this selection by presenting the reader with a tentative outline of what we consider to be the core processes of regional planning. It is these processes which, we contend, represent the tentative foundations for a concept of public intervention.

In this collaborative effort we are indebted to many individuals too numerous to mention, not least authors and publishers who have kindly agreed to allow us to reprint and edit their work. To these individuals — including our friends and colleagues at Trent, the Institute and elsewhere — we proffer our thanks. At the personal level we would like to extend our gratitude and love to those who allowed us to start — and encouraged us to finish this study.

David Gillingwater
D. A. Hart

July 1977

Acknowledgements

Acknowledgements are due to the following for kind permission to reproduce the selected writings in this volume:

1   The University of Illinois Press, the Board of Trustees
2   *The Political Quarterly* and D. Donnison
3   *Journal of Regional Studies* and R. Rhodes
4   *Journal of Regional Studies* and P. Self
5   *Journal of Regional Studies* and J. Cousins
6   *Tavistock Institute of Human Relations* and J. Friend
7   *Public Administration* and C. Painter
8   *Local Government Studies* and D. A. Hart
9   *International Social Development Review* and J. Friedmann
10 Her Majesty's Stationery Office, the Controller
11 *Pergamon Press* and D. Hart

PART I

PERSPECTIVES ON REGIONAL PLANNING

Introduction

Regional planning, like many other forms of public planning, is currently in a state of turbulence if not crisis. It has not achieved those things which its early protagonists claimed for it, nor does it appear to have been a consistently successful vehicle for the translation of considered intent into actual impact. Given the levels of resources, power and means of communication and control, potentially at the disposal of those political administrations responsible for regional planning, this is a matter for concern.[1]

One reason for this problem — not the only reason, the best reason, or in itself an adequate reason — is rooted in the implicit philosophy which, more often than not, is to be found supporting the 'current best practice' of public planning generally, and which is particularly well illustrated by regional planning. This philosophy has been forged by a process of bringing together the critical assumptions which underpin the rational model of decision-making with those of the integration-consensus model of social change. The rational model, more often than not, provides the basis for the methodology and management of the 'internal' processes of regional planning; the 'external' image of the reality of societal relations — and the processes of change which regional planning seeks to influence — is supported by the model of social integration-consensus.[2] The fusion of these two strands has created a 'rational-consensus' philosophy which, it could be contended, forms an important part of the foundations of public planning.

There are a number of conceptual and practical difficulties associated with the operationalisation of this particular philosophy; it is based on assumptions which are at best misconceived and at worst positively misleading. For implicit in this rational-consensus philosophy is a model of intervention — a philosophy of planning — which, when translated into processes of 'current best practice', suggests that regional planning is concerned with the operationalising of at least three critically important and universal prescriptive qualities: (a) that planning is concerned with decisions and the concern of decision-makers — but more importantly with the making of decisions according to the axioms of rational choice; (b) that society *per se,* on whose behalf such planning is undertaken, is somehow structured, highly integrated and cohesive; and (c) that planned intervention can be successful in the accepted sense, that is, initially stated intent can equal actual outcome.[3]

These almost ubiquitous, but implicit, assumptions apparently lie at the core of 'current best practice' in regional planning, at both conceptual and practical levels. With some exceptions most contemporary planning studies are examples of the attempt to apply natural rules associated with what can be termed the rational-consensus model of intervention. A problem with this professed wisdom is that such rules are about as natural as, for example, the comparatively recent and

3

widely-held view which conceptualised man as an inherently objective and rational being searching for objective truth via the application of instrumental reason.[4] If this view is being increasingly regarded as questionable, if not untenable, then why should it be accorded such an apparently high and uncritical status in 'current best practice'? But more importantly, how can regional planning, using this model of intervention, seek to realise expectations when the very foundations upon which those expectations are based are so weak?

Some of the important implications which follow from this brief assessment suggest that regional planning, and many if not most types of public planning, can very rarely, if ever, be successful in the accepted sense: that is, in the continuous and perfect translation of planned intent into actual impact through time; secondly, that reliance on the rather dubious equation of planning as decision-making ignores crucially important contextual processes, especially those associated with the political administration of regional planning; finally, that policies which are initiated and promo etl according to the mythical Paretian 'first-best' principle (which implies that society *per se* will somehow benefit as a result of planned change, so long as no individual member of it is left in a worse-off position — however defined) are, it is tempting to add almost certainly, doomed to the inevitability of failure.[5] For this belief ignores the consequences associated with such actions — those impacts, perceived or imagined, which in the complex processes of implementation destroy the very principles on which the 'first-best' criterion is based — and in so doing opens up the need to question the relevance of this philosophy, but (more importantly) to consider critically the utility of other competing and alternative philosophies of intervention.

Whilst this book is not directly concerned with many of these issues, each of the selected writings which follow indicates in some way the consequences which are likely to ensue if avenues of exploration into alternative types of planning processes, and hence into philosophies, are not continuously and internally undertaken. It is little short of amazing that planners and planning theorists who seem to accept the wisdom of rational-consensus are apparently often inconsistent in applying their own principles to themselves, and in considering the consequences which follow as a result. If one objective of regional planners is to systematically and continuously seek ways to improve the quality of planning processes and actions then, according to the axioms of rational choice, every conceivable alternative approach which may meet such an objective should be explicitly stated, subjected to rigorous evaluation, and hence to the development of a preferred approach which meets the demands associated with the objective. Perhaps the critics of the rational-consensus school adhere more closely to the principles of rational choice than do the protagonists themselves.

Assumptions and problems

The critical assumption upon which this book is based concerns the crisis in which

4

regional planning, as an important strand of public planning, currently finds itself. Contemporary planning practice appears to have an underpinning philosophy of processes but, as we have begun to point out, it is a philosophy with a dubious pedigree. A cursory evaluation of the planning literature implies that the development of this philosophy did not begin until at least the late 1950s or early 1960s, further implying that before this era a philosophy of planning processes did not exist.[6] This was simply not the case. Before the almost universal acceptance of the rational-consensus model there was indeed the semblance of a philosophy — albeit a very tentative and embryonic one, as the writings of Benton MacKaye and Patrick Abercrombie begin to display.[7] Indeed it is possible to argue a case that one of the reasons why regional planning currently finds itself in a situation approaching crisis proportions is precisely because of its almost dogmatic reliance upon, and universal acceptance of, a set of philosophical foundations which are at best misplaced and questionable, and at worst positively misleading. As a consequence, other emergent and potentially more viable foundations have been pushed to the periphery of concern or, worse still, ignored.

Of the principal problems with which the rational-consensus school does not concern itself, the problem of politics and, in particular, the political administration of public planning must represent one of the most significant. Their model creates the impression that the political context within which public planning is inextricably interwoven is of less importance than the technical ability required to produce the basis for good decisions. The logic behind this good currency approach is deceptively simple: if only policies can be forged in the best possible manner, which is according to the axioms of rational choice, then it only remains for the technical decision-makers to present their case to the political decision-makers for the rational implementation of that policy, other things being equal, to follow automatically. This impression is compounded further by the view that the political context is often regarded as an obstacle hindering the inexorable progression of good policy, but an obstacle of significant importance which has to be tolerated and overcome. One problem with this argument is that, by definition, the political context includes those very planners who consider it to be an obstacle! For there are no such creatures as public planning or political administration *per se* — rather there are a multiplicity of competing types of public planning and political administration, all with different emphases, serving disparate interests, and operating at different spatial scales.

Regional planning and its administration is only one of a number of varieties of public planning; indeed it is possible to argue a case that there is no such thing as regional planning *per se* but rather, to use the United Kingdom as an example, regional economic policy, regional strategic planning, and regional administrative planning (health, education, water, utilities, etc.).[8] Each variety operates and is operated within a disparate and differentiated political context — formal and informal, party and technical, overt and covert, short run and long term, at national, regional and local levels. It is therefore no exaggeration to claim that public planning is rooted in politics, and its political administration is rooted in planning. It is a lamentable fact, in turn, that the conceptual linkages between the processes of public planning, their derivatives, and the political administrations within which these processes operate, remain largely neglected and to a limited extent ignored or assumed away by at least some of those with an interest in the nature and practice of regional planning.[9]

Aims of the book

The aims of this book are related to these kind of issues. First and foremost the book attempts to present the reader with a critical examination of the problems, processes and prescriptions facing regional planning, from the perspective of its political administration. The reader will search in vain for an assessment of contemporary problem regions, quantitative or otherwise; such assessments are readily available elsewhere.[10] Similarly the book is not chiefly concerned with an account and description of the ways in which regional planning bodies actually operate. The selected writings which follow are all broadly conceptual accounts of the political administration of regional planning – the processes of regional planning. Here the emphasis is placed upon ideological, institutional and administrative aspects of the continuing processes of initiation, development and effectuation of public policies at the regional scale, howsoever defined.

The other principal aim of this book is to continue the emergent debate surrounding the legitimacy of public intervention, but from the perspective of regional planning. This is the concern of a more general problem: that of the development of a philosophy of public interventionism. It is not the intention of this book to present the reader with a fully formulated philosophy of regional planning in this essentially edited volume. Rather the aim is to bring together and present a number of selected writings on regional planning which may be regarded as potential starting-points or bench-marks for just such an attempt: a tentative exploration into the feasibility, relevance and utility of developing an alternative to the rational-consensus philosophy of interventionism.

Structure of the book

The material which follows divides into four reasonably distinct parts. First is an attempt to provide some 'Perspectives on regional planning': an outline of what may be referred to as the core processes of regional planning, looked at from the perspective of its political administration.

This part is also an attempt to provide a framework for the selected writings which constitute the other three and substantive parts of the volume. It is perhaps worth adding a cautionary note here of the 'goodness of fit' between the outline of these core processes and the selected writings which follow from it. The relationship is tentative, and the developing links are often not completely drawn;

6

the 'fit' between this framework and its emerging subject matter is necessarily far from perfect.

This 'Perspectives' section concludes with two selected writings: Benton MacKaye (1928, Chapter 1) and David Donnison (1974, Chapter 2). The former stresses the philosophical idea of 'planning as revelation', along lines not dissimilar to the philosophy of pragmatism as developed by John Dewey;[11] the latter the political and institutional nature of regional planning, with reference to the United Kingdom.

The second part of the book considers 'Problems of regional planning'. Three selected writings follow a brief introduction and overview: R. Rhodes (1974, Chapter 3) on the problems of the political administration of regional planning; Peter Self (1964, Chapter 4) on problems besetting the concept of regional planning itself, and his critical conceptual distinction between national/regional and regional/local planning;[12] and the Rowntree Research Unit, University of Durham (1974, Chapter 5) on problems which underpin the political and development assumptions upon which regional planning practices are so often based.

The third part of the book concerns 'Processes in regional planning', and in particular political and administrative processes. A brief introduction and overview is followed by three selected writings: J. Friend, J. Power and C. Yewlett (1974, Chapter 6), C. Painter (1972, Chapter 7) and Douglas A. Hart (1976, Chapter 8). The first emphasises administrative and managerial processes of regional planning; the second, processes of its political administration; and the third, an evaluation of the notion of planning as an iterative set of administrative and institutional processes — based on a critique of the rational-consensus model and its corollary, disjointed incrementalism.[13]

The fourth and final part of the book considers some 'Prescriptions for regional planning'. It is an attempt to bring together dominant themes suggestive of ways in which current regional planning practice might evolve and be recast, if not transformed. Three selected writings follow a brief introduction and overview: John Friedmann (1972, Chapter 9), the North West Joint Planning Team (1974, Chapter 10), and F. Wedgwood-Oppenheim, D. A. Hart and B. Cobley (1976, Chapter 11). Friedmann equates regional planning with implementation, whereas the North West Joint Planning Team, in an extract from the *Strategic Plan for the North West* of 1974, suggests the need to institutionalise what they call 'continuous regional planning', and the Wedgwood-Oppenheim et al. contribution calls for a regional 'performance evaluation and policy review unit'.

The core processes of regional planning

If planning has a *raison d'etre* it is, we are told, to assist with the steering and management of change.[14] Regional planning is no exception to this generally accepted rule. What makes it a reasonably distinct form of intervention is the

7

priority which is accorded to administrative processes operating between the principal levels of political administration – central/national and peripheral/local. In this sense regional planning is perceived as a framework for the steering and management of change at some intermediate level between central ('top-down' approach) and local political administrations ('bottom-up' approach).[15]

A number of problems arise from this interpretation: for example, what does the framework consist of? How does it manage to steer change? The answer to these questions, and to others of a similar nature, is that a framework is in itself not capable of a management or steering capacity. It is not the framework *per se* which is of interest or importance, therefore, but rather the manner in which it is given instrumental meaning; that is, how it is operationalised. This is the crux of the problem, for a framework implies the superimposition of artificial constraints and restrictions on the ability to manoeuvre, according to certain set rules or principles or assumptions as to what is or is not legitimate intervention. To an extent a framework implies some degree of control and direction; if it does not then the whole concept is of little utility in a planning context.

How then is a framework operationalised? In the case of regional planning it more often than not takes the form of a number of key or core processes, and processes of an essentially political and administrative nature. It will be suggested in what follows that it is possible to identify at least three different and general ways of operationalising the meaning of regional planning, and that each of these approaches has played an important part in steering the philosophy and practice of regional planning to its current position. An attempt will be made to examine each of these approaches in terms of their internal configuration, but more importantly to see how, when taken together, they interrelate to form a more substantive set of core processes for regional planning.

Policy and regional planning

The first set of core processes suggests that regional planning is primarily, though by no means exclusively, concerned with, and the concern of, the initiation, articulation and implementation of public policy between central and local political administrations. This particular approach, which is the one often employed in 'current best practice', adheres to the philosophy of the rational-consensus model of planning. Overgeneralising and simplifying, the policy approach argues that the principal concern of regional planning is with the making of strategic policy to enhance the steering capacities of its political administration.[16]

The primary focus of political attention is with attempts to initiate demands for administrative devices and to mobilise support for them, once determined. These devices are by definition of an anticipatory, *ex ante* nature, and are devised with the aim of enabling decision-makers to better order change (and hence improve steering capability). The administrative style generally associated with this policy approach is more formal and discrete, in the sense of occurring at stipulated

8

intervals. Since institutional control over events external to the environment within which regional planning operates is much less than total, it follows that a policy approach is concerned with the identification and specification of policy problems in this external space, in as comprehensive a form as possible.[17]

The aim of this approach to regional planning is seen to be to achieve some measure of consensus as to what these problems are, together with agreement over the objectives for their solution. The administrative orientation of the planning processes is therefore towards a consultative forum for decision-making. The *raison d'etre* for this approach is to induce change, primarily, though by no means exclusively, along pre-determined and preferred routes, — be they spatial, functional or temporal. Indeed the temporal emphasis of concern is generally more with the longer term than the 'here and now'; with a broad overview of remedying structural problems rather than with precise details of adaptation at the margin. The forms of intervention and action are a trend projection of recent changes in the planning environment, together with an evaluative analysis of the likely consequences of non-intervention, and the presentation of a limited number of alternative potential devices for intervention.

The administrative objective of this policy-orientated exercise is to create and sustain the legitimacy associated with the unquestionable need to intervene in the exercise of proposing authority.[18] This objective is operationalised by the medium of strategic coordination — the fundamental ability to harness available resources and cooperation to maximise the comprehensiveness necessary for a total approach. Because of the multiplicity of uncertainties surrounding and permeating the original specification of the problems to be resolved, and the need for agreement for, and coordination of, action, the output of such deliberations is typically cast in the form of the strategic policy statement, consultative or otherwise. The ideological roots, stressing consensus formation, are to be found in the argument that we need to know before we can act, but before we can act we need to agree about what we need to know.[19] The structure plans component of the new-style development plans system provides perhaps the best example of the policy approach;[20] similarly the Mark III regional strategies typified by the *Strategic Plan for the North West* of 1974;[21] a good example is also provided by the initial paper of the Labour Government's *Industrial Strategy* of 1975.[22]

It is possible to identify a number of explanatory levels associated with the policy approach to regional planning on the basis of this summary, as Fig. I.1 illustrates. This approach, which is an oversimplification of the 'current best practice' model, has a certain coherence about it, but it is a coherence based on dubious foundations and questionable assumptions as to what are the actual core processes of regional planning and the corresponding control capabilities. Too great an emphasis is placed on only one part of the intervention equation, that of planning as the forging of expectations; it says little, for example, about the idea of planning as controlling such expectations.[23]

Explanatory level	Characteristics of policy approach
Focus of political attention	*Ex ante* control
Decision-making emphasis	Anticipatory
Institutional control	Partial
Problem orientation	Specification
Orientation of planning processes	Consultation
Temporal emphasis	Long term
Basis for intervention	Consequences of past change
Prescriptive objective	Inducement of change
Organisational output	Strategic policy statement
Implementation procedures	Comprehensive — 'open'
Ideological values base	Consensus formation

Example: *Strategic plan for the North West*, 1974

Fig. I.1 The policy approach to regional planning.

Control and regional planning

The second set of core processes suggests that regional planning is less concerned with the initiation or articulation of public policy, and more with political and administrative processes associated with the exercise of control between central and local political administrations.[24] By utilising the same explanatory levels as employed in the analysis of the policy approach it is possible to develop an alternative, indeed competing, control-based model for regional planning.

At the risk of overgeneralising and simplying the argument, the central idea of the control approach hinges on the notion that the principal concern of regional planning is with the use of strategic control instruments to enhance the steering capacities of its political administration. The primary focus of political attention is therefore not so much the development of control devices *per se*, but rather their application and implementation, that is, the planning of their use. Regional planning is seen not so much as an administrative system attempting to anticipate future events but much more as a set of continuous and *ad hoc* procedures of influence and control concerned with the exercise, application and maintenance of political and administrative authority within its previously acceptable legitimation space. Institutional control tends to be substantial, but is never total: the legitimate action space is well-defined, implying that the political administration of regional planning has more than an adequate perception of the problems which it seeks to resolve. The emphasis is therefore almost exclusively orientated towards problem-resolution rather than with the prior specification of problems, the planning processes being grounded more in procedures to ensure direction rather than consultation.[25]

The *raison d'etre* underpinning this approach is the crucial assumption that regional planning is concerned with intervention to ensure the sequential ordering of desired change. An important qualification is attached: regional planning is not concerned with the ordering of any or all such change but only with that change which is within its legitimate concern and hence responsibility. This legitimation space is tightly defined according to successes and failures of past action and demands for current intervention. The temporal emphasis of the control approach is therefore predicated on the perceived need for action and intervention in the short run, with concomitant pleas for short run pay-offs.[26]

The manner in which the control approach is operationalised and given instrumental meaning is by the operation of administrative or contextual control. The political administration of regional planning disposes authority; and organisational output is typically cast in the form of statements of instrumental control, buttressed with the prospect of legal, budgetary and organisational sanctions if not implemented. Because of the very complexity of these tasks, procedures for implementation are more piecemeal and partial than complete and comprehensive; if the control approach to regional planning strives for comprehensiveness it is of a very limited form, and confined to action within the previously-defined legitimation space. It implies a trade-off between comprehensiveness on the one hand and certainty on the other: attempts to increase one suggest an inevitable reduction in the other, for control implies certainty over outcomes, and comprehensiveness inevitably reduces the prospect.[27]

Examples which bear some correspondence to the control approach are confined, at least in the UK context, more or less exclusively to the economic policy strand of regional planning: for example, the extensive controls operated over the location of the manufacturing and commercial office sectors as operated by the Department of Industry, or the original formulation of the 'planning agreements system';[28] other examples include the development and implementation of capital investment programmes of the 'regionalised' public sector agencies — water, gas, electricity and, to a lesser extent, health and transport. Examples of control devices are provided by the many and varied department-initiated statutory instruments and regulations (formal directives) and circulars (formal advice) to dependent agencies, especially local authorities; and by planning's statutory framework — for example, the provisions contained in the Community Land Act of 1975, the Land Compensation and Control of Pollution Acts of 1974, and the Town and Country Planning Acts of 1947 through to 1972.

As with the policy approach to regional planning, the control model can be similarly structured (Fig. I.2). This model also has a semblance of coherence about it, but it is a coherence which is at best partial; for example, this form of regional planning assumes that the control devices which are employed are communicated to it, are somehow given by or handed-down from some other or higher authority. The

11

analogy with the functional approach to public planning is clearly quite strong.[29]

Explanatory level	Characteristics of control approach
Focus of political attention	*Ex post* planning
Decision-making emphasis	Authoritative
Institutional control	Substantial
Problem orientation	Resolution
Orientation of planning processes	Direction
Temporal emphasis	Short run
Basis for intervention	Ordering future change
Prescriptive objective	Dynamic equilibrium
Organisational output	Control instruments
Implementation procedures	Complete — 'closed'
Ideological values base	Central guidance

Example: Regional economic policy, UK

Fig I.2 The control approach to regional planning.

Communication and regional planning

The third approach as to what constitutes the core processes of regional planning develops from the argument that it is neither explicitly concerned with the derivation of policy statements nor the explicit concern of the exercise of control. If regional planning is concerned with anything substantive then it is with communication, and in particular with the initiation and opening-up of communication and information channels between central and local administrations. The objective underpinning this particular approach concerns the problem of matching central policy intentions to local implementation capability and policy impact. Regional planning is seen to provide this link, thus enhancing the steering capacities of the political administration by controlling or influencing information flows from centre to periphery, and back again, in some continuous fashion.[30]

By employing the same set of explanatory levels as those utilised in examining the policy and control approaches, it is possible to derive a communication-based alternative. Unlike both the former approaches, a communication approach to regional planning emphasises the importance of political and administrative coordination. The focus of political attention is geared towards the coordination of policy with the means to control its effectuation; that is, *ex ante* control with *ex post* planning at some intermediate level between central and local administrations.

In terms of the ability to influence events, the emphasis of decision-making is to be found in attempts to improve and control, to facilitate, the quality and quantity of information passing between levels. The administrative style of the communication approach is therefore more informal than formal and, almost by definition, of a continuous nature. Institutional control is very limited; there is little or no power or authority for regional planning to specify or resolve problems which lie beyond the boundaries of its limited legitimation space, only the ability to articulate problems between agencies. The processes associated with this type of planning are rooted in the ability to negotiate; reticulist skills are the predominant attributes of the communication approach. The time-horizons are present-orientated, and if there is a specific administrative objective it is to mediate between agencies in conflict situations. The ability to intervene is almost exclusively limited to the provision, expansion or restriction of channels for communicating change. If there are organisational powers available then they are restricted in the main to the exercise of administrative discretion. This particular attribute, political leverage, is arguably the most significant in the limited armoury of the communications approach; it is extremely difficult to assess in any systematic way.[31]

The ability to implement these clearly limited, but often powerful, procedures is in turn partial, rather than complete or comprehensive. The problem in this context is not so much uncertainty surrounding the ability to intervene, but the fact that its role is somewhat restrained by the substantive authority associated with the centre and the periphery; the image of reality may be very broad or narrow, and it may or may not correspond to the dimensions of the legitimation space, but the fundamental ability to operate within the boundaries of that image is substantively constrained by the activities of both central and local political administrations.[32] The channels for implementation are therefore a complex and continuous attempt to iterate between 'opening-up' and 'closing-down' the boundaries of the legitimation space.

Perhaps the best example of this approach to regional planning is provided, in the UK context at least, by the configuration of advisory regional economic planning councils and boards currently operating in England; other examples include the regional offices of central government departments, the many regional standing conferences of local planning authorities, and the revised 'planning agreements system' contained in the 1975 Industry Act.[33]

The communications approach can be structured in similar fashion to the competing alternatives of the policy and control models (Fig. I.3).

Explanatory level	Characteristics of communications approach
Focus of political attention	Coordination
Decision-making emphasis	Facilitative
Institutional control	Marginal
Problem orientation	Articulation
Orientation of planning processes	Negotiation
Temporal emphasis	Present-orientated
Basis for intervention	Awareness of current change
Prescriptive objective	Conflict resolution
Organisational output	Communication channels
Implementation procedures	Partial – 'iterative'
Ideological values base	Continuous information mediation

Example: regional planning councils/boards, UK

Fig. I.3 The communications approach to regional planning.

Regional planning: policy, control, communication

Three alternative, competing and stylised arguments have been put forward as to what constitutes the core processes of regional planning – policy, control or communication. An outline of the internal configuration of each of these models has been advanced, examples approximating to the respective approaches cited, and a hint of the principal weaknesses noted. It is demonstrably clear that, when considered in isolation, each is an incomplete and partial, and therefore untenable, explanation; but it is unlikely that a pure form version of the policy, control or communications approach would, or indeed could, be found in reality. Nonetheless each model is indicative of a particular emphasis or bias which is readily identifiable in both the literature and practice of regional planning. It is the set of assumptions upon which these emphases are based which are of singular importance in this context for, when given some explicit internal coherence, each set constitutes an alternative outline for a philosophy of interventionism. In these respects it is possible to bring out some tentative conclusions which emerge from a comparison of these three competing philosophies.

The first point which can be made is that the core processes of regional planning are more substantive than those necessary for simply making policy, or in the application of control devices, or in the promotion of channels for communication. Regional planning is about the continuous processes concerned with the making of policy, the application of control devices and the promotion of channels for communication, however limited the role and place for each may be in those processes. Regional planning constitutes, and is constituted by, processes of policy, control and communication operationalised at some intermediate level between central and local political administrations. For example, the making of policy implies some measure of control and communication, if only in the ability to control the manpower and resources necessary for the preparation of a strategic policy statement, and the ability to articulate that policy once formalised. Indeed, the application of control assumes an existing policy and the means (i.e. a communication base) by which it can be implemented; similarly, communication does not exist in a vacuum, for it implies a bringing together, a synthesis, of policy intentions with the processes of control over implementation. Policy can exist independently of control and communication (as indeed may control and communication) but whether it can be wholly effective is another, and more important, matter.

Over-reliance on any one or two models is unlikely, except under the most extreme conditions and almost unique circumstances (for example, where regional planners have near-total control over their immediate planning environment), to achieve anything more than limited success in the translation of planned intent into actual impact. Thus regional planning cannot be satisfactorily accounted for as if it were only the making of strategic policy statements, or the application of instrumental control devices, or the operation of political leverage through communication channels. It is the interlocking of all three of these components which gives meaning to the idea of regional planning. The reason is quite simple, for the political administration of public planning being divided into large functional parts, rather than being wholly collective or atomised, no single political administration has the basic ability to effectuate its proposals without the prospect of having them changed by other administrations with an interest in the policy field. This is an almost continuous prospect for regional planning because, as we have previously argued, it is to be found located somewhere in the opportunity space between the two principal tiers of government — central and local.

The second point which emanates from this brief evaluation of alternative approaches is that each is not strictly a discrete alternative; rather each could be complementary. If the core processes of the political administration of regional planning are to be associated with a combination of policy, control and communication devices and procedures, then the assumption which was employed in outlining the three approaches as free-standing models is no longer necessary. A revised and arguably more satisfactory approach coalesces around the notion of the interdependence of policy, control and communication. The three approaches merge and shade imperceptibly into a common set of core processes, structured along similar lines, which can be illustrated by utilising the same set of explanatory levels. This revised schema is illustrated by Fig. I.4.

Explanatory levels	Characteristics		
	Policy	Control	Communication
Focus of political attention	*Ex ante* control	*Ex post* planning	Coordination
Decision-making emphasis	Anticipatory	Authoritative	Facilitative
Institutional control	Partial	Substantial	Marginal
Problem orientation	Specification	Resolution	Articulation
Orientation of planning processes	Consultation	Direction	Negotiation
Temporal emphasis	Long run	Short run	Present-orientated
Basis for intervention	Consequences of past change	Ordering future change	Awareness of current change
Prescriptive objective	Inducement of change	Dynamic equilibrium	Conflict resolution
Organisational output	Strategic policy statement	Control instruments	Communication channels
Implementation procedures	Comprehensive - 'open'	Complete - 'closed'	Partial - 'iterative'
Ideological value base	Consensus formation	Central guidance	Continuous information mediation
Example:	*Strategic Plan* for *the North West*, 1974	Regional economic policy, UK	Regional economic planning councils/ boards, UK

Fig. 1.4 Regional planning — policy, control, communication

However, an impression which is equally in danger of being created is that somehow these three ingredients, rather than free-standing entities, are all of equal importance, status and utility. This would be misleading: regional planning is not a simple mix of policy, control and communication — although it may be considered and evaluated in such terms — but rather a more complex mix of policy, control and communication devices and procedures which overlap one another, which are in a state of continuous interaction, and which will be emphasised at different stages in the broader procedures of regional planning. It is the contention here that this overlapping and interacting set of processes constitutes the political administration of regional planning — its core processes — which, when considered interdependently, could provide a tentative platform upon which an alternative to the rational-consensus philosophy of interventionism could be based. It is this continuous interaction between policy, control and communication, forming procedural chain and substantive spiral, which gives shape, meaning and dynamics to the core processes of regional planning.[34] It is around this particular conception of regional planning that the following eleven writings have been selected for inclusion. Each illustrates and reinforces a particular aspect or theme which can be found running through this 'Perspectives' section — from the viewpoints of problems, processes and prescriptions.

Notes

[1] This interpretation has been suggested by Gunsteren, 1976, p.iii; on crisis tendencies, see Habermas 1976a, pp. 45-92.

[2] See Gillingwater, 1975, Chap. 3, for a fuller treatment; also Dahrendorf, 1959, Chap. V.

[3] See Hart, 1976, especially Chap. 1; also Gunsteren, 1976, op.cit.

[4] For a phenomenological approach to the concept of 'naturalness', see O'Neill, 1974, p.v; for an extended discussion and particularly powerful critique, see Habermas, 1976b.

[5] For an incisive account of the relationships between 'first best' and planning, see Self, 1976; for a more fundamental philosophical argument see Habermas 1976a, op.cit., Part One; for a 'second best' critique of 'first best', see the seminal paper by Lipsey and Lancaster, 1955/56; for a more general treatment related to public intervention, see Rees, 1976.

[6] One of the original and most influential books on the rational-consensus model as applied to organisational processes — the 'scientific management' approach — is March and Simon, 1958; for an indication of the ways in which this approach percolated its way into public planning, see Chadwick, 1971, McLoughlin, 1969 (both urban planning), or Hall, 1970 (regional planning); for a particularly formal and formalised treatment relating to the US experience, see Boyce, Day and McDonald, 1970, and Boyce, McDonald and Farhi, 1972.

[7] MacKaye, 1928 (Chapter 1 in this volume), and Abercrombie, 1945.

[8] For a brief outline of the organisation of British public planning, see Gillingwater, 1975, op.cit. pp. 122-6.

[9] For evidence of this general neglect, see Glasson, 1974, or Alden and Morgan, 1974; this has led Chadwick, 1975, to remark that: 'the conceptual basis of regional planning is the Achilles heel of pretty well every book which attempts the subject ... time would be more fruitfully spend on improving the conceptual basis of regional planning than on refining some esoteric aspects of regional science'

(p. 332); for evidence of the importance of this link, see Crossman, 1975, on the contextual elements surrounding the designation of the Central Lancashire New Town, and Crossman, 1976, on the Regional Employment Premium; also Derthick, 1974, for a US comparison.

[10] For example, see Keeble, 1976, or Manners (ed.), 1972; also Holland, 1976a/b.

[11] See Dewey, 1927, especially the last chapter — the links are uncannily close; for an extended treatment, see Scheffler, 1974.

[12] On the importance of this conceptualisation, see Hall, 1970, op.cit., Hall, 1974, and Gillingwater, 1975, op.cit.; for a somewhat narrower interpretation, see Alden and Morgan, 1974, op.cit.

[13] The argument that disjointed incrementalism is a corollary of the rational choice model is one which is a matter of some dispute — see Reade, 1976; it is quite clear that the protagonists of disjointed incrementalism developed their alternative out of a critique of the rational choice model. In this narrow sense disjointed incrementalism may be interpreted as a logical outcome, or 'natural consequence' (O.E.D.), of rational choice; its corollary in fact.

[14] For a particularly congent account of the concept of steering capacity, see Habermas, 1976a, op.cit., especially pp. 4-5; with respect to regional planning, see MacKaye, 1928, op.cit. (Chapter 1 in this volume).

[15] On this 'top-down'/'bottom-up' concept, see Self, 1974 (Chapter 4 in this volume); for a codified version, see Hall, 1970, op.cit.

[16] See, for example, the North West Joint Planning Team, 1974 (Chapter 10 in this volume); also Wedgwood-Oppenheim et al., 1976 (Chapter 11 in this volume).

[17] See, for example, Wedgwood-Oppenheim et al., 1976, op.cit. (Chapter 11 in this volume); also Friend et al., 1974 (Chapter 6 in this volume).

[18] For evidence, See Rowntree Research Unit, 1974 (Chapter 5 in this volume); also Painter, 1972 (Chapter 7 in this volume).

[19] See, for example, Hart, 1976 (Chapter 8 in this volume); also Friedmann, 1972 (Chapter 9 in this volume).

[20] See in particular Circular 66/74, on Structure Plans, Department of the Environment, 1974; also the *South Hampshire Structure Plan*, Hampshire County Council, 1972.

[21] North West Joint Planning Team, 1974 op.cit. (see also Chapter 10 in this volume; see also *Stratetic Choice for East Anglia*, East Anglia Joint Planning Team, 1975.

[22] Treasury/Department of Industry, 1975.

[23] On this relationship in general, see Hart, 1974.

[24] The meaning of control in this context fol.ows Popper, 1966 (and included in Popper, 1972) and his notion of 'plastic control' : that is a kind of control intermediate between 'iron' control and no control. On control in regional planning see, for example, Wedgwood-Oppenheim et al., 1976, op.cit. (Chapter 11 in this volume); also Rhodes, 1974 (Chapter 3 in this volume); for an alternative view, see McLoughlin, 1973, and for a critique, see Gunsteren, 1976, op.cit.

18

[25] For evidence, see Hart, 1976, op.cit. (Chapter 8 in this volume).
[26] See Friedmann, 1972, op.cit. (Chapter 9 in this volume); also Rowntree Research Unit, 1974, op.cit. (Chapter 8 in this volume). j[27] For further discussion, see Wedgwood-Oppenheim et al., 1976, op.cit. (Chapter 11 in this volume).
[28] On regional economic policy as control, see Button and Gillingwater, 1976. Introduction; on 'planning agreements', see Bromborough and Smyth 1975.
[29] On this relationship, see Gillingwater, 1975, op.cit., especially pp. 88-90.
[30] See in particular Donnison, 1974 (Chapter 2 in this volume); also Friend et al., 1974, op.cit. (Chapter 6 in this volume) and Painter, 1972, op.cit. (Chapter 7 in this volume).
[31] For evidence, see Wedgwood-Oppenheim et al., 1976 op.cit. (Chapter 11 in this volume).
[32] For an example of an institutional response to this problem, see the seminal contribution by Abercrombie, 1945, op.cit.: for a contemporary response, see North West Joint Planning Team, 1974, op.cit. (Chapter 10 in this volume); also the response to that response, the proposal for setting up a performance-evaluation-policy-review (Chapter 11 in this volume). It is perhaps of interest to note that to date (1977) this type of unit has not been operationalised.
[33] For an excellent review, see Donnison, 1974, op.cit. (Chapter 2 in this volume; also, with respect to the West Midlands, Friend et al., 1974, op.cit. (Chapter 6 in this volume) and Painter, 1972, op.cit. (Chapter 7 in this volume); on revised planning agreements, see Department of Industry, 1975.
[34] These concepts of a 'procedural chain' and 'substantive spiral' are to be found in Hart, 1976, op.cit. (Chapter 8 in this volume); see also Hart, 1974, op.cit. p.40; the treatment here is seen to complement this earlier, essentially urban-orientated, approach.

References

(* included in this volume)

Abercrombie, P., *The Greater London Plan 1944*, HMSO, London 1945.
Adorno, T., Albert, H., Dahrendorf, R., Habermas, J., Pilot, H. and Popper K., *The Positivist Dispute in German Sociology*, Heinemann, London 1976.
Alden, J. and Morgan, R., *Regional Planning: A Comprehensive View*, Leonard Hill, Heath and Reach 1974.
Boyce, D., Day N. and McDonald, C., *Metropolitan Plan Making*, Regional Science Research Institute, University of Pennsylvania, Philadelphia 1970.
Boyce, D., McDonald, C. and Farhi, A., *An Interim Report on Procedures for Continuing Metropolitan Planning*, mimeo, Regional Science Research Institute, University of Pennsylvania, Philadelphia 1972.
Bromborough, J. and Smyth, D., *Planning Agreements in Practice, Labour*

Economic Finance and Taxation Association, London 1975.

Button, K. and Gillingwater, D., *Case Studies in Regional Economics,* Heinemann, London 1976.

Chadwick, G., *A Systems View of Planning: Towards a Theory of the Urban and Regional Planning Process,* Pergamon, Oxford 1971.

Chadwick, G., 'Review of *An Introduction to Regional Planning',* Town and Country Planning, June 1975, p. 332.

Crossman, R., *Diaries of a Cabinet Minister,* vol. I, Cape/Hamilton, London 1975.

Crossman, R., *Diaries of a Cabinet Minister,* vol. II, Cape/Hamilton, London 1976.

Dahrendorf, R., *Class and Class Conflict in Industrial Society,* Routledge and Kegan Paul, London 1959.

Department of the Environment, 'Structure Plans', Circular 66/74, HMSO, London 1974.

Department of Industry, 'The Contents of a Planning Agreement', *Trade and Industry,* 8 August, 1975, p.337.

Derthick, M., *Between State and Nation: Regional Organisations of the United States,* Brookings Institution, Washington 1974.

Dewey, J., *The Public and its Problems,* Swallow Press, Chicago, 1973 edition.

*Donnison, D., 'The Economics and Politics of the Regions', *The Political Quarterly,* April-May 1974, pp.179-89.

East Anglia Joint Planning Team, *Strategic Choice for East Anglia,* HMSO, London 1975.

*Friedmann, J., 'Implementation', *International Social Development Review,* No. 4, 1972, pp.95-105.

*Friend, J., Power, J. and Yewlett, C., *Public Planning: The Inter-Corporate Dimension,* Tavistock, London 1974.

Gillingwater, D., *Regional Planning and Social Change: A Responsive Approach,* Saxon House, Farnborough 1975.

Glasson J., *An Introduction to Regional Planning.* Hutchinson, London 1974.

Gunsteren, H. V., *The Quest for Control: A Critique of the Rational-Central-Rule Approach in Public Affairs,* Wiley, London 1976.

Habermas, J., *Legitimation Crisis,* Heinemann, London 1976a.

Habermas, J., 'The Analytical Theory of Science and Dialectics', in Adorno, T. et al., *The Positivist Dispute in German Sociology,* Heinemann, London 1976b.

Hall, P., *The Theory and Practice of Regional Planning,* Pemberton, London 1970.

Hall, P., *Urban and Regional Planning,* Penguin, Harmondsworth 1974.

Hampshire County Council, *South Hampshire Structure Plan Draft Written Statement,* South Hants Plan Advisory Committee, Winchester 1972.

Hart, D., 'Ordering Change and Changing Orders: A Study of Urban Policy Development', *Policy and Politics,* vol. 2, no. 1, 1974, pp.27-41.

Hart, D., *Strategic Planning in London: The Rise and Fall of the Primary Road Network,* Pergamon, Oxford 1976.

*Hart, D., 'Planning as an Iterative Process', *Local Government Studies,* vol. 2, no. 3, July 1976, pp.27-42.

Holland, S., *The Regional Problem*, Macmillan, London 1976a.

Holland, S., *Capital versus the Regions*, Macmillan, London 1976b.

Keeble, D., *Industrial Location and Planning in the United Kingdom*, Methuen, London 1976.

Lipsey, R. and Lancaster, K. 'The General Theory of the Second Best', *Review of Economic Studies*, vol. XXIV, no. 1, 1955/56, pp.11-32.

McLoughlin, J., *Urban and Regional Planning: A Systems Approach*, Faber, London 1969.

McLoughlin, J., *Control and Urban Planning*, Faber, London 1973.

*MacKaye, B., *The New Exploration: A Philosophy of Regional Planning*, Harcourt Brace, Illinois 1928 (reprinted 1962, University of Illinois Press).

Manners, G., (ed), *Regional Development in Britain*, Wiley, London 1972.

March, J. and Simon, H., *Organisations*, Wiley, New York 1958.

*North West Joint Planning Team, *Strategic Plan for the North West*, HMSO, London 1974.

O'Neill, J. (ed.) *Phenomenology, Language and Sociology*, Heinemann, London 1974.

*Painter, C., 'The Repercussions of Administrative Innovation: The West Midlands Economic Planning Council', *Public Administration*, Winter, vol. 50, pp.467-84.

Popper, K., 'Of Clouds and Clocks: An Approach to the Problem of Rationality and the Freedom of Man', Compton Memorial Lecture, University of Washington, St. Louis 1966, in Popper, K., *Objective Knowledge: An Evolutionary Approach*, Clarendon, Oxford 1972.

Popper, K., *Objective Knowledge: An Evolutionary Approach*, Clarendon, Oxford 1972.

Reade, E., 'Review of *Regional Planning and Social Change*', *Journal of Regional Studies*, vol. 10, 1976, p.336.

Rees, R., *Public Enterprise Economics*, Weidenfeld and Nicolson, London 1976.

*Rhodes, R., 'Regional Policy and a "Europe of Regions": A Critical Assessment', *Journal of Regional Studies*, vol. 8, 1974, pp.105-14.

*Rowntree Research Unit, University of Durham, 'Aspects of Contradiction in Regional Policy', *Journal of Regional Studies*, vol. 8, no. 2, August 1974, pp.133-44.

Scheffler, I., *Four Pragmatists: A Critical Introduction to Peirce, James, Mead and Dewey*, Routledge and Kegan Paul, London 1974.

*Self, P., 'Regional Planning in Britain: Analysis and Evaluation', *Journal of Regional Studies*, vol. 1, no. 1, May 1964, pp.3-10.

Self, P., *Econocrats and the Policy Process: The Politics and Philosophy of Cost-Benefit Analysis*, Macmillan, London 1976.

Treasury/Department of Industry, *An Approach to Industrial Strategy*, Cmnd. 6315, HMSO, London 1975.

*Wedgwood-Oppenheim, F., Hart, D. and Cobley, B., *An Exploratory Study in Strategic Monitoring*, Pergamon, Oxford 1976.

Overview

The two selected writings which follow this introduction and overview are by Benton MacKaye (1928, Chapter 1) and David Donnison (1974, Chapter 2). MacKaye's contribution is included to illustrate the point that regional planning did, indeed, have an emergent philosophy — albeit rooted in a form of pragmatism akin to John Dewey — which can be traced back to the early 1920s; but more importantly it is included for the many profound insights it offers into the nature and practice of regional planning — such as the idea of 'planning as revelation' — as indicated by the sub-title of the book from which this extract is taken: *A Philosophy of Regional Planning*. The Donnison article focuses attention on a survey of the UK dimension, and in particular with the experience of British regional planning. It offers an explicit contribution towards a critique of regional planning from the perspective of political administration.

1 Planning as revelation

Excepts from Benton MacKaye, *The New Exploration: A Philosophy of Regional Planning,* The University of Illinois Press, 1928, pp.146-58 and pp.208-14.

What is the essence of a good plan? I recall the words of a certain civil engineer while seated around the evening camp fire during a surveying trip into the hemlock country of western Pennsylvania. Absorbed in thoughts of the day's work, he sat gazing into the embers. Suddenly he came to life with an expression of relief: 'Well, I can't help it, I didn't make the country!'

We were running a line for a logging railroad which was to cross a divide and dip over into an adjoining valley. We hoped the line could reach the bottom on a 6 per cent. grade. But we discovered that this could not be. The grade must be steeper, or else switchbacks must be put in. The engineer was disappointed. His first plan could not be carried out. The reason was that his plan did not fit nature's. Nature had moulded the country in a certain way. The job of the engineer was to find out that way: it was not to inflict a plan of his own, but to uncover nature's plan. And so it spelled relief to the engineer to realise that after all it was not for him to 'make the country'.

'To command nature,' said Plato, 'we must first obey her.' That is what this engineer did. He desired to command nature by locating a railroad whereby the hemlock timber could be removed from a certain valley. This he wanted to accomplish by means of a railroad having the easiest possible grade, and so he ran a line to see if he could get into the valley on a 6 per cent. grade. He discovered that nature would not allow this. And so he yielded to nature (he 'obeyed' her) by finding another line — a line which suited her, a line which required a grade of 6½ per cent. instead of 6. Having made this adjustment, the engineer was enabled to build his railroad into the valley and remove the timber: having thus obeyed nature, he was able to command her.

Here we have the function of every sort of planner: it is primarily to uncover, reveal, and visualise — not alone his own idea but nature's; not merely to formulate the desire of man, but to reveal the limits thereto imposed by a greater power. Thus, in fine, planning is two things: (a) an accurate formulation of our own desires — the specific knowledge of what it is we want; and (b) an accurate revelation of the limits, and the opportunities, imposed and bequeathed to us by nature. Planning is a scientific charting and picturing of the thing (whether logging railroad or communal centre) which man desires and which the eternal forces will permit.

The basic achievement of planning is to make potentialities visible. But this is

24

not enough. Visibility is only part of revelation. The mould must be rendered not only visible but audible. It must be *heard* as well as *seen*. The regional planner, in revealing a given mould or environment, must portray not alone for the sense of sight, but for that of hearing also. Indeed he must portray in terms of all the senses. If he would portray for us a possible colonial village in New England, he must portray it in terms of the three dimensions — and of the five senses. He must in his imagination see the common, and hear the church bell, and smell the lilac blossoms, and contact the green-shuttered houses: he must also see and contact the human activity. The individual art of painting consists in revelation in the realm of eyesight; the individual art of music consists in revelation in the realm of hearing; but the synthetic art of developing environment consists in revelation in the realm of all the senses. Planning is revelation — and all-round revelation.

The function of planning is to render actual and evident that which is potential and inevident. The potential image on the exposed camera film requires the chemical of the photographer to develop it and make it actual; the potential images and worlds lying within the surface of a region require the chemical of the imagination to develop them and make them actual. This action of the imagination has already been described under the term of psychologic conversion. This is closely related to biologic conversion: the action of the human brain cell is akin to that of the cambium layer. The cambium is that layer of perpetual fluidity which in the tree converts the ethereal substance of carbon dioxide into the solid substance of wood and timber. It represents the realm of creative action (call it art or engineering): it represents the eternal present — that fluid twilight zone between the ethereal future and the solid past wherein our destiny is moulded. Planning takes place in this cambium, twilight zone.

There are two particular potential images and worlds lying within practically every region: these are the indigenous world and the metropolitan world. The contrast between them is obscure and inevident. The most important revelation to be made by the chemistry of the imagination, in our own particular problem of regional planning, is the rendering evident of this inevident contrast.

The notion is dawning in the public mind, apparently, that something is wrong with the way in which our towns and countryside are being treated. The cry grows louder against billboards, hot-dog stands, and the motor slum which is pushing its way along the rural waysides. 'Slum flow' is what a friend of mine has called it, a term which we might well use as a short name for 'metropolitan flow.' Now and again the cry strikes directly toward the contrast itself between the indigenous and metropolitan environments. Note these interesting comments made by John H. Bartlett, First Assistant Postmaster General, in his speech in Newport, New Hampshire, on the occasion of the centennial celebration of Sullivan County: [1]

An appealing cry for help comes from the small and fast-vanishing villages of our small towns and can be heard from every hilltop in the County. . . . If the present course of human events in these places continues, is it possible that we will finally have in Sullivan County only two towns, or so-called cities

25

[Claremont and Newport]? And I conjecture that then the chain stores would prevail here — those monopolistic 'strings' that are bossed by outside capital, and stocked up and cashed up by machine-made boys shot here from distant headquarters. . . . It seems to me that we are afflicted with pernicious myopia if we cannot see this tendency of things, this toboggan of events against the little villages. . . .

Concentrated business, concentrated capital, concentrated power, concentrated politics, concentrated everything! Where does this process of concentration leave the individual? And where, forsooth, does it leave the poor little town? Where does it deposit the power that governs our State and shapes the destiny of our old-fashioned New Hampshire civilization?

Mr. Bartlett, a high Government official, is expressing here a deep undercurrent in public consciousness: it is an arraignment of the metropolitan mould and an appeal for the indigenous — an arraignment of 'concentrated everything' and an appeal for the 'New Hampshire civilisation.' Yet along with this desire for the innate life there goes, as Mr. Mencken has pointed out, the seemingly deliberate effort for the opposite — the lust (the 'libido' as he calls it) to build loathsome towns and to 'make the world intolerable.' The confusion in men's minds regarding the underlying nature of the indigenous and metropolitan worlds is entertaining, but it is tragic. These worlds, these environments, represent in their essence the antipodes of human experience: one is inherent, the other is intrusive; one is natural, the other is mechanised; one is art, the other is artifice; one is symphonic, the other is cacophonous.

But unfortunately it is not in their essence that we experience these environments; we experience them instead in what might be called in very truth a complex. We get the two essences in combination. The titanic turreted skyscraper viewed through evening lights from New York harbour combines national power in repose and majesty with imperialistic affront and sinister contemptuousness. The down-town shopping district of the average small American city, with its left-over shade trees, combines the home-coming thrill of the stately elm-lined village roadway and common meeting-ground with the rotary excitement of the typical Main Street. The journey by motor through the American countryside combines the elixir of the stage-coach drive through hill and dale with the melancholia inflicted by a wayside architecture glorying in the heyday of its drabness. There is a hankering lure about each one of these phenomena: there is in them, as Mr. Mencken would say, 'a voluptuous quality' of almost ecstatic ugliness.

The metropolitan environment, taken as a whole, is a sort of modern inorganic siren. She is the mistress of our outreaching yet befuddled senses. We are like the man who is attracted towards a courtesan. To get an ounce of solid living he endures a pound of the meretricious. And we do likewise — those of us who 'fall for' metropolitanism. If we would admire suggestion of majestic power, we must grovel before display of imperial contempt; if we would attain a little thrill of village hominess, we must submit to the blasts of Main Street blatancy; if we would

26

snatch a whiff of verdant countryside we must tear through a stench of tenemented roadside. To get an ounce of the native and indigenous we must take a pound of the foreign and exogenous. This is so in the courtesan environment; and it is so in the metropolitan environment.

The roué endures the courtesan because she contains a tiny element of the innate woman; most of us endure the metropolitan life — the exogenous life — because it contains an element of the innate life — the indigenous life. The drop of peppermint flavours the whole of what would otherwise be a stale and flat concoction.

The revelation of a contrast (as that between the indigenous and the metropolitan) makes one fundamental aspect of regional planning. There is another fundamental aspect. This is the revelation of potential conditions in preparation for some possible occasion or event. This is best illustrated perhaps in the case of military planning, where the expected event is an emergency — something requiring immediate yet comprehensive action.

Supposing our friend the civil engineer, mentioned previously, had been a military engineer. Supposing his problem had been, not to bring a railroad into the valley, but to bring an army in. The problems are much alike: in each case some manner of road would be required; that is, some means of access. One is an industrial problem, the other a military problem. Each requires preparation and mental forethought. Neither the railway nor the army could properly enter the valley until the scouts had gone ahead and charted (mentally) the way.

Every deliberate action, big or little, good or bad, military or industrial, starts in the mind. It must be conceived and rehearsed in the realm of thought before it can take place in the physical. It must be created before it can be done. So-called doing is only half the job.

Nobody knows this better than the military engineer, or strategist. Witness Napoleon and his maps. Not that he charts in advance each particular campaign or movement. Usually there is not time for that. But he has charted, perhaps many times, the general military situation. He has studied the ground, and the armies, and a multitude of potential actions. He has directed a dozen battles in his mind before one battle on the ground. By thinking through the dozen battles that never do take place, he equips himself to handle the one which comes to pass.

Military strategy is one kind of regional planning. It is the charting and visualising of deliberate, coordinated action over an extended territory. So also is industrial regional planning: it is the charting and visualising, within a region, of coordinated action for the purposes of industry. So also is regional planning in general: the visualising within a region of coordinated action for the purposes of general human living.

Planning with respect to expected or possible events is a matter of mental preparation: it is revelation plus elasticity. This applies to war, to industry, and to general living; it applies to a military invasion and to a metropolitan invasion. As with the small affairs of life, so with the large; all we can do is to know our mind and watch our chance. We plan for various contingencies — A, B, C, and D. And then E happens! Four precious plans we must cast aside, but on the strength of these (the knowledge attained in framing them) we can forthwith frame a plan for meeting E. We can never foresee with surety our particular actual opportunity: we can, however, if we will, foresee a series of potential opportunities. And we can prepare ourselves mentally for each. By preparing for several things which may happen, we indirectly prepare ourselves for what does happen. Planning is strategy: it is the revelation of a number of possibilities in order to control a single actuality.

Our immediate particular job, with respect to preparing ourselves mentally for the vicissitudes of the metropolitan invasion, is the charting, revelation, and contrasting of the indigenous and metropolitan moulds. For into one or the other of these the future population is bound to flow. Population, like water, follows the channels that have been laid for it. That mould which is most in evidence is the one which will control the currents of the population. If, therefore, we are in favour of one mould as against the other (as we are) then it is for us to reveal that mould – to bring it out and develop it and make it strong – to make it resistant to the intrusion and the invasion of the other mould.[...]

The subject of the birth rate lies at the bottom of every social question known to man. It is obviously related to regional planning, and not only to the problems of the regional planner but to those of other workers for the common good – the social worker, the political reformer, the economic reformer, the labour leader. But none of these allows his particular line of evolution to wait on the solution of the riddle of population. It might be maintained that this is what he should do: that the regional planner, for instance, wastes his time when he visualises the mould for the distribution of the flow of population, while the source of the flow itself remains unchecked. This point appears to be well taken, especially so since we are stoutly maintaining within these pages that the regional planner should deal with the sources and not the 'mouths' of the population's flow. Our position can be clarified perhaps by means of the same analogy which we used before – that of controlling water-flow.

A civil engineer is given the large problem, let us say, of controlling the flow of the Mississippi River and of preventing or reducing floods such as those which have made such havoc during recent years in the lower reaches of the valley. He should not, in our opinion, depend wholly on the construction along these lower stretches of revetments and levees whose only function can be to hold intact a flood wave which has already got started: he should, instead, build in the regions of the headwaters a series of storage reservoirs such as the Pittsburgh Flood Commission projected to control the floods at Pittsburgh. Furthermore, he should take steps to maintain on the upland watersheds above the reservoirs sufficient forest-cover to make for equable flowage and for reducing the process of silting up the reservoirs. In short, he should catch the flood wave before it gets started, by controlling the flow in the highest portions of the land.

But is this enough? Why stop at the land? Why not go into the sky? For the rainfall in the sky is the source of all waters on the land. But perhaps you will maintain that we know very well that man has no control of rainfall. We know nothing of the kind. It is an open question whether the maintenance of a continental forest-cover affects the continental climate. There seem to be good reasons for thinking that it does: that the influence of forest-cover tends toward equability of rainfall. Such are the tentative conclusions of Raphael Zon, of the United States Forest Service, the most eminent American authority on the subject. It is the opinion of a number of foresters and meteorologists that if investigation were extended far enough, the tentative working hypothesis formulated by Zon would be established.

Our civil engineer in charge of controlling the flow of the Mississippi River might be one of those who believed in this hypothesis: if so, would he be warranted in delaying his project (of control by reservoirs) until Zon's hypothesis was established and then acted on? That would be like waiting for the millennium or (to quote the vernacular) 'until hell freezes over.' It might well take a generation to establish the hypothesis and then a full century to establish the required areas of forest. The reservoir could be launched in a decade. The ultimate source of river-flow lies, of course, in rainfall; but the immediate source of river-flow, and the source which now we can control, lies in the streams which constitute the headwaters of the river's system. Some day, perhaps, man will be able to control the rainfall itself the world over, but today he knows he can control the headwater streams region by region. The engineer who controls the headwater streams within a region is working with the most fundamental source of river control within the range at present of the art of engineering.

The control of America's population is quite as deep-seated probably as the control of America's floods and rivers. America's flow of population is part of the world flow of population. The ultimate source of population flow within any region in America lies in the flow of population the world over, but the immediate source of the region's population-flow lies in the various communities distributed throughout the country. The flow of population issues from the communities — especially from the larger communities. The regulation of this flow is the immediate problem of the regional planner: he deals with the problem of controlling not the total quantity of people within a region, but the distribution of the quantity which is already there. The regional planner makes no attempt to control the flow of population into his region from other portions of the world; no more than the engineer attempts to control the flow of water into his river basin coming through rainfall from other portions of the world. The regional planner and the engineer, each within his region or his river basin, accepts a given amount or quantity of flow, and then distributes it according to some plan. Each one works with the immediate source of flow and not with the ultimate source. The civil engineer works not to control the world's rainfall, and the regional planner works not to control the rate of world population.

Each of these technicians works within the present range of his particular technique. The physician may be able in time to control the rate of world population and thereby to extend the range and influence of regional planning and of every other social service; indeed, the Western European countries have all made a distinct advance in this direction; but the regional planner who in the meantime guides the flow of population issuing from the communities within his particular region will, like the engineer, be 'working at the sources' within his present range.

Again we maintain that the control of any kind of 'flow' — whether of water or of population — must take place at the source of the 'stream' rather than at its 'mouths.' This applies alike to the civil engineer and to the regional planner, but it applies only to the sources which lie within their particular art or technique. It does not apply to the sources which lie beyond and outside of such art or technique. The relation between the world-wide flow of water known as rainfall and the local flow within a single river system is similar to the relation between the world-wide 'flow' of population and the 'flow' within any single region. The relation in each case is between a general and a local flow. Control of the general flow is more fundamental, of course, than control of a local flow. But an effective local control, though not complete, should not be forsaken for the pursuit of a promised general control: the latter pursuit should be carried on and the art of man thus widened, but an art already developed should be utilised to the full measure of its range. Control of the world's rainfall and control of the world's birth rate should both be studied, but not to the neglect of developing the known possibilities of civil engineering and of regional planning. [...]

The job to do in each one of these developments is not to plan but to reveal — to seek the innate design of forces higher than our limited powers. [...] Planning is fundamentally revelation. Let us never forget this. The true planner is a seeker — a revealer: he must guard himself from dogma as he would from poison. This is a special admonition to the technical planner. And the best guard he can procure is the amateur planner. The point may be made that the technician unsupported by the people and a public consciousness is a head without a body, and that the public at large, unguided by technical advice, is a body without a head. The amateur in any line is a representative of the best thought of the public at large — he is the forerunner of the ultimate conviction of an advancing public opinion: for this reason he is the ally *par excellence* of the technician. Let the technical planner or 'revealer' ally himself closely with a body of amateur revealers: then shall we have a body with a head. We have just been referring to certain types of amateur revealers: [..]* let us make a closer canvas of these amateur assistants.

There is the amateur revealer of Mother Earth herself — of the earth's surface as carved and uplifted and carved again by the cosmic forces. This is the would-be geographer and geologist — the 'Little Humboldt,' if you please. There is the revealer of the earth's wild life, as it has evolved out of that 'indefinite past' of which Lincoln spoke. This is the student of natural history, the botanist, the ornithologist, and the others — the little 'Darwins' and 'Audubons.' The special province of these amateurs is the primeval environment; they stand high among the real users of the cabin and the trail: their field of activity and romance lies within sight of the camp fire.

There is the amateur revealer of the story of mankind — the past story and the future story. This is revealed to us in its human intimacy through the local history of a region's settlement, and in the general community life springing from such settlement. Here is the field of the local historian, the historical writer and dramatist, and the 'Egglestons' and 'Hawthornes' of the region. I refer not to mere delvers in the past. I refer to the seekers of that which 'belongs to the ages' and not to any special generation. Eggleston has preserved for us a chapter of American life, that of the Hoosier town. Hawthorne has given us, in *The Scarlet Letter* and *The House of the Seven Gables,* a picture of colonial New England; and Owen Wister, in his *Virginian,* has captured the primitive western utopia of the cow-puncher. Through each of these and through every other indigenous American story (whether captured or yet at large) there runs a stream of permanent American purpose (and world-purpose). The historian or dramatist whom I have in mind is the one who, like the authors just named, would aspire to reveal that 'stream' – he who would develop a portion, however tiny, of that stream's potential 'horse power' towards the upbuilding of a future world. Let us, to get down to a prosaic and utilitarian example, reveal and restore the colour and atmosphere of the old colonial mansion, built perhaps upon a cellar hole exuding tradition, and then, in our plans, install a modern bathroom. Let us, in short, combine the virtues of the ancient and permanent wih those of the modern and permanent. Thus may we keep abreast of the 'stream' and develop its full 'horse power.'

Next there is the revealer of the community's play life. I refer especially to the folk-play – the song and dance and the various outdoor sports going with the season and the time of day. Here is another vital opportunity for the would-be dramatist, and particularly the musician-dramatist. Here is a field of permanent rhythm and melody awaiting the hand of the 'little Wagner' or the coming of another Gilbert and Sullivan. Through the skillful tuning up of the strains latent in 'Lady Walpole's Reel' and 'Turkey in the Straw' there is opened a way toward a 'listening in' on what seems to be a portion of that basic symphony itself lying at the bottom of indigenous life and comradeship. Here is an outlet for youthful sensibilities which, when shorn of ancient Puritan inhibition, is charged sufficiently with its own intrinsic joy and healthful abandon to elude safely the short-circuiting indulgences of a metropolitan – and courtesan – environment.

The field of activity and romance belonging to the two last-named 'revealers' – to the 'embryonic Hawthornes' and to the 'little Wagners' – emanates from the village green. Its sphere of influence embraces the community as such, the unit of humanity with its starfish symmetry of structures and its latent symphonious human function of all-round social contact. Its special province is the communal environment.

There is no class of revealer that I known of whose special province is the urban environment The life of the true city is one of numerous specialties and groups. But there is a class of revealers whose province might be said to be the environment of the thing which can be described under the term of 'regional city.' These revealers consist of a class of what we can refer to as 'general appreciators' – those persons who, motivated usually by an artistic sense, instinctively seek a symmetric and symphonious setting both for the community and for the national life. They rank high in numbers, but thus far have not been integrated in any common movement. They are found in the ranks of such movements as those for establishing parks and forests, and for the eradication of city slums. They consist largely of fighters against specific evils, though for the most part they are not lacking in constructive sense. They are at bottom positive artists, not negative fighters. The particular value of such revealers with respect to our present problem would lie in their possible interest in the general framework of the regional city. This framework is in a sense the cement which binds the three elemental environments within a region. The heart of this framework lies in the inter-village highway, or 'intertown.' Here is an environment all its own — the wayside environment. The wayside is a cross-section of the countryside. And right here we have the special province of this class of would-be, or amateur, landscape-makers. Their special field of activity would come, not from the camp fire nor from the village green, but from the wayside.

There is one class of revealer whose field of activity emanates from all three environments — that of the camp fire, that of the village green, and that of the wayside. This is the artist proper, the landscape painter or even the amateur photographer. He brings the comprehensive notion to the eye as the musical artist brings it to the ear. Each of the revealers we have mentioned — naturalist, historian, dramatist, artist, is engaged in the imaging, on paper or canvas or other vicarious medium, of the vital forces, rhythms, and aspects of definite desirable environments. Could their efforts, properly mobilised and focused, achieve a revelation of these selfsame forces in a medium more vital and more real? This apparently was the query in the back of Thoreau's head when he pointed out the latent consummation which in these pages has been emphasised. He says:

> It is something to be able to paint a particular picture, or to carve a statue, and so to make a few objects beautiful; but it is far more glorious to carve and paint the very atmosphere and medium through which we look. . . . To affect the quality of the day, that is the highest of arts.

'The very atmosphere and medium through which we look.' Here is the common mind which we have called environment; it is the quality of the day: to affect it is the highest of arts. Such is the consummation awaiting the combined vision and sensibility of the various classes of 'revealers' we have mentioned. The art of the drama came about as a synthesis of the other arts. The art of developing environment, of 'living in the open,' of 'affecting the quality of the day,' seems by natural and inevitable steps to be forthcoming as another and greater synthesis.

Another name for art is culture. To this particular type of culture I have elsewhere adapted a term once used by Chauncey J. Hamlin of Buffalo, New York. His term is 'Outdoor Culture.'[2] Outdoor culture is the dramatisation of the countryside. But it is not so much an affecting of the countryside as of ourselves who are to live in it. After all, it is ourselves and not the land, whose happiness is affected. The way to get more fun and zest out of playing and living within our native land and field is the same way as to get more fun out of playing on the football field: it is to know the game better — to know the art better. In developing ourselves in the man-to-man contact of football, we develop the whole environment of virile athletic sport in developing ourselves in other tangible contact — by the camp fire, in the village gathering, and along the wayside — we develop other tangible environments whose combined power constitutes the day itself. In this wise, in developing ourself to demand the best in life, we build the kind of world that the human mind ultimately seeks.

Lewis Mumford [...] has pointed out to us two distinct type of utopia: the utopia of escape and the utopia of reconstruction. Here is our choice: between the make-believe and the real. Shall we go to the play and for the time being become a big vicarious Cyrano and let it go at that; or shall we, in addition, capture the spirit of our hero and resolve to become real, if diminutive, Cyranos? Our job in the new exploration is nothing short of making a utopia of reconstruction - the remodelling of an unshapen and cacophonous environment into a humanised and well-ordered one. This is something which the technical planner cannot do alone: he requires the close alliance of the amateur revealer of life's setting, and above all of human life itself. To remodel our house properly, we must live in it. To remodel 'the open,' we must learn the art of 'living in the open.' This art is in the making. It is the coming synthetic art — call it outdoor culture or what you will — which, from camp fire and village and wayside, is now radiating its vital influence and beginning to find itself. And so we begin to realise Thoreau's dream and prophecy, and to take part each in our humble path in affecting the quality itself of our common mind and day.

Notes

[1]   Reported in *The Boston Herald*, 6 July 1927.
[2]   Hamlin coined this term at a meeting in 1925, in Washington, of the President's Conference on Outdoor Recreation.

2 The economics and politics of the regions

D. Donnison, 'The Economics and Politics of the Regions', *The Political Quarterly*, April-May 1974, pp.179-89.

For many years British regional policies were essentially economic, producing few political innovations. More is now heard of political regionalism, but its ideas lack firm economic foundations. We should try to reconnect discussion of these two aspects of Britain's problems by asking what regional policies are for and what political institutions we need for these purposes.

What are we trying to achieve?

During the last century, social reformers like Charles Booth — and before him, Thomas Chalmers — were concerned about small, inner urban areas and the problems of public health, poverty and disorder which afflicted the communities living in them. Such policies as the country had for particular areas were generally directed to neighbourhoods of this kind. Things were transformed by the decline of Britain's basic industries which set in about the turn of the century. The tide of migrations which had drawn people to the centres of these older industries turned. Areas like South Wales which had steadily gained migrants for years,[1] began to suffer continuing decay and its social repercussions were high among the priorities of every British Government.

Regional policies to help these much larger 'depressed areas' were a central feature of the broad consensus on which the postwar town and country planning legislation of the 1940s was launched. Other members of this loosely organised coalition were spokesmen of the public health movement originating in the nineteenth century, the conservationists, the Labour movement with its memories of the hunger marchers, and those concerned about congestion in the growing conurbations or about the target offered to bombers by the concentration of productive capacity in the South Eastern corner of the country. All of them agreed that the sprawling growth of the wealthiest regions must be reined in, and that the industries of the depressed regions must be revived and diversified and their old cities renewed. Regional policies were strongly industrial and physical, calling first for new jobs and new houses.

To these concerns were added, by the early 1960s, growing anxiety about economic stagnation and Britain's failure to keep pace with her continental neighbours. When Labour was returned to power in 1964 with the crucial support of Scottish, Welsh and North English votes, regional policies were expected to play a central part in the programme that would enable Britain to escape from the cycle of 'stop-go-stop' — a cycle that was itself due to the recurring need to halt expansion whenever full employment began to overheat the economy by driving up wages in the prosperous midland and south-east regions. The problems of the depressed and the prosperous regions came to be regarded as opposite symptoms of the same fundamental disorders.

Next it looked as if this essentially economic formulation of regional problems was to be given a more explicitly political dimension. The tentative political innovation of setting up nominated regional advisory planning councils in 1975 was carried further when the Crowther (later Kilbrandon) Commission was appointed in 1969 to consider the possibility of bolder constitutional changes. When it reported four years later the Commission was still doubtful about the strength and the significance of regional patriotism.[2] With the Scottish National Party capturing a Labour stronghold a few weeks later it was clear that such loyalties were not a negligible force. But although revolts of this kind may be expressed in nationalist forms, they may be due to more deeply rooted economic and social grievances. The Royal Commission implicitly acknowledged this possibility when reporting on its own research. In the course of hour-long interviews with the public about dissatisfaction with government 'the only specific "solution" put to those being interviewed was some kind of devolution. . . . It must be recognised, however, that if a person is dissatisfied, and he is presented with only one suggested remedy, then he may be expected to take a generally favourable view of that remedy, whatever it is, even if he has given no previous thought to it.'[3] Despite these doubts the Commissioners went on to recommend bold (though diverse and conflicting) devolutions of power to regional assemblies of various kinds.

Regional policies in Britain are predominantly economic. They are designed, as they always have been, to reduce the differentially high rates of unemployment in the ailing regions — both for the sake of these regions, and for the sake of the general development of the whole economy. Only in Northern Ireland (and there only since 1968) have Westminster's policies been directed primarily to civil rights, power sharing, public order and other essentially political questions.[4]

Strategies for the future

We have achieved considerable success in bringing work to the poorer regions and promoting new industry there. In many respects South Wales, Yorkshire and Humberside, and more recently the Scottish Highlands, have begun to catch up with the rest of the country. Ulster was doing well too, till 1968. Even to prevent further decline of areas depending so heavily on declining industries and on agriculture might be acclaimed a success. But we pay a continuing price for these achievements, for we have failed to generate the self-sustaining growth which would enable the central government to wind down its regional policies. That does not mean these policies are merely a drag upon the economy: they benefit the prosperous regions too, by maintaining demand for their products while reducing competition for their congested land. Nevertheless regional policies have failed to attain their ultimate objectives. What more must we do?

It is not enough to give people more and better jobs in an expanding economy. We must attend to the whole, complex, social and economic 'mesh' of the society they live in. The human race can survive incredible hardships, but it tolerates very little disappointment: indeed it is a mark of the intelligent that they switch, quicker than most, from activities which are unsatisfying to those which seem likely to be more satisfying. That means we must try to ensure that more rewarding opportunities are within easy reach — financially, spatially and culturally speaking. The rungs in the ladder, to adopt a metaphor, must be close together without major discontinuities between them. Moreover, each ladder of opportunities must be sustained by others in neighbouring sectors of the economy. These points can be illustrated in a homely fashion. Why should we expect children to sacrifice opportunities for earning in order to stay on at school and continue their education unless they are convinced by the experience of their families, friends and neighbours, that by so doing they can get better jobs? And why should young people do the extra work, take the extra training and assume the extra responsibilities which bring promotion unless they believe this will open up new opportunities and earn them more money? And why should they bother to earn more unless they can see — again within easy reach — better houses and other goods and services which they want to buy for their families? Often people do achieve these things despite adverse circumstances; but the achievement must have been harder and rarer than it need have been.

If this over-simplified psychology is fundamentally sound, it suggests that we must beware of discontinuities, where the rungs of a ladder are missing or lead nowhere, and disjunctions, where neighbouring ladders are not available to provide mutually supporting opportunities. The poorer regions appear to have more than their share of these discontinuities and disjunctions owing to long term changes in the pace and direction of their economic and social development. Too often these have been exacerbated by clumsy public intervention in the region's affairs.

Where are the lowest council rents, and where — after the South-East — are the most expensive owner-occupied houses? Both are generally to be found in Scotland. There the middle rungs of the housing market are often missing, making it unusually difficult for people to secure a better or more conveniently located house. This pattern must reduce incentives to earn the money which could secure a better home and must encourage enterprising people to go elsewhere — and it is partly due to the Government's policies.

Where is the highest educational attainment to be found — the largest proportions of seventeen-year-olds still in school, and the largest proportions securing 'A' level successes and moving on to higher education? Wales usually comes at or near the top of these lists. In this case the ladder works well, but neighbouring ladders are often missing: there are too few jobs for well-qualified young people and too few houses of the sort they later want to buy. Thus the most able often

36

have to leave the region, or remain there as underemployed workers and housewives. Meanwhile, people who do want to set up new industries in underemployed regions may be deterred from doing so by other disjunctions such as the lack of skilled workers, managerial talent, sub-contractors, merchant banks and risk-taking lenders.

Too often regional policies have tended to exacerbate these disjunctions and discontinuities, rather than to diversify and enrich the economy. Aluminium smelters, steel works and oil refineries − the typical show-pieces of such policies - employ very few people in relation to the capital invested in them or the subsidy they attract from the taxpayer. At Hunterston, in Scotland, planning permission is being sought for a refinery which might employ 400 people. It will cost about £150m., of which £30m. will come from the Exchequer − amounting to £75,000 per job.[5] Often these workers turn out either to be semi-skilled, with few opportunities for promotion, or highly qualified outsiders with few roots in the area. Anglesey's aluminium smelter presents the same picture. Thus regional policies add new discontinuities to those already afflicting such areas. Meanwhile the arrival of these monster plants often discourages tourism and halts the development of holiday and retirement cottages which are built, provisioned and repaired by local people in small local firms.

This analysis suggests it is not enough for government to provide the infrastructure of roads and public services and large subsidies for capital investment in the ailing regions. These regions also need more skilled work, more labour-intensive enterprise, more service industries (including tourist services), more training, and more opportunities for managerial, technical and professional work. They should rely less on costly subsidies for capital-intensive manufacturing industries unless they offer opportunities of this sort for local people, and they should be cautious about recruiting branch plants unless they bring managers and headquarters staff with them.

There is nothing new about these ideas. Many politicians and their advisers are well aware of the inadequacy of current strategies. They probably know that manufacturing industry employs a declining proportion of the labour force in advanced economies, and thus offers less leverage as an instrument of regional policies. They know, too, that some of the country's biggest employers who set up new works in under-employed regions during the past decade had their fingers burnt and are reluctant to repeat the experience, while others have been tempted to leave once the temporary advantages conferred by generous depreciation allowances are exhausted. Recent research shows that even when such enterprises succeed, their multiplier effects often 'leak' to the more prosperous regions, and generate little further local growth. These are now the common-places of debate about regional economics. But they seem unfamiliar to those concerned with regional politics who are engaged in an entirely different debate.

The Kilbrandon Commission's Report and its accompanying Memorandum of Dissent say very little about the economic and social structure of the regions or the opportunities they offer to their people. 'The defects to be remedied', according to the majority, are 'centralisation' 'the weakening of democracy', and the failure to recognise 'national feeling.'[6] The minority tell the same story:

> The essential objectives of any scheme of constitutional reform must be:
> (a) to reduce the present excessive burdens on the institutions of central government;
> (b) to increase the influence on decision-making of the elected representatives of the people;
> (c) to provide the people generally with more scope for sharing in, and influencing, governmental decision-making at all levels;
> (d) to provide adequate means for the redress of individual grievances.[7]

This is a middle-class, rather donnish formulation of regional problems. The questions posed are important enough, but anyone who has seen Govan, in Glasgow, the seat which a Scottish nationalist has just captured from Labour, can envisage more pressing and practical deprivations which are likely to motivate its electors; and those electors are not so naïve as to believe that 'the redress of grievances' can be brought about by reducing the 'burdens on ... central government' – quite the contrary. Their grievances about unemployment, bad housing, poverty and the politicians who fail to remedy these things, could be explained without references to 'national feeling', and may not be satisfied by wholesale devolution of powers to regional assemblies.

Institutions

Some will conclude that the Commissioners' proposals are a colossal *non sequitur*. But that should not obscure the need for a more relevant reorganisation of regional government. I do not have solutions to offer – only a few suggestions which may point us in the right direction. We need regional authorities capable of gathering and relating information about the different 'ladders of opportunity', and monitoring the economic and social development of their territory. For a start, the boundaries of existing regional authorities – for Health, Employment, Education, Police, Social Security and other services – should be reconciled. The officials responsible for them cannot talk to each other till they are talking about the same people in the same areas. Related to this administrative system we need political assemblies capable of providing a forum for debate about trends and policies in these and other fields. That will call for stronger regional offices of central government, more representative planning councils, and some further devolution of powers to both; but it would fall a long way short of the wholesale, legislative devolution to 'democratic assemblies' throughout the country – each with their own civil service, law-making and taxing powers – which some of the Kilbrandon Commissioners call for.

We have to consider whether this country has room for another layer of government; and if so, where it should be fitted in. Britain is similar in size and output to the State of California. Its population is about twice the size of California's, but has less ethnic, linguistic and cultural diversity. Britain's industrial, commercial cultural and political life is centred on one urban region, California's on two – neither of which is the State's political capital. In comparison with California and many other places, Britain already has strong central and local government. The latter is currently being recast to produce fewer and stronger units to which more powers are to be devolved from the centre. (That, at any rate, has been the continuing theme of more than fifteen years of debate about this reorganisation, and of the Government's case for the current reforms.) There is scarcely room for another tier between the two.

Meanwhile, an increasingly vigorous under-layer of 'micro-politics' has been developing in this country. Repeated studies[8] have shown that local loyalties tend to focus most intensely on small areas, often of about 5,000 to 20,000 people. It is this sort of localism which has helped to create the neighbourhood councils, community action projects, legal advice centres, tenants' associations, amenity societies and local pressure groups concerned with civil rights, education, conservation and many other matters. Meanwhile, it is often forgotten that within the conventional system of local government it is the parish councils – the smallest units of all – which have been expanding their activities most rapidly over recent years.[9] We are witnessing, in new forms, a revival of spatially oriented programmes dealing with areas similar in their small scale to those which concerned Charles Booth and his nineteenth-century contemporaries.[10]

To justify the insertion of a new layer of regional authorities into this system, it must be shown that government has to deal with quite a lot of problems which are important enough to retain the attention of good politicians, which should be considered together, not in separate agencies, which are too large in scale to be given to the enlarged local authorities of the future, and too small in scale to require decision by the central government. In Northern Ireland there would be an unanswerable case for strong regional government (quite apart from the arguments derived from current conflicts) because local government has been virtually destroyed. Ulster's new district authorities have practically no powers over housing, education, social services, police or any of the other things which make local government in Britain a reality. Without an effective regional government there would be no means of co-ordinating these powers or formulating policies for the development of the province.

But how about Britain? Decisions to open a major new museum, a nature reserve, a large sports centre or a hypermarket might fall into the category we are looking for – too large for a local authority but too small for central government. But are they important enough to recruit good politicians – a very scarce resource? If we turn to consider decisions such as the closure of a major pit or shipyard, a twenty-mile extension of a motorway, or the founding of a new university or teaching hospital (which are regarded as more important) it is clear that they would benefit from better evidence about regional needs and from debate in a more effective regional assembly. But could that assembly decide such questions? If spokesmen of the major interests at stake (such as the National Union of Mineworkers, Vickers, the University Grants Committee, or the Association of Municipal Corporations — all with their headquarters in London) were aggrieved at the outcome, each could secure an interview with the relevant Minister within a week, no matter how formidable a layer of regional government was interpolated below him — and that is not because people enjoy talking to Ministers, but because the resources of money and power required to implement decisions of this kind come from the centre. And no one insists more vociferously that the national taxpayer and his government should continue to provide these resources than the spokesmen of the most deprived regions.

The Kilbrandon Commissioners aim to cull the powers of a strengthened regional government from the centre. That would pose dilemmas for anyone attempting to equalise opportunities among the regions. For egalitarian policies call for a redistribution of resources that benefits the regions which need help most, and that implies restriction of growth in the more prosperous regions, at least in the short term. Thus the central government would not in practice give much autonomy to assemblies in the more prosperous regions which used their powers to grab more growth for themselves. Neither would the electors take much interest in — or long re-elect — politicians who consistently subordinated their interests to those of voters in other regions. The majority of the Kilbrandon Commission recognise this dilemma, and propose a legislative devolution of powers only for Scotland and Wales. There the dilemma is resolved — for vigorous advocacy benefits the poorer regions. I will return the to economic implications of Celtic regionalism in a moment. But first we should briefly consider England, which has different regional problems.

Current trends in employment, transport and the location of jobs and housing are creating, over much of England, a continuous, low density urban system linked by a network of predominantly car-born communications between homes, work, shopping, education, recreation and other activities. The urban patterns now taking shape here may be less 'regional' in the old-fashioned sense. People no longer look to a regional capital for so many of the goods and services they need: they travel longer distances, and in different directions for different purposes. The centres of some of the biggest cities — London, Manchester and Liverpool, for example — are being deserted by industry and people at such a rate that some planners fear it will become increasingly difficult to rescue them from urban decay, municipal impoverishment and social disorder. It is much too soon to say that this American-style 'crisis of the cities' is upon us, but such dangers are not to be dismissed.

Such problems must be tackled on a regional scale because their solution calls for policies for the location and mix of employment, the building and allocation of housing and the development of public and private transport which expand beyond the territory, powers and resources of local government. But the problems to be resolved arise partly from conflicts between the interests of city and surburban authorities. Thus they will frequently call for final decision by the central government. This amounts once again to a case for institutions capable of gathering and analysing regional data, formulating regional plans and creating a forum in which they can be debated — possibly a strengthening of the regional institutions we already have — but not the creation of new, autonomous regional authorities.

If steps are taken to strengthen regional government, at least in Scotland and Wales, will they make it easier or harder to enrich and diversify the opportunities which life offers to people in the more deprived regions? To achieve that we may need development agencies, armed with a budget and powers to act, and working in collaboration with central governments, the nationalised industries and local authorities. (The Highlands and Islands Development Board was an early attempt to create such an agency.) They should be staffed by people with a flair for picking and backing entrepreneurs in the public and the private sector. Such agencies need regional focal points for the inter-change of information and the formulation of plans, but it does not follow that they must be all crammed into a regional mould. Some will deal with parts of a region such as the Highlands and Islands or particular centres of growth or redevelopment such as the London Docks. Others may deal with particular industries, such as tourism, on a nationwide basis. Their relationship to the political system is vital, but delicate — and it is to that I must now turn.

The successful development agency is innovative rather than defensive, seeking new talents and fostering new enterprises, wherever they are to be found. It selects, discriminates and backs success rather than failure. Elected authorities do not do these things well. Politicians are necessarily and properly obliged to look after the largest and most vulnerable groups in their constituencies, which in failing economies means the long-established failing industries and communities — very conservative interests in many ways. Politicians have to be chauvinistic, preferring their own people to newcomers and outsiders. They should give priority to the poorest groups — and will, if these groups are large enough to count, electorally. They tend to spread resources thinly to please the maximum number of voters, and allocate them according to rather rigid, publicly defensible rules. All of that is good politics, but very bad development policy. In the ailing regions of the United Kingdom it tends to be one-party politics too, for opposition is weak in these areas. That makes things worse still. In Northern Ireland fifty years of one-party government ultimately provoked conflicts which destroyed, along with much else, all the gains that economic planners were beginning to achieve. It is dangerous rhetoric to advocate the devolution of powers to Scottish and Welsh legislatures, in which opposition is likely to be even weaker than it was at Stormont, as a means 'to enlarge democratic accountability'.[11]

This argument, I appreciate, sounds undemocratic. Our dilemma is that the institutions needed for regional policies must be publicly accountable because they will have to wield too much money and power to survive for long if they are not; yet the regional and national assemblies to which they should account must be no more than vigilant shareholders — prepared to withdraw their support if progress towards the general objectives of enlarging and diversifying opportunities is not made. Progress is unlikely to be made if regional development becomes the direct responsibility of elected assemblies, or if it is not constantly supported by central government.

41

Conclusion

As this country develops its regional institutions and devolves more power to them we must not lose sight of the complex human realities of regional development. Hitherto, Britain's regional policies have been directed to simple but pressing needs – particularly for work and wages. In future we shall require more discriminating policies, based on a wider understanding of the social and economic processes which enlarge or restrict people's opportunities. Those policies cannot be sustained unless they gain wise political support. They will not get it from wholesale devolution of powers to a countrywide system of competing regional assemblies, often dominated by one party. Between regions, that would provoke conflict, strengthening the hands of the most prosperous and making it harder for the poorest to secure the help they need. Within regions, it would strengthen the hands of all the most defensive conservative forces and make innovation and the expansion of opportunities harder than ever.

Notes

[1]   D. Friedlander and R. J. Roshier, 'Internal Migration in England and Wales 1851 to 1951', *Population Studies,* vol. XIX and XX, March and July 1966.

[2]   Royal Commission on the Constitution, 1969-73, vol. I Report; vol. II, *Memorandum of Dissent,* Cmnd. 5460 and 5460-1 1973.

[3]   Cmnd. 5460, para. 268.

[4]   For fuller accounts of the development of regional policies in Britain see Gavin McCrone, *Regional Policy in Britain,* Allen & Unwin 1969; and Harry W. Richardson, *Elements of Regional Economics,* Penguin Books 1969.

[5]   The example is Professor Donald Mackay's *A New Approach to Regional Policy,* Poland Street Paper, no. 1, 1973 (PEST; 9 Poland Street, W.1).

[6]   Report, chap. 23

[7]   *Memorandum of Dissent,* p. xiv.

[8]   John Baker and Michael Young, *The Hornsey Plan,* The Association for Neighbourhood Councils (18 Victoria Park Square, E.2), 1971; *Report of the Royal Commission on Local Government in England, 1966-69,* Cmnd. 4040, vol. III, App. 7; F.W. Boal, 'Territoriality on the Shankill Falls Divide, Belfast', Irish Geography, vol. VI, no. I, 1969, p.30.

[9]   *Report of the Royal Commission on Local Government in England, 1969,* Cmnd. 4040, vol. III, App. 8.

[10]   For a fuller discussion of these developments, see 'Micropolitics of the City', in David Donnison and David Eversley (ed.), *London: Urban Patterns, Problems and Policies,* Heinemann, 1973.

[11]   Cmnd. 5460, para 122.

An earlier version of this paper has been published in Morgan Sant (ed), *Regional Policy and Planning for Europe,* Saxon House, Farnborough, 1974.

PART II

PROBLEMS IN REGIONAL PLANNING

Overview of Part II

The three selected writings which follow this introduction and overview are by R. Rhodes (1974, Chapter 3), Peter Self (1964, Chapter 4) and the Rowntree Research Unit, University of Durham (1974, Chapter 5). The Rhodes paper is concerned with the problems associated with the political administration of regional planning — or rather with an evaluation of the problems of alternative competing models, proposed and in existence, for administration at the regional level of government.

Peter Self's original contribution, although published more than a decade ago, remains one of the most important essays yet written on the problems of regional planning. It is important for at least two reasons: for the insights it offers into the clarification of many of the contradictions and ambiguities which so characterise regional planning, and for the codification it offers — the dualism of regional planning as *national-regional* and *regional-local* planning. This dualism is now firmly embedded in many, but by no means all, of the contemporary accounts concerned with the problem of what regional planning is and what it is not.

Where Self concentrates on the overt political and administrative context, the Rowntree Research Unit have attempted to get beneath such formality. Their focus of attention is the North-East of England, and combines an outline of the historical development of 'regional politics' with a conceptual model which attempts to account for the rise of such a creature. Their argument suggests that localised social and political issues have in many instances been covertly 'regionalised' to defuse and ultimately depoliticise them.

3 Regional policy and a 'Europe of Regions'

Modified from R. Rhodes, 'Regional Policy and a "Europe of Regions" : A Critical Assessment', *Journal of Regional Studies*, vol. 8, no.2, 1974. pp. 105–14.

Introduction

The subject of regionalism places almost impossible strains on the flexibility of the English language. This one word is used to cover such diverse subject areas as national economic planning, political devolution, administrative deconcentration, and local government reform. As a result there is considerable confusion surrounding the subject. The purpose of this paper is ostensibly a simple one – to explore the semantic confusion and to make a number of suggestions which will enable the topic to be discussed more precisely. And some clarity is essential because a number of policies of key importance are about to emerge from the European Community (EC). Foremost amongst these is the EC's regional policy and the attendant suggestion for a 'Europe of Regions'. What is this 'Regional Policy'? What is the 'Europe of Regions'?

In order to answer these questions my attention cannot be focused exclusively on the supra-national level. In Britain local government has been reformed and the Kilbrandon Commission on the Constitution has reported. Both of these developments will affect any European initiatives on regionalism. Nor is Britain the only country making such changes. For example, France has a long history of regional experimentation. It is important, therefore, to ask what is meant by 'regionalism' in the various member states of the European Community and what is the significance of such variations in meaning for the proposed 'regional policy' and the 'Europe of Regions'. By examining these variations and suggesting some clarifications in terminology, I will be able to critically examine the recent policy proposals and identify some key weaknesses.

Towards a 'Europe of Regions'

The proposed regional policy of the EC and the concept of a 'Europe of Regions' are discrete policies with only the former being EC official policy. But both ideas are intertwined in a number of ways. As a first step, I will describe their main features before turning to examine their inter-relationships.

The final communiqué of the Conference of Heads of State or Government held in Paris in October 1972 stated that:

> The Heads of State or Government agreed that a high priority should be given to the aim of correcting, in the Community, the structural and regional im-

balances which might affect the realization of Economic and Monetary Union.

The Commission was invited, as a result, to prepare a report analysing the EC's regional problem and to create a Regional Development Fund by 31 December 1973. In May 1973, the Commission produced its *Report on the Regional Problems in the Enlarged Community* (Thompson Report) (Commission of the European Communities, 1973). [1]

The Report delineates the moral, environmental and economic case for a Community regional policy, provides statistical material for identifying regional disequilibria, and lays down a number of guidelines for a Community regional policy. Chief amongst these guidelines is the recognition that EC policy cannot be a substitute for national regional policies. Finally, the Report discusses the establishment of a Regional Development Committee and the mechanism of the Regional Development Fund.

There are two points to be made about this policy. First and foremost it must be emphasised that the EC is talking about regional economic policy — about measures to reduce disparities in the economic prosperity of regions within the Community. Moreover, in proposing such measures, national regional economic policy remains paramount. Second, it should be clearly appreciated that the development of the EC's regional economic policy is a prime goal of British government policy. British membership involves substantial costs to her balance of payments because of the Common Agricultural Policy (CAP). The development of a regional policy is seen as an important means of offsetting these costs. The concept of a 'Europe of Regions' is considerably more nebulous and, at the same time, more emotive. The flavour of the idea is captured in the following quotations:

> A shift of authority away from the nation state both upwards and downwards would be the best way of combining the technological needs for larger units with the human demand for smaller ones. (Brittan, 1972).
> For so many modern purposes, the nation is either too big or too small. For technological industries, for defence, for transport, for energy, it is too small. For welfare, for cultural loyalties, or for any real sense of belonging it is too big ... it is a dream of many Europeans that the continent may be retreating to a medieval pattern. (Sampson, 1968, pp. 430.)
> An extended regionalism may indeed provide the key that unlocks the door to further European integration. (Banks, 1971, p.287.)

It should not be thought that the idea has no serious support. Ernest Wistrich, Director of the European Movement, has advocated ' ... maximum devolution to those levels of government which are closest to the citizens ... ' (Wistrich, 1973, p.31).

And the Liberal Party has supported ' ... the development of direct links between regional authorities and the Community ... ' (Liberal Party, 1973).

Similarly, Jean Monnet's Union of European Federalists have urged that 'from the smallest village up to the federal government, all matters in a federal constitution ... that can be adequately settled by a lower tier of government must be settled at that level.' (European Federalists, 1972.)

Finally, a number of regional politicians, for example from Scotland and Bavaria, have expressed interest in a special direct relationship with the Community and they have received a sympathetic hearing from the Commission.

Moreover, there are echoes of these ideas in the Commission's pronouncements. The Thompson Report recognises the cultural aspects of regionalism when it talks of the 'moral basis' of regionalism; of 'sustaining local communities' and of 'historical and cultural values which are the moral wealth of each region'. But, the idea of a 'Europe of Regions' is only implicit in the report. It is not developed or even clearly articulated.

There is, however, a stronger link between the two ideas than the Thompson Report's implicit recognition of the moral basis of regionalism. Although no firm proposals have been put forward, the manner in which the EC's regional policy will be administered has been under discussion (IULA, 1973). There are some obvious advantages in having the administrative machinery for the policy as near to the point of implementation as possible. Central governments are by no means the sole repository of information about the regions. Administering the policy at a regional level carries the possible advantages of more direct access to better quality local information and greater capacity to adapt to local circumstances. The development of regional machinery to implement the EC's regional policy has strong *prima facie* affinities to the idea of a 'Europe of Regions'.

But, the description to this point has been without a framework. I have offered no definition of regionalism. Nor have I critically discussed the ideas described. I turn to the question of what is 'regionalism' in the next section with a brief survey of what is meant by regionalism in Britain. But, one point should be clear at this juncture. Future policies of the EC make the discussion of regionalism of key importance. Clarity in the use of the concept is clearly essential if these policies are to be carefully evaluated – and careful evaluation is essential given the probable importance of EC regional policy not only for Britain, but for all EC member states.

Regionalism in Britain

Regionalism in Britain has a long history (Smith, 1964; Thornhill, 1972) and I do not propose to give a synopsis of it in this paper. I have one, relatively simple, objective – to delineate the various uses of the term 'regionalism' in Britain. But, in order to classify the uses of the term, it is essential, as a first step, to specify the bases of classification. I want to suggest that the term regionalism differs in terms of:

(a) the objectives regionalism is intended to serve; and
(b) the number of functions it encompasses.

The rest of this section attempts to justify this basis of classification.

In Britain, it is possible to distinguish four objectives underlying regionalism:

(a) the administrative deconcentration of the departments of central government [2]
(b) the regionalisation of national economic planning;
(c) the reform of local government;
(d) the recognition of cultural nationalism.

In this ranking, the concept of regionalism becomes increasingly complex. Thus for (a), administrative deconcentration, there is a single objective and usually only one function is involved; whereas for (d), cultural nationalism, a number of objectives and a wide range of functions are involved. Moreover, at each level the problems of regionalism become more complex. I now consider each of these objectives in more detail.

Regionalism in the form of administrative deconcentration has a long history in Britain (Smith, 1964) and it is still a feature of the organisation of most central government departments (for examples see Cross, 1970). Because only one function is involved and because the main objective is administrative convenience the definition of a region is a relatively easy task.

The regionalisation of national economic planning requires more extensive discussion. As before, it is primarily an extension of the functions of central government but the problems surrounding the definition of a region are more complex. The basic question centres on the areal distribution of economic prosperity within the country. Which areas are economically disadvantaged? Which areas should be economically developed? As McCrone has pointed out, 'Many of the most important decisions of regional planning involve choosing between regions' (McCrone, 1969, p. 243). These are deceptively simple questions which often involve difficult political decisions about the allocation of national resources. But ignoring this particular aspect, a second question must be faced — should only economic criteria be employed to define the regions? Clearly any economic action has social repercussions and the underlying motives of regional economic planning involve the idea of social, as well as economic, justice. In addition, the term 'economic planning' is a broad one encompassing a number of more specific functions (e.g. agriculture, industrial location). These have to be coordinated for effective planning, and yet they have separate administrative arrangements. In other words, the attempt to define a region, when the key objective is the re-distribution of national resources to promote economic development on an areal basis, is a difficult task because the objective is a complex one — involving social as well as economic goals — and it requires the coordination of a number of governmental functions.

The regionalism which aims at the reform of local government is different in kind from the two forms discussed so far. It is not an extension of the functions of central government but an attempt to strengthen another unit of government. For many years local government has been criticised because, it was argued, there were too many authorities with limited resources. One solution, it was suggested, was to increase the size of local authorities by replacing them with a small number of large regions. A variant of this argument focused on land use planning which it was argued required large areas to be effectively carried out. But this was just a particular aspect of a more general problem.

Regional reform of local government raises a number of problems. The basic question to be answered is what can be achieved in terms of economy and efficiency by creating large new authorities? This in turn raises the question of why does a particular service require a larger administrative area? But, how large should that area be? Will that area be suitable for all services? The basic problem centres on the fact that the larger the number of functions the more intractable the problem of defining regional boundaries. Moreover the objective of strengthening a unit of government below that of the central government is a complex one.

This point will become very apparent if I now turn to examine regionalism as a means of giving governmental expression to cultural nationalism.

Regionalism as cultural nationalism is not simply concerned with economic development, administrative convenience or even local government reform. It encompasses all of these and also aims to give expression to an identifiable homogeneous sociological/demographic/cultural area (Mackintosh, 1968). In other words, the objective is an extremely complex one. To the extent that an area is homogeneous the problem is not intractable (e.g. Scotland). But for heterogeneous areas such as England, defining the boundaries becomes highly arbitrary. In the context of reforming local government, the concept of the 'city region' (Senior, 1965) has been influential because it is one means of de-limiting boundaries which recognises an area's demographic/sociological characteristics. For large areas of the country, however, such city regions are difficult to identify.

With complex objectives and large numbers of functions the criteria for defining regions become not only greater in number but they also become mutually contradictory. For example the demographic considerations may not give areas particularly suited to the efficient administration of services. But, apart from these problems, there is an even greater difficulty to be surmounted. Any comprehensive regional reform will create a strong intermediate unit of government. Or, to state this problem slightly differently, regionalism which attempts to give governmental expression to cultural nationalism necessarily aims to redistribute political power from the centre to the regions.

The popularity of regionalism as regional economic planning and as a form of administrative deconcentration can be attributed to the fact that they do not involve any question of altering the areal distribution of powers (ADP) [3] (Maass, 1959). Regionalism as local government reform involves strengthening existing units of government. Regionalism as cultural nationalism involves creating a new unit of government. A common approach to regionalism is to identify two major problem areas, namely the definition of areas and the form of regional machinery. The former I have touched upon already. I would like to suggest that although it poses a problem, it is by no means the major one. Nor is the form of regional machinery a problem — it is a symptom. The prime problem in the discussion of regionalism is not what are the boundaries of the regions or what form of regional machinery but what is the desirable areal distribution of powers?

50

At this juncture it will be helpful to turn to examine the recent reorganisation of local government because it illustrates the central importance of the ADP. In an earlier paper (Rhodes, 1974) I have discussed already the defects of the reorganised local government structure. I do not propose to cover this ground again. But it is important to look at the Royal Commission's analysis of the defects of local government. There is one crucial omission. Although it was specifically excluded from the Commission's terms of reference: 'The primary issue is still how much real devolution of power will be conceded.' (Mackintosh, 1970, p. 55.)

In particular, it is crucial to examine the division of functions between central and local government. No assurance that the government wants a strong system of local democracy [4] can be plausible, when, on the one hand functions are removed from local government (e.g. personal health services, water supply) and, on the other, there is no analysis of the appropriate division of functions between central and local government. Strong local government is a government with a wide range of responsibilities.[5] Any attempt to strengthen local government must examine the nature of its responsibilities. Any thorough-going analysis of this question must, logically, cover the distribution of functions between centre and locality. No proposals for the reform of local government which leave this particular question waiting in limbo can be adequate.

The irony of the situation stems from the recognition of the importance of this question by the appointment of the Kilbrandon Commission on the Constitution. But local government was reorganised on 1 April 1974, and although the Kilbrandon Commission (Royal Commission on the Constitution, 1973) recommended some measure of regional devolution, its proposals were too late (this point is developed in Rhodes, 1973b). Local government has been reorganised without the central issue ever emerging to real prominence.

This state of affairs seems likely to affect the prospects of Kilbrandon's recommendations. Any new regional tier will have to carry out functions it inherits from somewhere. It will be as much a nonsense to create a regional tier without examining the division of functions between region and locality as it was to reorganise local government without examining the distribution of functions between centre and locality. And, although the reorganisation of local government may be a decisive step backwards, it is highly improbable, now it has been reorganised, that all will be thrown into the melting pot in a further reorganisation following on the publication of the Kilbrandon Report. In other words, the ADP is central to both local government reform and the discussion of regionalism as a means of giving governmental expression to cultural nationalism. But, in spite of its importance, it has been peripheral to the debate about local government reform and as a result the possibility of regional reform is diminished.

A number of conclusions can be drawn from this survey of the regionalism in Britain:

(a) The objectives and functions of regionalism differ greatly.
(b) A region can only be defined after the objectives have been specified because the objectives determine the criteria for drawing the boundaries.

(c) The more comprehensive the concept of a region, i.e. multi-functional/ multiple objectives, the greater the problems of definition.

(d) Comprehensive forms of regionalism presuppose decisions about the desired ADP within the particular political system.

Regionalism in Europe

The discussion of regionalism in Britain has revealed some of the complexity surrounding the subject. But this complexity could be a characteristic found only in Britain It is relevant at this stage to broaden the scope of the discussion and examine the various uses of the term regionalism amongst our EC partners To what extent is the complexity found in the UK repeated in the EC? To what extent is the ADP a feature in the European debate about regionalism?

One problem facing any writer attempting to survey the forms of regional government and regional administration in Europe is the patchy nature of the information. There has been one valuable survey however, carried out by Dr. E. Kalk on behalf of the International Union of Local Authorities. I draw heavily on his work for the information in this section (Kalk, 1971. See also Leemans, 1970; Council of Europe, 1972).

Kalk defines a region as any level of government between local (lowest general purpose) level of government and federal/central level of government. The various forms of regionalism are classified by the level of government (local, intermediate, central-regional, and local regional) and by purpose (planning, planning and other (few) purposes, general purposes). These two bases are combined to give:

Table 3.1 Forms of regionalism in the European Community*

---

1 Local general purpose level of government†
2 Local-regional level of government
  (a) Planning.

      Belgium (Fédération des communes), Germany (Associations in urban areas), Italy (piani intercommunal), Netherlands (Jt. Authority for the Eindhoven Conurbation).

  (b) Planning and other purposes:

      France (Communautés Urbaines), Netherlands (The Rijmond Authority).
  (c) General purposes.

3 Intermediate general purpose level of government

  Belgium (provinces) Denmark (Amter, Bykommuner), France (départements), Germany (Bezirke, Ireland (counties). Italy (provincie), Netherlands (provinces)

4 Central-regional level of government
  (a) Planning:

      France (regions), Germany (Regionale Landesplanungsgemeinschaften), Italy (regioni, UK (Economic Planning Regions).

  (b) Planning and other purposes.
  (c) General purposes.

---

* The table is compiled from Kalk (1971, pp. 11-51, Annexe 1, Annexe 2 and the sections on the individual countries). Luxembourg has no regional level of government and it is not included as a result. The information on Ireland is from Chubb (1970).
† Examples are given only for the regional level.

Two conclusions stand out in this table. First, that regionalism in Europe takes many forms notwithstanding the fact that Kalk uses a different basis of classification; and second, this regional reform is never comprehensive. There are no examples of general purpose units at either the local-regional or central-regional levels. There are also very few examples of other functions, albeit a restricted number, being added to that of planning. The only reservation to this latter conclusion concerns the intermediate general level of government. But this category is a confusing one. In many countries this intermediate level would be considered local government (e.g. France, UK). They are called regions by Kalk because they are the second (top) tier of local government and he reserves the term local government for the lowest general purpose level of government. In addition, this category includes units of field administration (administrative deconcentration) but it specifically excludes the state level in federal systems (e.g. Federal Republic of Germany). These various inclusions and exclusions seem highly arbitrary and the confusion of local and regional government is undesirable. There are other weaknesses in Kalk's classification.

The classification used earlier in this paper is based on the objectives underlying regional reforms as well as the number of functions (Kalk's 'purpose'). The advantage of this is that it provides the basis for an explanation of why reform took place at a particular level of government. Just as the question of the ADP is logically prior to the question of the form of regional machinery, so decisions on the objectives of regional reform are prior determinants of the governmental level at which reform will take place. Where local government reform is the underlying objective to the reforms at the local-regional level other functions are added to that of planning. Conversely, where centrally initiated regional economic planning is the prime objective, the regional machinery is (a) central-regional, and (b) unrelated to other functions (e.g. UK). Another defect of Kalk's classification is that it is not inclusive. For example he mentions only some of the forms of administrative deconcentration in Britain. Nor does his classification encompass the variety of forms of administrative deconcentration in Europe. Fried distinguishes between the functional (UK), integrated prefectoral (France), and the unintegrated prefectoral (Italy) systems of deconcentration (Fried, 1963). All three involve areas of administration larger than the lowest unit of general purpose government (Kalk's definition of a region) but nowhere are these variations identified or discussed.

But, the main criticism of Kalk's scheme of classification is that it does not explicitly take into account the basic problem of the ADP. It is clear from this table that no general purpose regional institutions have been created. It is not clear in what way his scheme of classification points towards an explanation of this fact. But the ADP is crucial. Jack Hayward has pointed out that the initiative for a closer link between regionalism and economic planning in France came from the regional economic expansion committees (REEC) and not from the centre. The REECs were unofficial, voluntary bodies which owed their strength to support from local authorities and economic interests. But the reforms of 1964, rather than welcoming this local initiative, attempted to domesticate and neutralise the REECs by turning them into *Commissions de Dévelopement Economique Régionale* (CODER). CODER were part of the state administrative machine, with a membership the product of government nomination, and the traditional role of suppliant to the prefect (Hayward, 1969). These developments reflect the continuing distrust between centre and locality (Kesselman, 1967) — a distrust which has been frequently identified as a characteristic of the French political tradition (Almond and Verba, 1963; Hoffman, 1959; Wahl, 1962). In other words, French beliefs about the appropriate ADP reject the idea of strong units of government below the national government.[6] As a result, regional reform has been at the central-regional level and has been restricted to the function of regional economic planning.

It is perhaps worth noting at this point that the terms areal distribution of power and political tradition are used in preference to that comparative terminology which talks of the difference between federal and unitary states. The French example I have just discussed could be said to illustrate one of the features of a long-standing unitary state. But this terminology suffers from the disadvantages of being both legalistic and having an almost exclusive focus on institutions. For example, the term federalism encompasses such a variety of governmental forms that a precise definition for the purposes of comparison is virtually impossible. As M.J.C. Vile has pointed out: '. . . there has been an extensive, and intensive, discussion of [the problem of defining federalism] , and there has been a progressive movement away from the relatively formal and restrictive definition used by K.C. Wheare in 1943, until current writers on federalism have eroded the concept to the point where it has become so vague, so all-inclusive, and so meaningless that their formulations have become quite useless as analytical tools . . .' (Vile, 1973, p.2 and pp.34-5). Moreover, focusing on the constitutional aspects of federalism and describing its particular institutions tells us very little about how those institutions actually work (cf. Wheare, 1946; Sawyer, 1969).

The term ADP does not suffer from these limitations. Rather than starting from the assumption that the distribution of powers takes a particular form between particular sets of governmental institutions (i.e. federalism), the term ADP assumes the need to ask *what* is the distribution of powers between the various governmental institutions.

But governmental institutions (and the decisions about the ADP they reflect) do not come into being overnight. They have evolved, often over centuries. The concept of political tradition is used to draw attention to the importance of examining the historic evolution of the ADP in a particular country. In other words no ADP can be understood without examining the history of ideas about the form of government and the development of governmental institutions in the country under consideration (for an exemplification of this argument, see Hoffman, 1959).

Although the information on forms of regionalism in Europe is not entirely satisfactory, this brief survey of the forms does enable a number of conclusions to be drawn. First, the approaches to regionalism in Europe do encompass (a) a variety of objectives, and (b) different numbers of functions. Second, the greater the number of functions and objectives involved in any regional reform, the more prominent the question of the ADP. Finally, the approach to the question of the ADP is heavily conditioned by the political tradition of the particular country. In other words, this survey corroborates and adds to the conclusions arrived at in the survey of regionalism of Britain. In the light of these conclusions, it should be possible to remove some of the semantic confusion surrounding the concept of regionalism before returning to evaluate the policies summarised at the beginning of this paper.

Regionalism — some definitions

The discussion of the forms of regionalism in Europe illustrates the major problem facing any attempt at definition — there is no single way of defining the entity 'a region'. It depends upon the objectives of regionalism, the functions it encompasses, and the ADP of the particular country. Any benchmark for the concept of a region must recognise the different uses between countries. I suggest that the only way out of this difficulty is to define a region as the governmental/administrative unit larger in geographical area than the top tier of general purpose local government but smaller than the central/federal level of government in the particular country under consideration. But this definition is only a benchmark. It does not encompass the variations in objectives and numbers of functions. It only recognises that any definition of a region must take as its starting point the existing structure of government (and the ADP implicit in this structure) of the country under consideration. In order to move beyond this benchmark it is not possible to use the word region (or regionalism) in an unqualified way. To make sense of the complexity I have identified, it is essential to elaborate the terminology. I have suggested already the bases for this elaboration - the differences in objectives and functions. The weakest form of regionalism refers to the deconcentration of the central administration. The level of government is central-regional, the objective is simple and clear (administrative convenience), and usually only one function is involved. This form of regionalism can be termed regional administration.

One very common form of regional administration focuses on national economic planning. But the complexity of national economic planning requires the coordination of a number of functions at regional level and the ostensibly simple economic objective involves the complex question of social justice. As before, the level of government is central-regional but, in order to recognise the greater complexity of this form of regional administration, I shall call it regional economic planning.

The remaining forms of regionalism approximate to the common usage of the term. The reform of local government is local, involves multiple objectives and a large number of functions and, above all, involves a redistribution of governmental power from centre to locality. For the first time, therefore, it is possible to talk of regional government.

Regionalism as cultural nationalism is a form of regional government under these terminological conventions, but there is one major difference. It encompasses the reform of local government. In other words, regionalism as cultural nationalism incorporates regional government but it is not itself only regional government. The difference is, of course, one of scale and degree, but it is an important difference and I use the term regional devolution to describe it.

This terminology raises the question of how does regional devolution differ from federalism. Most writers would agree that the independence of the two levels of government is a distinguishing characteristic of federalism. But, in practice, it is clear that federalism implies also a high degree of interdependence and it is at this point that many of the definitional problems arise.[7] Livingstone argued: 'Federalism is thus not an absolute but a relative term; there is no identifiable point at which a society ceases to be unified and become diversified . . . All communities fall somewhere in a spectrum which runs from what we may call a theoretically wholly integrated society at one extreme to a theoretically wholly diversified society at the other.' (Livingstone, 1956, p.4.) The spectrum of federalism concept had led to a *reductio ad absurdum* in which W.H. Riker has argued that federalism does not exist. (Riker 1969). I suggest that this difficulty has arisen because the term federalism has been used to describe a particular form of governmental inter-relationship — constitutional independence — and to describe a variety of forms of governmental interdependence. The confusion of describing both one state and a variety of states with one concept can be overcome if federalism is seen as a specific form of regional devolution — that form characterised by 'the co-ordinate division of powers.' (Wheare, 1946). The term regional devolution is thus used to describe the various forms of governmental interdependence.

The major objection to this terminological convention lies in the statement that no existing form of government can be called federal under this strict definition. But Weber's concept of the 'ideal-type' provides an answer to this problem. The point is not that the ideal typical characteristics of federalism are descriptively inaccurate in a specific case but that the concept so defined is a useful 'tool for the historical comparison of two or more real situations.' (Mouzelis, 1967, p.49).

The definition of federalism I have suggested coupled with its ideal type methodological status carries the implication that there are a variety of other forms of governmental interdependence. My discussion of regional devolution emphasises the importance of the ADP. It thus follows that, if federalism is precisely defined, it is necessary to ask what is the ADP of a particular country. In other words, the approach not only gives the concept of federalism a specific meaning but it encourages also the need to analysis the various other forms of governmental interdependence. Moreover, it does this without distorting the analyses in the direction of certain constitutional forms irrespective of their applicability. The question posed is a precise one — 'What is the ADP?'. And it is crucial that any discussion in this area get away from an emphasis on legal definitions to an examination of how the ADP actually functions.

In conclusion a number of points can be made about these terminological conventions. First, the differences are not absolute but ones of degree, each form of regionalism being more comprehensive than its predecessor. Second, the utility of this kind of exercise depends upon (a) the extent to which it makes sense of past uses of the words; and (b) the extent to which it clarifies our thinking on the subject. There can be no advantage in striving for fixed meanings. The aim is only to increase our understanding of a particular concept at a point in time. I think these conventions do enable us to be more precise in our thinking about the concept of regionalism — a point I will try to demonstrate by returning to examine the policies I described at the beginning of this paper.

Regional policy re-examined

The examination of the concept of regionalism in this paper enables any review of the EC's regional policy and the idea of a 'Europe of Regions' to be brief because the terminology I have suggested reveals some glaring inadequacies. First, neither the Commission's regional policy nor the Federalists' 'Europe of Regions' is consistent or clear in its use of the term of regionalism. Although the Commission is talking almost exclusively of regional economic planning, nonetheless vague references to 'living communities' (regionalism as cultural nationalism?) can be found. The Federalists are even less precise. Their argument presumably refers to regional devolution and yet there is (a) no recognition of the difficulties of identifying culturally/sociologically/demographically/homogeneous areas; (b) no discussion of the problems of defining an area suitable for administering a large number of functions; and (c) a confused suggestion that regional economic planning can provide the underpinnings for a 'Europe of Regions'. The last point highlights a second major problem. The shift from regional economic planning to regional government/regional devolution is a dramatic one — it raises the issue of ADP. There is no reason to anticipate that national governments will allow regional government/devolution to come about through the gradual transformation of regional economic planning — the overspill theory that economic interdependence will lead to political interdependence has scarcely had the most dramatic confirmation during the 16 years of Community existence (Coombes, 1970, Hoffman, 1966; Shonfield, 1973). In fact to be more categoric, national governments will not permit the EC to take decisions about their ADP. The history of the EC is a history of national governments asserting their primacy over supra-national considerations. But EC decisions about the ADP are crucial for a 'Europe of Regions'. The policy is a non-starter. It is not clearly articulated and it fails to recognise the basic fact of Community existence — the primacy of national governments.

There is a danger, however, that regionalism will become the new dogma — the flag to be waved on all public occasions irrespective of its relevance. This can be seen in the Thompson Report's references to 'living communities'. Such comments are virtually irrelevant to the subject matter of the report. Its concern is with a

57

regional economic policy. It barely touches on the means for implementing that policy within the individual member states. Moreover, because the policy is solely concerned with regional economic planning, the question of the appropriate machinery of implementation does not require reference to cultural/demographic factors. By itself no regional economic policy is capable of tackling the larger problems of regionalism as cultural nationalism. Nor is it self evident that a regional level of administration is the best. It is possible that the existing machinery of government (i.e. local government) is more than adequate for the task. But the point underlying these comments is that confusions and problems are raised because the Thompson Report wanders away from its basic starting point of regional economic planning without ever being clear about its objectives in so doing. Regionalism is generally thought to be a 'good thing'. It may well be. But its merits are not enhanced by vague genuflexions in the direction of cultural nationalism. Policies will become more explicit and our analysis of their implications more precise, when we are clearer in our use of the term regionalism. Advocacy of the merits of regionalism does not benefit from subsuming its many forms under a single, unqualified term.

Conclusions

I have argued in this paper that:
(a) Clarity in the use of the term 'regionalism' is essential given the importance of EC regional policy and the idea of a 'Europe of Regions'.
(b) The definition of regionalism is a function of (1) its objectives, (2) the number of functions, and (3) the ADP of the particular country under consideration.
(c) On the basis of (b), it is possible to distinguish between regional administration, regional economic planning, regional government and regional devolution.
(d) These distinctions reveal ambiguities in the EC policies which suggest (1) that the idea of a 'Europe of Regions' is a non-starter, and (2) that the EC's regional policy, especially as regards its implementation, has adopted the banner of 'regionalism' without assessing whether it is appropriate.

The relationship between the EC and the administrative structure of its member states is an important area of investigation. (Rhodes, 1973a; Wallace, 1971, 1973; Wallace and Wallace, 1973). The whole question of the means for implementing the EC's regional policy is central to the relationship. But it does not mean that regionalism is the only viable link between the EC and sub-national units of government for administering the policy. We know very little about the links between the EC and local governments in the member states. Such links exist. They have been important in the past (Rhodes, 1973a; Patterson, 1973). It would be premature to conclude that a new tier of government is required for the regional policy, especially in view of the complexity surrounding the term regionalism and the key importance of governmental objectives in determining its form. It is equally essential to ask if there are other ways of achieving these objectives. Regionalism should not become the dogma of the next decade. What is being attempted is more important that rigid adherence to a way of doing it.

Notes

[1] For a brief history of the EC's regional policy see Lind and Flockton (1970).

[2] My use of the term deconcentration follows Maddick (1963).

[3] The term ADP refers to techniques for the distribution of governmental power on an area basis.

[4] The Government's White Paper, *Local Government in England* (Cmnd. 4584, HMSO, 1971) talks of creating a 'vigorous local democracy' (p. 6) and of giving 'every encouragement . . . to local democracy' (p. 15).

[5] A strong local government system does not depend solely on the possession of a wide range of responsibilities. It depends also on the willingness of local government to accept, fulfil, and develop its responsibilities. For a development of this argument see Rhodes (1973b).

[6] For an examination of the problems surrounding the attempts to reform regional and local government in France see James (1967), Mawhood (1972), Pallez (1967), and Swetman (1965).

[7] Vile, 1973, pp. 2-3 distinguishes between independence and interdependence but does not recognise that it is this very distinction which generated the move onto the slippery slope of the spectrum of federalism. As a result, he insists still that 'federalism' must encompass both ideas.

Bibliography

Almond, G.A. and Verba, S., *The Civic Culture*, Princeton University Press, 1963.

Banks, J.C., *Federal Britain?* Harrap, London, 1971.

Brittan, S., 'The balance-sheet for the new Europe', *The Financial Times*, 26 October 1972, p.25.

Chubb, B., *The Government and Politics of Ireland*, Oxford University Press, 1970.

Commission of the European Communities, *Report on the Regional Problems in the Enlarged Community*, Commission of the European Communities, Brussels, 1973.

Coombes, D., *Politics and Bureaucracy in the European Community*, Allen & Unwin, London, 1970.

Council of Europe, *Regional Institutions and Regionalisation in Member States*, Council of Europe, Strasbourg, 1972.

Cross, J. A., 'The regional decentralisation of British government departments' *Public Administration*, vol. 48, 1970, pp. 423-41.

European Federalists, *Political Declaration of the Committee of European Federalists,* The European Movement, London, 1972.

Fried, R.C., *The Italian Prefects*, Yale University Press, New Haven, 1963.

Hayward, J. E. S., 'From functional regionalism to functional representation in France – the battle of Brittany', *Political Studies*, vol. 17, 1969, pp. 48-75.

Hoffman, S., 'The areal division of powers in the writings of French political thinkers', in Maass (1959), pp. 113-49 (see below).

Hoffman, S., 'The fate of the nation-state', *Daedalus*, vol. 95, 1966, pp. 862-915.

IULA, 'Memorandum on regional development in the European Communities', *Europinform*, nos. 10/11, 1972, pp. 225-8.

James, P. B. M., 'The organization of regional economic planning in France,' *Public Administration*, vol. 45, 1967, pp. 353-67.

Kalk, E., *Regional Planning and Regional Government in Europe*, International Union of Local Authorities, The Hague, 1971.

Kesselman, M., *The Ambiguous Consensus*, Knopf, New York, 1967.

Leemans, A. F.,*Changing Patterns of Local Government*, International Union of Local Authorities, The Hague, 1970.

Liberal Party, *Report of the Working Party on the Machinery of Government*, The Liberal Party Organisation, London, 1973.

Lind, H. and Flockton, C., *Regional Policy in Britain and the Six/Community Regional Policy*, PEP/Chatham House (European Series No. 15), London, 1970.

Livingstone, W.S., *Federalism and Constitutional Change*, Oxford University Press, London, 1956

Maddick, H., *Democracy Decentralization and Development*, Asia Publishing House, London, 1963.

Maass, A., *Area and Power*, Collier-Macmillan, London, 1959.

Mackintosh, J.P., *The Devolution of Power*, Penguin, Harmondsworth, 1968.

Mackintosh, J. P., 'The Royal Commission on local government in Scotland', *Public Administration,* vol. 48, 1970.

McCrone, G., *Regional Policy in Britain*, Allen and Unwin, London, 1969.

Mawhood, P. N., 'Melting an iceberg: The struggle to reform communal government in France,' *Br. J. Pol. Sci.*, vol. 2, 1972, pp.501-15.

Mouzelis, N. P., *Organisation and Bureaucracy*, Routledge and Kegan Paul, London, 1967.

Pallez, G. 'France's new 'Communautes Urbaines', *Stud. Comp. Local Govt.*, vol. 1, 1967, pp. 28-39.

Patterson, W., 'European policy in Germany', *Public Affairs*, vol. 5, 1973, pp. 3-6.

Rhodes, R. A. W., 'The European Community and British public administration: The case of local government,' *J. Common Market Stud.*, vol. 11, 1973a, pp. 263-75.

Rhodes, R. A. W., 'Anaemia in the extremities and apoplexy at the centre: An examination of the European dimension to the Kilbrandon report' *New Europe*, vol. 2, 1973b, pp. 61-77.

Rhodes, R. A. W., 'Local government reform: Three questions' *Soc.Econ.Adm.*, vol.

8, 1974, pp. 6-21.

Roker, W. H., 'Six books in search of a subject or does federalism exist and does it matter', *Comparative Politics*, vol. 2, 1969, pp. 135-46.

Royal Commission on the Constitution, *Report* (Cmnd. 5460), HMSO, London, 1973.

Sampson, A., *The New Europeans*, Hodder & Stoughton, London, 1968.

Senior, D., 'The city region as an administrative unit', *Political Quarterly*, vol. 36, 1965, pp. 82-91.

Shonfield, A., *Europe: Journey to an Unknown Destination*, Penguin, Harmondsworth, 1973.

Smith, C., *Regionalism in England*, Vol. 1 *Regional Institutions: A Guide*, Vol. 2 *Its Nature and Purpose 1905-1965*, Acton Society Trust, London, 1964.

Swetman, L. T., 'Prefects and planning: France's new regionalism', *Public Administration* vol. 43, 1965, pp. 15-30.

Thornhill, W., *The Case for Regional Reform*, Nelson, London, 1972.

Vile, M. J. C., *Federalism in the United States, Canada and Australia.* Research Paper No. 2 for the Royal Commission on the Constitution, HMSO, London, 1973.

Wahl, N., 'France', in S.H. Beer and A. B. Ulam (eds), *Patterns of Government*, pp. 275-305, Random House, New York, 1962.

Wallace, H., 'The impact of the European Communities on national policy-making', *Government and Opposition*, vol. 6, 1971, pp. 520-38.

Wallace, H., *National Governments and the European Communities*, PEP/Chatham House, (European Series No. 21), London, 1973.

Wallace, H. and Wallace W., 'The impact of Community membership on the British machinery of government', *J. Common Market Stud.*, vol. 11, 1973, pp. 243-62.

Wheare, K. C., *Federal Government,* Oxford University Press, London, 1946.

Wistrich, E., 'Democracy in a federal Europe', *New Europe*, vol. 2, 1973, pp. 29-37.

4 Regional planning in Britain: analysis and evaluation

P. Self, 'Regional Planning in Britain: Analysis and Evaluation', *Journal of Regional Studies*, vol. 1, no. 1, May 1964, pp. 3-10.

Foreword

This paper starts with a brief historical review of developments in regional planning in Britain up to and including the creation of a system of regional boards and councils for economic planning.

Its main purpose is to ask and analyse some questions about the future of regional planning in the light of recent events. This is done in the three subsequent sections which deal with the nature of planning regions, of regional plans, and of regional administrative machinery.

History of regional planning in Britain

The history of regional planning in Britain largely consists of two active movements, concerned with tackling two different kinds of regional problem. I have written some of this history elsewhere (Self, 1964; Self, 1961), and in this paper I will summarise the history briefly. In addition, we should remember the regional theories of geographers and political scientists,[1] which exerted little influence when first produced but which have considerable relevance still to current issues. I return to these in the second section.

One of the two movements in regional planning has focused upon the problems of the city or urban region. Its original motivations were largely social: to eradicate congested and blighted living conditions in the big cities through redevelopment schemes, density controls, and the provision of garden suburbs or garden cities (earlier phase) and satellite or new towns (later phase). Technical aims of rationalising and improving public services in large urban areas have also played a growing part in this movement, particularly in relation to gas and electricity supply (early phase), water supplies, housing and (of rapidly growing importance) transportation. The limitations of local government structure have stimulated these pressures for urban regional planning.

Concepts of the urban region have also changed. Originally the focus was on the large city or provincial capital, viewed both as having severe internal problems (congestion, etc.), and also as providing the regional focus for a variety of services to its hinterland. In the second phase the emphasis shifted to the internal problems of the few large conurbations, with their hinterlands, viewed mainly as reception areas for overspill population. (This phase of thinking has just been reached in the local government reorganisations for London and Tyneside.) More recently attention has shifted back to broader concepts of urban region, because of the simultaneous factors of economic concentration within broad zones and population diffusion in and around these zones. This calls for new kinds of planning and service provision.

The first steps towards urban regional planning were taken by joint advisory committees of local authorities. The next, highly influential step was the preparation during the 1940s of a series of advisory regional plans by distinguished town-planning consultants, notable among whom was Sir Patrick Abercrombie. These plans were strongly motivated by the social aim of accelerating urban redevelopment and dispersal, and by aesthetic concepts of new regional forms typically conceived as the location of new developments against a 'green backcloth' of protected green belt and countryside. These plans made relatively little contribution to subsequent problems of transport planning and city centre renewal. They assumed a static or declining national population, and treated employment location as subsidiary to social aims. In their inspirations and limitations (not all of which were, of course, the planners' faults) these plans remain a monument to the town-planning ideology of the 1940s.

However, these plans, despite their advisory status, had great practical impact through their influence upon governmental measures and decisions, and upon local development plans. The New Towns Act (1946) and Town Development Act (1952), particularly the former, were major instruments for promoting urban regional dispersal, although their main effects were confined to two urban regions (London, Clydeside). Aided by the Town and Country Planning Act (1947) and the 'Sandys Circular' (issued by Ministry of Housing, 1956), county councils struggled to create closely drawn green belts around conurbations and some other cities. Massive public schemes of urban redevelopment got under way in all the large cities. But difficulties mounted, as general population growth and an increasing divergence between the location of employment and of population defied the town planners' assumptions, and also added to transport problems.

The long-drawn, frustrating 'overspill' controversy between cities and counties was a witness to these difficulties, and to the breakdown of regional planning concepts. By the late 1950s, urban regional planning had lost its direction.

There have been some recent efforts to revive a sense of direction. Most important of these is the Ministry of Housing's South-East Study (1964), which does not so much break new ground in policy as apply the Abercrombie thesis of urban dispersal to a much vaster region, which covers the area south and east of a line from Wash to Solent, plus Dorset. This exercise, however, departs from Abercrombie policy in recognising or assuming the 'inevitability' of further substantial increases in long-distance commuting to work in London, and in proposing general land allocations for meeting this development. The study is thus a mixture of boldness and compromise. Its greatest weaknesses are the failure to analyse possible trends in employment growth and location, or to examine

63

alternative development strategies in any detail. Its economic component is weak.

A further response to the same problems has been the creation of a Standing Conference on London Regional Planning, covering Greater London, eleven counties and ten county boroughs. This body is only advisory, but has produced some excellent technical reports. Similar developments have not yet occurred in other urban regions, but the Ministry of Housing has floated the idea of tackling county-city dilemmas by a series of 'sub-regional' plans. The Ministries of Housing and Transport are also cooperating in a series of land use-transportation studies for the conurbations, and the study for Southampton—Portsmouth (where expansion is proposed under the South-East Study) provides an illustration of the kind of plan to be produced for an incipient urban region.

An alternative approach to the treatment of urban regional planning is provided by the report of the Crowther Steering group to the Buchanan Report ('Traffic in Towns', HMSO 1963), which takes the urban commuting zone as its regional planning unit, and suggests the creation of a Government-appointed development agency for each such zone, with powers both to coordinate and to undertake highway improvements and urban redevelopment. This proposal puts the stress upon regional transport planning. Its business-minded approach would require a departure from present systems of town and country planning and local government.

The other main regional planning movement has been concerned with the problems, not of urban regions but of regions suffering from unemployment and industrial stagnation. This movement has followed a continuous course since the 'special areas' legislation of the 1930s. Its methods have been to steer more industrial growth into the backward regions, through the techniques both of industrial location controls (provided under the Town and Country Planning Act of 1947), and of financial and physical incentives, including tax concessions, building grants and the provision of subsidised industrial estates (provided under the Distribution of Industry Acts 1945 and 1950, the Local Employment Act 1960, and various budget concessions).

The force of the programme has varied from time to time, largely according to levels of regional unemployment and political considerations. The areas qualifying for assistance have also varied. After 1945 the 'development areas' included some fairly broad regions; the Local Employment Act of 1960 concentrated assistance on much more narrowly defined development districts; and recently there has been a swing back to a regional definition of the areas where special assistance is available. Throughout, however, the techniques used have been *ad hoc* pressures on the decisions of individual firms, and the only criterion has been the relief of unemployment. There has been little attempt to foster co-ordinated plans of industrial development, or to set broader goals for regional economic development. A good illustration of this is the small proportion of Government-sponsored research establishments located in unfavoured regions.

Recently the aims of regional economic planning have broadened. Government White Papers for Central Scotland and the North-East (1963) promised these two regions a differentially high share of public investment, and also proposed to concentrate new development in a number of 'growth zones', including several new towns. The same idea has been followed in the recent Government decision to choose Leyland-Chorley as the next new town in Lancashire.

In December 1964 the Labour Government announced its intention to create a system of regional economic planning under the general control of its new Department of Economic Affairs. England was subsequently divided into eight economic planning regions. Scotland, Wales and Ulster each functions as a separate region. In each region there has been set up an economic planning board of departmental officials assisted by an economic planning council of nominated members drawn mainly from local government, industry and the Universities. This machinery will primarily be concerned with the preparation of regional economic plans which (when centrally approved) will eventually become part of the national economic plan that is also to be produced. This new machinery is intended to produce a more comprehensive approach to regional development, with particular attention to the needs of 'backward' regions.

The brief account shows that the two strands of regional planning in Britain have interacted from time to time, but have largely been differentiated. Their interaction was apparent at the time of the Barlow Report of 1940 when the relationship between the decline of the older industrial areas and the overgrowth of London was strongly asserted. Subsequently, the Board of Trade's 'work to the workers' programme was pursued in a way which entailed pumping new employment into crowded conurbations which schemes for urban regional planning were trying to decongest. Some reconciliation of aims has come with the adoption of a 'growth point' philosophy for regional economic development. This philosophy, however, was pioneered in Scotland, where the various strands of regional development have been integrated into a single Scottish Development Department. The acceptance of similar policies in England is still doubtful. Even in the case of the North-East, the Board of Trade has continued since the White Paper to pump new industry into the small part of that region which lies outside its supposed growth zone.

The new regional economic planning machinery covers Britain comprehensively, but recent developments in urban regional planning have been sporadic with a particular focus on the problems of the South-East. Nor is it clear how far the problems of urban regions will or should be assimilated by the new regional economic planning machinery. The 'chosen instruments' of urban dispersal and 'development areas' policies are respectively new towns and industrial estates: both have a big influence upon industrial mobility and growth and upon inter-regional balance: but they are controlled by different Government Departments with different objectives. Integrated regional planning may be on the way but it has hardly arrived yet.

What kind of region?

I can now turn to the questions which have continuing importance for regional planning. First, let us consider the nature and size of the regions which it is desired to plan.

The history of regional planning gives us only clues to the answer. This is because, as already noted, the focus has been upon particular problem areas (urban regions or depressed areas) which have been defined in an *ad hoc* way. No official comprehensive system of planning regions existed until the Government's present exercise, which does not resolve all the problems.

Any system of planning regions will have to take into account the following criteria:

(a) *Economic planning*. If there are to be economic regional plans worth the title, the regions covered must be reasonably large and (at least potentially) economically diversified. To focus simply upon a narrow depressed industry zone means abandoning broader economic goals (such as increases in regional productivity and income, and a diversified economic structure) and settling for blood transfusions from the national Exchequer. As Hirschmann points out, if only we could in some respects treat a region as though it were a country we would indeed get the best of both worlds, but this is dependent upon the region having adequate development potential.

Some claim that Britain (or the UK) should be treated as only one economic region. Geographic size may support this argument, but population density, industrial scale and inter-regional differences in industrial and employment structure justify a regional approach. But the present Government is right in stipulating fairly large economic regions.

(b) *City or urban regions*. There is no one adequate way of defining city region. It depends upon the criteria used. If the focus is upon the provision of services by a city to its surrounding hinterland, then there is one national centre in a category of its own, about a dozen major provincial centres, and many more minor ones. Many of these service areas overlap.

It is interesting that many geographical-political plans for a devolution of power to regional units have concentrated upon the catchment areas of major provincial centres. Thus the plans of C. B. Fawcett, E. W. Gilbert, and E. R. C. Taylor roughly agree in proposing eleven English regions based upon Newcastle, Manchester, Leeds (or York), Nottingham, Birmingham, Plymouth, Bristol, Oxford, Norwich, Southampton (or Winchester), and London.[2] Other schemes (such as the early heptarchic plan of the Fabian Society) follow similar lines. What is especially interesting is the considerable degree of resemblance between these older concepts of the city region and the new economic planning regions. The chief differences relate to the recognition of additional city regions in the extremities of England (Carlisle, Plymouth), and in the South-East (Southampton, Oxford, Norwich). These last three city regions always had less scale and substance than the others, and the growth of London has squeezed them further.[3]

A second approach to the definition of the urban region concentrates upon its growth function. Here we are in the familiar field of population and industrial spread, and of overspill schemes. It is these criteria which led to such a wide definition of the region taken for the South-East Study, and the same factors *could* justify very broad definitions of urban region elsewhere. Glasgow has overspill links with the Highlands, and Liverpool and Birmingham may colonise North Wales. However, small and distant overspill schemes do not really define an urban region satisfactorily, because much the more important factors are population density and the concentration and linkage of industrial activities: while associated with high density and concentration are all the functional problems of transportation, housing, recreation, water supply, etc. On this vital basis, the key urban regions cover a radius of 20-30 miles from the centre of the major conurbations (the London region may be larger, but that is a matter for argument).

Finally, there is a third definition of urban region which includes smaller and also potential urban regions, and which employs the additional criterion of the size of population needed to sustain a full range of facilities, other than those which only the very largest centres can provide. This is a forward-looking definition because it envisages a time when the population of Britain will be both much larger and more evenly spread, i.e. the smaller and potential urban regions will have gained ground at the expense of the largest ones. This approach has been pioneered by Mr. Derek Senior, who recognises about thirty-five urban regions of this type in England and Wales,[4] which should become not only planning units but units of a reformed local government system. There is much merit in this concept, as it applies to local government. However, many of the urban regions as thus defined are (and probably always will be) extremely small in comparison with those based on the major conurbations, and the extent of influence of the big centres is rather artificially reduced. Mr. Senior recognises that this kind of unit would not serve for economic planning, but pleads reasonably enough that economic planning regions should not cut across the lines of these urban 'sub-regions' (as they have done in the case of Sheffield or Stoke-on-Trent).[5]

(c) *Administrative and cultural factors.* Briefly, administrative factors point to large regions because of problems of staffing and coordination. Cultural factors require respect for the boundaries of Scotland and Wales, although in the case of Wales this runs contrary to other criteria. The institutional and sentimental loyalties attached to countries and cities must also influence regional structure.

What conclusions follow from this analysis? Economic and administrative factors dictate large, diversified regions and, although criticism in detail can be plentiful, the economic planning regions recently selected follow these criteria.

It is the approach to urban regions which creates dilemmas. Our first definition (the 'old' city-region concept) accords tolerably well with economic planning regions, although it would favour rather more regions in the rural extremities and the South-East. The second (conurbation region) definition applies to only a part of Britain, because many areas lie well outside urban regions as here defined.

Conversely, however, some of these conurbation regions lie so close together that a question arises of integrating them. Manchester and Merseyside, Tyneside and Teeside, Clydeside and Edinburgh: the centres of each of these pairs are only about 40 miles apart. Integration would stress their growing interaction and membership of an economic region (North-West, North-East, Mid-Scotland). Separation stresses their different civic roots and character, and the link with centrifugal overspill areas (Merseyside links to North Wales, etc.). Finally, the third (Senior's) definition covers the whole country with variable urban regions potentially capable of becoming sub-units of the economic regions. This is tidy.

My own views are that the problems of regional economic planning and the conurbation regions are so entwined, that regions need to be selected which comprehend both: and that it would not be satisfactory to treat economic planning at one regional level and physical planning at another (lower) level. Thus, I would favour broad regions for both economic and physical planning, while accepting Mr. Senior's areas as desirable local government units wielding substantial town planning powers.

The West Midlands (Warwickshire, Worcestershire, Staffordshire, Shropshire, Herefordshire) comes nearest to a model unit for regional planning, because it satisfies all the criteria save Senior's. It is a diversified and well-marked economic region, and it is also a city and urban region based on Birmingham. Elsewhere, reconciliation of criteria is harder, but I think that the economic regions now selected also offer (in principle) a reasonable framework for physical regional planning, with provisos: (a) that special supplementary plans are desirable for certain remote but potentially substantial urban regions (Carlisle, Plymouth), and also for at least two 'secondary regions' within the South-East that would be based on Southampton and Norwich; and (b) that 'fringe' questions receive due attention: for example, there should be no splitting of any existing urban region, and the possibility of creating a new urban complex running across regional boundaries (for example, in the Crewe–Stoke-on-Trent area) must not be overlooked.

What kind of plan?

In theory a regional economic plan might set various targets for economic development and public investment: and physical planning could be a subsequent operation, done either on a regional or sub-regional basis, within the framework of the resources allocated.

Regional development, however, turns not only upon investment funds, but upon the human and natural resources available, and upon the kind of environment which can be created in the region. Regions vary in their capacity for providing an attractive environment for living and working, and the quality of the environment itself helps to attract or repel enterprise.

Again, development patterns vary considerably in the costs which they impose and the satisfactions which they yield. Town planning is replete with discussions about the relative values of higher and lower densities, optimum size of towns, methods of coping with traffic, etc., and much sense can be talked on individual issues. But it is far harder to evaluate the merit of a total 'package' of development proposals such as the plan for a big city or a region contains: problems exist not only in the techniques of measurement, but specifically in the weighting and combination of the different factors.

There is always, and rightly, room for the visionary who will hold up a picture of the city or region as it might become. But visions need to reflect real possibilities and to take objective account of costs and benefits.

Where knowledge is limited it is mistaken to demand uniformity. There has to be scope for regions to experiment with distinctive kinds of development pattern. There is too little variety and experiment in modern Britain.

We may distinguish between the national and regional contribution to regional plan making.

National contribution

A general overview of the prospects of different regions can only be provided in the first place from the centre. A first step is to consider the implications of likely developments in the size and structure of the national economy for the fortunes of individual regions. This can be supplemented by studies of particular industries and services in terms of their regional implications.

This kind of analysis is inevitably tentative and fallible. But it does help to give a preliminary objective basis for judging what would happen to the regional distribution of economic activity if (a) government is merely 'neutral', or (b) it continues only with its present policies, or (c) it applies new policies. Conversely, this analysis will help to show the feasibility of regional development targets, and a further stage can be the evaluation of different general measures for reaching them.

Because of the failure to analyse trends dispassionately regional planning suffers today from a certain intellectual confusion and dishonesty. It is politically difficult often to state regional prospects objectively: both because 'forecasts' and 'assumptions' are quickly taken as statements of Government intentions (which they are not), and because desirable regional targets may then be seen to call for more action than the Government is able or is prepared to take. This political problem will not diminish, it will increase with the creation of the new regional machinery which will bring (as it should) new regional demands to the attention of Whitehall.

The best solution would seem to be the creation of an independent Institute of Regional Studies, which can provide the basic framework of inter-regional analysis and also help regions with their own individual studies. In this way the regions will know better where they stand, and the Government can decide its own policies with the help of forecasts for which it does not have to take responsibility.

The Government has powerful tools at its disposal for influencing the pattern of regional development. These include: (a) distribution of industry incentives, (b) new towns, (c) investment in airports, ports, motorways, (d) the location of research establishments, (e) the placing of defence projects, (f) the location of the offices of central government and public corporations, (g) projects of public corporations, (h) housing subsidies, (i) the location of Universities, and institutes of higher education. It would be unrealistic to suggest that all these activities should be conducted primarily from the viewpoint of improving regional balance. But at least the whole field should be surveyed in an attempt to align these programmes in a general regional strategy and to avoid flagrant contradictions,* and so as to make the agencies concerned aware of regional goals.

A critical problem is the growing concentration of the middle-class salariat in the South-East, which explains much of the difference in economic growth patterns and prospects between North and South. This degree of concentration can probably only be broken by a major and very difficult government initiative, even though regional initiatives could help. If, however, this trend is to be allowed to continue, then regional policies (including that for the South-East) must be drastically altered accordingly.

Another critical central decision is whether and when to embark upon long-term development projects which will not 'pay off' quickly (hence they will always be politically very difficult), but which may be vital to social and economic well-being later. Examples are the creation of new urban complexes in relatively remote areas such as Cumberland or the South-West or parts of East Anglia.

Regional contribution

This needs to be aimed, not just at squeezing more aid out of Whitehall, but at demonstrating how the development of a region can also fit in with and help to realize national objectives.

This can be done by uncovering potential new resources, by showing how particular industries can hope to grow and flourish in the regional environment, by suggesting suitable locations for major new projects, and by indicating the special contribution which a region can make to national strategy. (For example a South-West Plan should show the ways in which this region might develop to take some of the load off the South-East.) It is right that national decisions, e.g. over the location of a new office complex, should be influenced by the vigour of regional initiatives: for the keenness of the regional leaders must be a prime factor in the success and workability of any project. It is also right that regional bodies should have a considerable say in public investment decisions, e.g. the precise location of a new town, motorway, or airport.

What kind of machinery?

Certain problems are posed by the new regional planning machinery in Britain.

1. The whole machinery is advisory only. The civil servants on the boards are primarily concerned with their departmental duties, and their loyalties are vertical (to departments) rather than horizontal (to regional boards).

2. Because departments have different views, concrete questions will tend to gravitate to Whitehall, there to be settled by 'the usual machinery' (including the

Cabinet or a Cabinet Committee if the issue is very controversial).

3. The regional advisory councils have no elective roots or staffs of their own, and occupy a generally inferior position to the boards of civil servants. They will have to struggle to exercise any political leadership at regional level.

4. There is a great lack of skilled staff specifically available for regional planning. The staff resources of the Department of Economic Affairs are limited, and the planning staffs of the Ministry of Housing and Local Government are primarily occupied with local and sub-regional planning.

This is to state the difficulties. It is something to have the new regional machinery at all. Britain has hardly yet embarked upon national economic planning, and quick results cannot be expected in the regional field.

The example of France is instructive, because the new regional machinery in Britain has a good deal of resemblance to its French counterparts. Thus:

1. In both countries regional pressures originated with *ad hoc* voluntary bodies, such as the North-East Development Assoc. (U.K.) and the 'committees for regional expansion' (France). In both cases these pressures have now been formalized into official representative advisory committees.

2. In both countries a regional inter-departmental board of civil servants initially acted as the key body for regional planning, although in France the regional préfet has now taken over much of its duties.

3. There is pressure to increase the size of the region, although there are still twenty-one planning regions in France, and eleven in the U.K. as a whole.

4. There has been the same general switch of emphasis from a more traditional town planning approach to an economic approach to regional planning. In France also the first regional plans emanated from the Ministry of Reconstruction and Housing, but now primarily form part of the general economic planning machinery.

5. There is a continuing problem of coordination. The new office of regional préfet, because of French administrative traditions, is much better placed to exercise a strong coordinating role than is the chairman of an English regional board; yet even the préfet's influence is much limited in practice by the 'know-how' of departmental representatives.

This resemblance with France certainly reflects a grappling with common problems. However, the much more experienced and effective national machinery for economic planning in France provides a major difference. It was not until the fourth and fifth French plans that much progress was possible with regional planning. In this sense, regional planning is bound to lag well behind national economic planning.

On the other hand, Britain is probably in the lead in actual programmes of regional development, and also has strong traditions of local self-government which might perhaps be built up to the regional level. These assets need to be used.

Clearly an essential step is to get regional plans which really have some teeth in them, and which will be followed in departmental and local government action, as well as providing an effective focus for regional aspirations.

This is anything but an easy task. In my view, necessary measures for reaching this goal may include: (a) creating a national Institute for Regional Planning (see last section); (b) harnessing the expert staff of the Ministry of Housing more closely to work on the physical planning aspects of regional plans; (c) strengthening the authority of the coordinating Ministry (now the Department of Economic Affairs); (d) improving the status of the regional advisory councils; make sure that they are able to influence effectively the studies which are made, and be prepared for them to be a nuisance to Whitehall.

Notes

[1] Usefully summarised in *Acton Society Trust* (1965).

[2] This is a slight simplification. Two of these writers add a Carlisle region, one adds a Cambridge region, and one treats Oxford and Southampton as 'sub-regions'. See the maps, *Acton Society Trust* (1965).

[3] However, Southampton and Norwich are certainly camong the major potential regional centres — in this respect resembling Plymouth and Carlisle. The claims of the Norwich or East Anglian region have also been recognised in the Government's appointment of a separate economic regional council and board.

[4] For map and brief description, see Lonsdale (1965).

[5] The terms city region and urban region have been used flexibly throughout this discussion, but it is clear that city region best expresses the older concept of a major city's service area, while urban region better describes an entity in which the emphasis is upon population size and spread. Also the diffusion of population and services is making the functions of the central city relatively less important, and this trend will continue.

Select Bibliography

Acton Society Trust (1965), *Regionalism in England*, vol. 2.

Lonsdale, C. (1965), *Town and Country Planning*, vol.33, pp. 83-90.

Self, P. (1961), *Cities in Flood: The Problems of Urban Growth* (2nd ed.) chs. 3, 4, 6.

Self, P. (1964), *Urban Studies*, vol. 1, pp. 55-70.

Self, P. (1965), *Town and Country Planning*, vol. 33, pp. 330-6.

5 Aspects of contradiction in regional policy

Rowntree Research Unit, University of Durham (J. Cousins, R. Davis, M. Paddon and A. Waton), 'Aspects of Contradiction in Regional Policy', Journal of Regional Studies, vol. 8, no. 2, August 1974, pp. 133-44.

Introduction

Spatial concepts hold a fatal fascination for the sociologist. The perpetual reappearance of the notion of 'community' in his vocabulary has invariably provoked discussions of its spatial or areal connotations despite attempts to divest it of any such significance (Stacey, 1969). Regions, in so far as they have attracted much attention, have been included within the general 'physical' framework of community studies. The most cited sociological discussion of regionalism asserts that 'if we do not mean by the term "region" to call attention to the fact that we are looking at life in terms of the space dimension and the interest in location and position which that implies, then the term "region" has no intelligible meaning whatsoever', and equates the spatial and sociological with the claim that 'Just as regions are physical facts of nature, so they are also facts of culture' (Wirth, 1964). The study of regions thus denotes a concern with 'forms of social organisation', 'customs' and institutions as they are distributed in space. It involves debates about the boundaries of these collectivities: whether an area constitutes a sociological region; the sorts of indicators used to assess the location of boundaries: and discussion of the degree to which regions are becoming less or more homogeneous (e.g. Mumford, 1927; McKinney, 1971). Such a general orientation is likely to generate large numbers of empirical enquiries around these and similar questions. But by the same token as this type of regional study enjoys an affinity with studies of community in general, so the fundamental critique of community studies is applicable to it; this maintains that sociological and spatial boundaries are not coterminous and any interrelationship which may exist between the two is complex and tenuous (Pahl, 1966; Stacey, 1969).

Nevertheless, irrespective of whether or not they constitute social collectivities, regions enjoy a position of some significance in the sociological analysis of Britain and other advanced societies. The concept of the region has been used to analyse some of the major social and economic problems engendered by the development of an advanced industrial capitalist economy, and *regional* policies have been employed in an attempt to ameliorate these problems. Indeed since the 1930s such policies have been a permanent feature of the political and economic life of the UK, but the picture is familiar in most Western Countries — those areas which are 'troubled' by a declining and outdated economic base are those areas within which, for instance, there is a greater proportion of manual workers than the national average, lower average *per capita* income, worse housing and other social facilities, and so on. These are the problems regional policies set themselves to solve.

The nature of the analysis set out is often technical and complex, but the causal reasons advanced for the 'backwardness' of an area are those which have often been documented with regard to the Third World — an imbalance in the industrial structure, technological backwardness, and certain of the psychological characteristics of the region's population: and such analysis retains its seductiveness despite the indications that policies based on these premises have at best been only partially effective in their own terms.[1]

The overt features of such a regionalism in Britain have been provided by a number of institutions arising from the local level or established by the Central Government. These institutions are significant in that firstly, by their very existence they formalise the interpretations of social problems as regional in character; secondly, they recruit members of organisations and social groups and provide them with privileged positions in respect of the regional social structure; and thirdly, they articulate causal analyses of the region's problem, and suggest policy measures.

Conventional wisdom has isolated two rather different sorts of institution; firstly, those organisations which have evolved locally and which are seen as evidence of the existence of the region as a social collectivity; secondly, those bodies and institutions formally established by, and owing primary allegiance to, Central Government, as either advisory or executive bodies. Nevertheless, both types of body are seen as pursuing a similar aim and to have been called into being to tackle the same problem.[2]

The basic vocabulary of regional policy is shared by both kinds of organisations, although regional economic policies and techniques have changed (and, still more, varied considerably) in short term ways. For example, a report prepared for a local development body in 1956 foresaw no difficulties for the coal industry for the next 20 years (Allen *et al.*, 1957). Eight years later the first review of the County Development Plan prepared by Northumberland County Council chronicled 6 years decline in that same industry. The geographical extent, and actual content of regional economic incentives, has changed rapidly for instance as it did between 1960 and 1963, 1965 and 1967 and again between 1970 and 1972, but, underlying these short term variations, there has been an actual increase in both the geographical coverage and the policy content of such policies, which has led to the adoption of a basically evolutionary perspective on the development of regional policy in the British context (McCrone, 1968). We have challenged this interpretation in respect of the national development of regional policy elsewhere (Rowntree Research Unit, 1972a). We intend here (a) to analyse the organisational structures of the long sequence of regional organisations that have existed in the North-East of England since the 1930s; and (b) to expose the basic models of the region's problems and the programme of solutions advocated by these organisations. The bodies, and their analytical models, have certainly lost and gained in apparent power and legitimacy with the variations of governmental

74

interest in regional policy; the nature of their activities has also varied sometimes being more based on lobbying and promotion, sometimes more on an attempt to 'plan' the region's development. However our approach is to analyse regionalism, regional organisations, regional plans and regional policies in a political way. From this perspective, the origins, style and objectives of regional organisations and policies have changed little for almost 40 years. In our last section we will therefore discuss the causes of the currency currently given to an 'evolutionary' approach, and will advance an alternative explanation based upon an analysis of the relationship between regional bodies and social structural features of North-East England.[3]

Table 5.1 Some selected key characteristics

	Northern Region	UK
Home resident population at mid-1969 (%)	6·2	100
Unemployment rate (total male registered unemployed as percentage of all male employees at 10 January 1972)	9·3	5·9
Unemployment benefits 1969-70 (as percentage of total unemployment benefit)	10·8	100
Occupation of head of household, 1971 (%)		
Professional, managerial, teaching and clerical	19	26
Manual, inc. shop assistants and armed forces	50	48
Retired and unoccupied	31	26
Average weekly household income (£) 1970 and 1971	34.3	37

Source: Central Statistical Office, *Social Trends* No. 3, HMSO, London 1972.

The organisations

History

Figure 5.2. shows, in outline, the broad history of the progression of bodies either constituted in, or composed of members from, the North-East. All of these bodies have had as their primary aim the economic regeneration of the North-East of England in relation to the rest of Great Britain.

The first regional organisation, the North-East Development Board (NEDB), appeared in 1935. It was not produced in a vacuum, for the concept of 'regional development' had by then got a foothold at local levels throughout the area — in bodies such as the Tyneside Development Board and the Teesside Development Board, which had been campaigning for the introduction of Trading Estates since the late 1920s. These bodies were financed mainly from the funds of local

75

North East

Northern

Yorkshire and
Humberside

North
West

East
Midlands

West
Midlands

East
Anglia

Wales
and
Monmouthshire

South East

South West

Fig 5.1 Planning regions of England and Wales

councils.[4] NEDB's primary achievement was in getting the local authorities on the Tyne, Tees and Wear and of the Durham Coalfield into a single organisation, although it marked a significant step forward in Governmental policies towards the Depressed Areas, being financed by Government grants, through the work of the Commissioner for Special Areas.

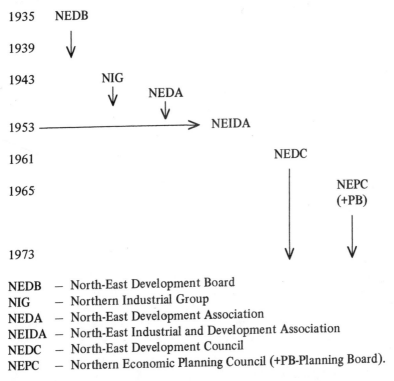

1935	NEDB				
1939					
1943		NIG			
			NEDA		
1953			→	NEIDA	
1961				NEDC	
1965					NEPC (+PB)
1973					

NEDB — North-East Development Board
NIG — Northern Industrial Group
NEDA — North-East Development Association
NEIDA — North-East Industrial and Development Association
NEDC — North-East Development Council
NEPC — Northern Economic Planning Council (+PB-Planning Board).

Fig 5.2 Schematic history of regional bodies in North-East England

The main aim was to provide for the 'exchange of opinions and concerted action on non-party lines by representatives of a great variety of interests, who have no other common meeting ground', and its major concern was to 'further on behalf of each and every part of the Area, the development of new industries and the revival and extension of existing industries in the area' (NEDA, 1949). It would do this by gathering and disseminating information, promoting research, and by lobbying Whitehall. Participation in the organisation was purely voluntary; it had no power to compel any local authority or private interest to join or contribute.

Part of the success in persuading the then Conservative Government (under Baldwin) to establish Trading Estates in the area was due to NEDB pressure. As in 1935, the year of NEDB's formation, the government appointed Major K. C. Appleyard — a member of the council of NEDB — as first Chairman of North-East

Trading Estates and, after discussions with the Commissioner for Special Areas, a non-profit making company was registered in early 1936, backed by £1½m. of Treasury money. Work began on the Team Valley site, Gateshead, in August 1936.

On the outbreak of war in 1939, NEDB ceased to function. Under the early war-time arrangements there was no such regional body, although the nature of war-time organisation served to reinforce the regional idea (McCrone, 1968). When, however, the need became apparent to organise for peace-time, thought turned firstly towards the reconstitution of a regional body, and in 1943, Lord Ridley, former chairman of NEDB, together with a group of five or six regional notables (including four industrialists), produced a paper concerning the region's post-war future and canvassed other industrialists, leading to the formation of the Northern Industrial Group (NIG). On the basis of its first publication (NIG, 1943) it secured the unity of the business interests of the North-East in one body, making itself a small ('so as not to be unwieldy') self-appointed advisory body, electing members for their knowledge of industry and because of their concern for the area as a whole, who served 'in their *personal* capacities, not as representatives of any particular body or organisation' (our emphasis). Its aims were:

(a) To develop and promote the prosperity of existing industry in the North-East, including the basic industries on which the region depends for the greater part of its employment;

(b) To encourage commercial, technical and industrial research with a view to developing ancillaries to the basic industries, and help establish new industries and so give a wider spread of employment by greater diversity;

(c) To advise and cooperate with the government and other bodies in respect of the industrial development and needs of the region in relation to local and national plans, with the object of maintaining a high level of employment throughout the region (NIG, 1953)

NIG was financed by industry, not government, 'so as to keep it as free as possible and avoid raising political issues'. Contributions did not confer any right of control, 'even though individual members may be associated with contributing organizations'. Cooperation with government departments, especially the Board of Trade, was good, and NIG saw itself as having a special role in advising government departments on the implications of policies as they affected the region.

The Group felt it could not function adequately, however, without the assistance of a 'democratic assembly' at the regional level, and so Ridley made moves to create such an assembly to 'continue the study of the general problems affecting the North-East and bring them continually to the notice of the government' (NIG, 1943). In October 1944, the North-East Development Association (NEDA) was formed for this purpose and to 'coordinate the activities of the many organisations concerned with employment and general and social welfare in the region, so it may advise the government'. The NIG would have a special relationship with the Association since, apart from sharing the same Chairman, it would be a 'constituent member of it, and one of its strongest

78

supporters'. NIG was formally represented on the Executive of NEDA and thus had a voice in its policy, although the reverse did not hold. NEDA would meet the need for a 'democratic' voice of the region to complement the activities of NIG, and thus its membership was drawn from all sections of the North-East — MPs, Local Authorities, Local Development Boards, Chambers of Commerce, the National Farmers' Union, NIG and the Regional River and Harbour Authorities were to be represented on its Executive. Its logic was 'unity' at the regional level, and it pursued this aim by gathering together experts in all fields to collect and analyse data and draw policy conclusions, making the results known via publications and reports (NEDA, 1949). NEDA had express approval from the President of the Board of Trade but no national financial backing, merely subscriptions from its members.

Until 1953, the two bodies continued parallel but separate and in that year NIG felt the time ripe for a merger with NEDA, as it felt that its tasks, set in 1943, had been completed and thus, in view of the favourable conditions in the region, it could no longer ask industry for funds. However, the need for a body specifically concerned with the state of the region and with research and publicity was still felt and so NIG merged with NEDA, drew up a new constitution, revised its membership and became the North-East Industrial and Development Association (NEIDA).

Under the old constitutions, no member of NEDA was taken from industrial and commercial undertakings *as such*, whereas NIG was composed of 60 members invited in their personal capacities, not as representatives of companies or unions. The constitution of NEIDA opened the membership to all companies and trade unions in the North-East, and to private individuals. The representatives of member bodies would be elected or appointed to committees as required. An Executive Committee large enough to represent all interests would be elected annually and would conduct the affairs of the Association. Detailed business would be done by three Standing Committees, those of Industry, Publicity and Research (NEIDA Report 1953-54). Simultaneously the activities of NEIDA began to assume the mantle of publicity and information.

The 1950s saw a marked decline of interest in both regionalism and regional policy, a decline both internal to the region and national in character (McCrone, 1968). Indeed in the mid-fifties the rate of national unemployment fell to around 1 per cent (1954: 1.1 per cent. 1955: 1.0 per cent, 1956: 1.0 per cent, 1957: 1.2 per cent), and the regional rate was rarely much higher than the national, falling as low as 1.3 per cent in 1956 (Rowntree Research Unit, 1972b). Little thought was given to future possible situations which might develop in the North, so that in the early and middle 1950s the main concern of planners when considering the coalfield was the provision of jobs for females and those males physically unsuited to mining. The contraction of the labour force in the mines was seen as a distant eventuality (it actually occurred in the late fifties and early sixties). NEIDA survived the period of quiescence in the 1950s, although not without financial difficulties and internal squabbles (NEIDA, 1960-61).

In 1961, NEIDA transformed itself into the North-East Development Council (NEDC) 'to assist in promoting the sound economic development of the region in the interests of the wellbeing of its people' (NEDC, 1961-62). It was to be a revitalised body based firmly upon the 11 local Planning Authorities and having minority representation of local MPs, regional industry and trade unions. This constitution provoked some criticism, from both local industrial interests and from some of the regional Planning Authorities (NEIDA, 1960-61), although by the end of 1962 all the Planning Authorities were represented on its Executive Committee. In its first Annual Report NEDC stated, 'The North-Eastern Development Council will take every action possible to publicize the merits of the North-East as an industrial location. It will encourage the further development of facilities and services which are essential for economic development. Its officers will go anywhere at any time in the pursuit of new industry. It will involve the people of the North-East directly and intimately in its work and so promote in their minds a justifiable sense of pride in their achievement.' In the course of its history it has undergone changes 'towards a market research organization' (NEDC, 1968-69), although its overall functions have remained the same.

1965 however saw the formation of the Northern Economic Planning Council (NEPC), a body constitutionally very different from NEDC. It serves the whole of the Northern Region, and more importantly its members are 'invited' to serve by the Minister. The Planning Councils were the idea of George Brown in the mid-1960s and their terms of reference were:

(a) To assist in the formulation of a regional plan, having regard to the best use of the region's resources

(b) To advise on the steps necessary for implementing the regional plan on the basis of information and assessments provided by the Economic Planning Board;

(c) To advise on the regional implications of national economic policies (Hansard, 1965a).

In this they were to be assisted by the Planning Board, a group of regional civil servants, who provided the resources for the collection of data relevant to NEPC's objectives, and technical assistance with regard to its analysis.

Although both bodies are distinct and constitutionally different, they do have a similarity of function — indeed when NEPC was formed it caused predictions that NEDC would soon be redundant, and forced the Officers of NEDC to consider the position of their body (NEDC, 1964-65). This similarity can be seen in their 'lobbying' relationship to Central Government, but whereas NEPC has privileged access to Central Government, advising the Minister in relationship to its region, NEDC has no such access. Its lobbying function is carried out by means of the usual channels open to 'private' minority interest groups — letters, meetings, publicity, questions from local MPs and so on. In this respect it is helped by its financial contributions from the regional Planning Authorities, and by a Government grant for publicity given on the proviso that a matching sum is obtained from the local authorities of the region. Both bodies continue to dominate the problems of economic development within the region in the 1970s.

Membership

When related in this way the history of regional development organisations seems to lend support to the thesis of those who promulgate an evolutionary perspective on the development of regional policy — an evolution from the first articulation of the problem, and the subsequent organisational response, by regional industrialists, to the theme being taken up separately by politicians within the region, the gradual merging of both groups to face the problems together, with eventually the task being taken over altogether by representatives of democratically elected Local Government. (National Government then appears, as ever, belatedly, cap-in-hand, with its own organisation.) However, an analysis of the membership of the respective bodies reveals, behind this apparent 'development' of bodies, a certain status within the ranks of those people in positions of authority. Lord Ridley (later Chairman of Northumberland County Council, who was a member of one of the famous coal-owning families of Northumberland, and had extensive business interests: according to the 1945 *Who's Who*, 'he owns about 10,200 acres') was not only the prime mover behind NEDB, NIG and NEDA, but was either Chairman or President of *all* of the respective promotional bodies from the formation of NEDB in 1935 to the transformation of NEIDA into NEDC in 1961. Major Appleyard, a founder-member of NEDB, became the first chairman of North-East Trading Estates, and Ridley was one of its first eight directors. Three of these eight signed the 1943 NIG document as did at least two members of NEDB. NIG had on the Executive Committee of NEDA, as of right, ten of its members. When NEDA and NIG merged to form NEIDA in 1953, the President, Vice-President, Chairman and Vice-Chairman of the Executive Committee were the same people who had previously held these positions on NEDA. NEIDA later came to have four Vice-Presidents, of whom three had held positions of executive authority in previous development bodies, and was thus dominated by the same people who had dominated the regional development bodies in the 1930s and 1940s. Even with the seemingly radical break in the histories of these organisations, the transition from NEIDA to NEDC, with the consequent resignation of all of the Executive of NEIDA, the unity is maintained, for in the dominance of the new Development Council by the Local Authorities, most of the 'new' personnel can be found to have served an apprenticeship with NEIDA (in its first year, 1961-62, 9 of the total of 13 local authority members of NEDC had served on NEIDA for at least one of the previous two years, eight of them had served in the immediately preceding year). Similarly two of NEDC's industrial representatives had been long-standing members of NEIDA, and one of them, appointed to NEDC in 1965 had been a Vice-President. At least five members of NEIDA have been invited to serve on NEPC since 1965 and there has been a similar overlap between NEPC and NEDC. The nature of the overlap can perhaps best be illustrated by the case of T. Dan

Smith,leader of Newcastle City Council during the early 1960s, and managing director of his own public relations firm, who was a member of NEIDA from 1959 to 1961, the Newcastle representative on NEDC from 1961 to 1964, and who was, from 1965 to 1970, the first Chairman of NEPC, or of George Chetwynd, MP for Stockton on Tees in the 1950s, who became first director of NEDC in 1962 and a member of NEPC in 1965. He has remained a member of the latter to date. Thus we can see that, within an overall picture of a fairly rapid turnover of representatives on these bodies, there remains within them a relatively unchanging central core, and it is this core who tend to occupy the most powerful positions of executive authority.

The analysis and the policies

During the 1930s an important shift occurred that changed the emphasis in the discussion of the problems of regional development in a decisively interventionist direction, and the dominant preferred modes of intervention themselves changed from labour transference and land settlement to regional economic development policies in the sense that they are presently pursued. This was a very significant shift as it involved the abandonment of earlier assumptions that the effects of industrial fluctuations were self-righting in the medium or long term, paralleling the simultaneous 'Keynesian revolution' in theoretical economics. 'There is no visible prospect of any considerable improvement. The most that is looked for is a recovery to something like the level of 1929' said a study survey of the North-East commissioned by the Board of Trade in 1931. 'It is highly improbable that any expansion of these (lighter) industries and services can take place on such a scale as to make up for a continued loss in the heavy or basic industries for which the Area is so favourably situated' (Armstrong College, 1931). 'We must not accept,' the Special Commissioner for Durham and Tyneside stated in a Report in November 1934, 'that the same forces which created the Depression will automatically readjust it, except after a lapse of time and at a cost of human suffering no modern government would care to contemplate. We can escape from this vicious circle' he went on 'only by some positive external assistance' (Ministry of Labour, 1934). 'It is now generally recognized that the Depressed Areas' said a second study survey in 1935 'cannot of themselves solve their problems and that positive action on the part of central government is necessary ... During the period of the world depression important internal changes were going on and the North-East Coast will, when the depression is over, be left with a very serious social and economic problem presented by a large permanent and disproportionate amount of unemployment' (Armstrong College, 1935).

We would not wish to overstress the radicalism of this transition. The older neoclassical economics of Marshall was not opposed to interventionism, and one of its sub-branches, welfare economics, was active in the theoretical rebuttal of laissez-faire. 'We have thus found that the creation of demand in bad times, and therefore also the transfer of demand from good times to bad, in such ways as to lessen the amplitude of industrial fluctuations is possible. We have now to consider the suggestion that whatever transfer is socially desirable in the sense that the gain in steadying industry exceeds the cost will already have been made under the influence of private self-regarding motives. It can easily be shown that this suggestion is incorrect,' wrote Pigou, in 1927. He went on, 'the presumption in favour of *some* creation or transfer beyond what comes about "naturally" is very strong.' In policy terms, then, important bridges existed between welfare economics and Keynesian economics. It follows that the inter-war experiments in regional policy and analysis cannot simply be assimilated into the development of regional policy as a pre-history. As McCrone admits: '(the powers of the Special Areas Commissioners by 1939) embraced a wider range than regional policy was to acquire again until 1960s' (McCrone, 1968), and much of the earlier and more theoretically primitive approaches to regional policy have been assimilated rather than discarded.

The only real casualty was the faith in the reagrarianisation of the working class by the conversion of the unemployed into peasant smallholders, a policy with obvious political implications, whose persistence as a serious theme during the 1930s is suggestive as to the social groups who were providing the political leadership in the North-East. The 1931 Survey thought that the North-East could produce more of its own food and urged improvements in agricultural marketing, and saw the development of foodpacking and glass jar making as fruitful outcomes of that improvement. The academics who were mainly responsible for the 1931 survey were sceptical of the value of settlement schemes; the repeat 1935 Survey gave it no consideration. Daysh, a Newcastle University economist, in 1937 remarked of South-West Durham: 'the suggestion has been made that the District should revert to agriculture, but that would not absorb a quarter of the unemployed. Meanwhile they tend their gardens and allotments and enjoy such recreations and entertainments as social service has been able to give them. That does not, however, answer the call for work.' Dennison in his classic study of regional problems in 1939 pointed out that nearly 20 per cent of the total expenditure of the Special Commissioners in the Distressed Areas had been devoted to land resettlement programmes; and that such schemes were (a) unlikely to provide for significant new employment, and (b) 'unsatisfactory in that they involve a method which depends on the subsidy from the rest of the economic system. To force workers into a depressed and declining industry must mean that they cannot be entirely self-supporting' (Dennison, 1939). Clearly the academics were aware that these schemes did have support in other quarters, notably from the industrial squirearchy of Captains, Majors, Colonels and Rear-Admirals who manned so much of the Special Areas Commission apparatus. In the 1934 report on the Depressed Areas, J.C.C. Davidson (later a Conservative MP), in his report on West Cumberland, actually suggested land settlement as one of his three main lines of attack on the unemployment problem (Ministry of Labour, 1934). Capt. E. Wallace, for Durham and Tyneside, devoted a section of his report to 'Employment on the Land', declaring that 'No comprehensive survey of the condition of the Durham coalfield can avoid the conclusion that the ultimate destiny of a large part of the country now industrialized must be a return to agriculture.' He quoted in his support a Tyneside Council of Social Service report in 1927; the evidence of a Major Pennyman of Cleveland ('the possession of even one acre of land could be combined with short-time working to provide a satisfactory level of subsistence'); Durham County Council's own efforts to create five-acre holdings; and the evidence of the miners' allotments (Ministry of Labour, 1934). These proposals have significant roots in early English social policy but by the end of the 1930s the academics had been successful in eliminating them. After 1939 they received no further mention.

The accompaniment to land settlement, the industrial transference schemes inaugurated by Baldwin in 1928 with the formation of the Industrial Transference Board to encourage labour migration from the depressed areas, seems to be another casualty. That is a superficial view. It is true that transference schemes reached their peak in 1930, collapsed in the Depression and were only partially revived in 1936/37. By the late 1930s this 'transference', now by spontaneous migration from the depressed areas, was seen to be not a solution but a key problem. The Barlow Commission of 1937-40 was specifically asked to calculate the social costs of such uncontrolled transference. We have elsewhere argued that the Barlow Report was deeply influenced by a conservative resistance to urbanism (Rowntree Research Unit, 1972b), and in that sense the abandonment of transference marked the continuance of the land settlement ideology in a new form.

But transference had a much more direct and obvious descendant. Transference between regions was, like land settlement, abandoned as a major national policy by the end of the 1930s, but transference within regions by the clearance of villages and concentration of population became a standard post-war element of local planning policy, in schemes like the village categorisation policy of Durham County Council and the similar (in practice as ruthless though much more vaguely stated) policy of Northumberland. Wallace stated of South-West Durham in 1934: 'the most optimistic forecast could hardly anticipate the possibility that new industries capable of employing even a reasonable number of inhabitants could be established in such communities' (Ministry of Labour, 1934). In 1937 Daysh wrote of the same area: 'Here live entire communities who can never hope to find re-employment in pits which will never reopen.' It was in fact the South-West Durham Improvement Association, a body which was set up by the Special Areas Commission in 1937, who first articulated the village concentration policy as a solution, whilst the Northern Industrial Group in its first statement in 1943 had a section entitled 'Rearrangement of population within the Area', noting that 'a scheme has been prepared by the South-West Durham Improvement Association . . . it involves moving the population away from abandoned collieries into groups centred on areas which can be regarded as suitable and prepared for modern industrial development, which in this case are suggested to be Bishop Auckland and Darlington.' Elsewhere they report that this policy has already begun to be implemented. Fogarty in 1945 stated that the Special Commissioner's First Report had seen some of the derelict mining villages as economically doomed; and elsewhere continued: 'The clearance and improvement of these derelict areas (N.B. not derelict land but "certain mining villages in West Durham where coal is worked out") . . . . is important as a means of attracting industry as well as for its own sake; the depressed appearance of parts of the North-East Coast has in the past acted as a definite deterrent to firms considering settlement in the region.' (Fogarty, 1945). Thus the two most apparently perishable elements in regional policy thinking of the 1930s have been assimilated into policy making.

For the rest, the problems and solutions assume a near-standard form at an early date, the problems being identified as:

(a) a 'Dual Economy' discrepancy based on the radical differentiation of 'heavy' or 'basic' industry and light industry, with an undue preponderance of the former in the North-East.

(b) the impossibility of heavy industry being any basis for growth; and with a perspective on heavy industry that varies from stabilisation at current levels of employment to the expectation of fairly imminent drastic further decline.

(c) the organisational and psychological backwardness of the North-East with a particular stress on the need to develop native entrepreneurial skills.

(d) the absence of 'new' industry partly attributable to remoteness, partly to the bad physical appearance of the area.

(e) the survival of obstructive localisms and favouritisms in the North-East.

(f) the unevenness of the economic prospects of areas within the North-East — some (e.g. South-West Durham) being regarded as lost causes, as 'derelict'; and some as having bright futures (e.g. Teesside).

No exhaustive exploration of these themes will be attempted here. They all occur in virtually all the regional surveys and reports to date, although on the whole, academic studies put the least emphasis on the motivational and attitudinal aspects of the region's problem. But this is only a minor source of discrepancy in the overall analysis. The North-Eastern economy, even if not the North-Eastern people, is predominantly seen as deviant (an undue preponderence of fairly heavy industry) and backward (the failure to develop 'light' or 'new' industry and services) and this failure is the failure to develop new native entrepreneurs and to promote itself to outsiders.

The 1943 NIG report assembles and summarises the proposals developed in the 1930s recommending policies of work to the workers; diversification of types of employment; the need to improve the outward appearance of the North-East and to provide executive housing in order to attract industry; government assistance for new factory building; Government control over industrial construction; the cheapening of transport to the North-East; the internal transfer of population; the extension of slum clearance and its linkage to industrial development; the construction of trading estates; and the need for a local development organisation. Despite the growth of such a regional organisation, the policy proposals of NEDC

(NEDC, 1962-3), and of NEPC (NEPC, 1969), in no sense go beyond advocating such steps, despite the acceptance of their orientation by the national government. The problem now is no longer one of persuading the national authority to accept such policies, but of the resources to assist in the solution of the problem. 'What is needed is money,' claim NEDC (NEDC, 1969-70) and, given this investment and national growth, the North-East will show itself to be what it really is, 'an area, not of decay, but of opportunity; not of the past, but of the future; not as a place apart, but as an integral part of Great Britain, contributing in full measure to the development and growth of our own region and also to the economic strength of the whole nation ' (NEDC, 1962-63). A strategy of regional development, the roots of which can be traced back to work done regionally and nationally over 30 years previously, and which has been unsuccessful (Rowntree Research Unit, 1972b), is thus trusted for the future.

Conclusion

We have thus argued that, despite a superficial historical accuracy, any attempt to construct an explanation of the development of regional organisations, and the policies they advocate, in the North-East in evolutionist terms is inaccurate, and in so doing we are extending and reinforcing work we have done previously on the national aspects of regional policy (Rowntree Research Unit, 1972a, 1972b). That the evolutionary view can still have widespread currency is understandable, for, in adopting this variant of the functionalist perspective, regional policy from the 1930s through to the 1970s can be represented as a series of policy responses to a changing situation in the region. That the situation has changed there can be no doubt, but, as we have shown, little reflection of this change can be found in the analysis and proposals put forward by the regional bodies. We would now like to turn to this problem of explanation, and advance, tentatively, an alternative hypothesis which fits the circumstances of a changing situation which has evoked a standard response.

We have shown that within the array of changing personnel who have manned the Executive Committees of succeeding regional bodies since the 1930s, a solid and relatively slowly changing core is to be discerned. We have demonstrated this above in terms of personnel (it can be represented metaphorically by Lord Ridley from the 1930s to the 1960s and by T. Dan Smith during the 1960s). This core can be seen not only in terms of these specific personnel, but in terms of interest groups, for within, and supporting, each long-standing figure on these Executive Committees lies an interest, or constellation of interests, which give their recipient a specific, and significant, place within the social structure of the region. The overall constellation of these interests is portrayed in the person of one of the key figures – Lord Ridley. A landowner and industrialist, chairman of one of the most powerful Local Authorities in the region, he had also by virtue of birth and connections a position of some influence nationally. When we consider the other long serving members of the bodies, the pattern emerges. Regional policies are pursued consistently by a group which represents a unified elite within the North-East.

Nevertheless these policies are presented as being policies in the interests of the area as a whole (rather than as interests of the elite), and they are pursued under the cloak of the democratic principle. Thus, even before the announcement of the membership of NEPC, William Rodgers, a junior minister in the Labour Government, assured the House that 'we shall certainly ensure that membership is representative of the region.' (Hansard, 1965b), and, four years later, Fred Lee, then Minister for the North, told the Commons in a written answer that 'The Council is composed of people intimately acquainted with the lives of the people [of the region]' (Hansard, 1969). Nevertheless, such a body has been criticised as *potentially* undemocratic. William Elliot, MP for Newcastle North, asked when the idea for the formation of the Council was first announced, 'Will he [the Minister] accept that there is a great deal of concern about the possibility of apparently unnecessary new bodies undermining democratically-elected local government' (Hansard, 1965c) and, when it was known that T. Dan Smith was to be its first chairman, Edward Heath asked Brown: 'Why it was found necessary to appoint such a controversial political figure to be Chairman of the Northern Regional Council as Mr. Dan Smith, who declared, as recently as last week, that "the democratic vote is no way to get the sort of changes we need in the North". Is this the sort of person to preside over a council such as this?' (Hansard, 1965d). Similar charges of political bias have been levelled within NEDC, especially over the ousting of the Conservative Ald. Grey of Newcastle as Chairman and the installation in his place of the Labour Ald. Allon of Durham Council. It has been such minor political disturbances which have tended to indicate the partial interests being served by the pursuit of regional policies from within, and on behalf of the whole, region. But such tensions do not affect the status claimed by the bodies. NEDC, having in the first 2 years of its existence 'succeeded in creating a regional self-awareness and . . . done much to restore a proud self-confidence to the North-East' (NEDC, 1962-63), began to speak as 'the Voice of the North-East, entrusted with the essential duties of pressure, promotion and publicity,' (NEDC, 1963-64), and, in later years, its most demagogic Chairman claimed that 'NEDC has a vigorous role to play in presenting "grass roots" opinion to central Government. We have spoken loudly and clearly to Governments in the past . . . and we will continue to do so in the future' (NEDC, 1971-72).

Regional policies as specific solutions to regional problems have certainly been advocated 'loudly and clearly' by the regional bodies, but, as we have suggested, regional problems are no more than a geographical constellation of social-structural problems. Seen in this context the regional problem changes its complexion, for its solution necessitates, not the geographical scheduling of areas and a policy of grants for improvements or to encourage firms to move into the area, but wider social structural reforms — perhaps heavier rates of progressive taxation to achieve income redistribution, perhaps more nationalisation of industry and the systematic planning of production by the State. Nevertheless, the main purpose of the regional organisations has remained constant – to persuade the people of the North-East to accept a certain range of policies and assumptions about policy, and to mobilise to achieve these aims in a socially comprehensive way, on 'regional' rather than on area, industry, party or interest basis. The significance of this policy-model of regional problems lies then in alternative approaches which have been repressed; the significance of the regional organisation lies in its repression of a spatial or social lack of homogeneity in the North-East. Each kind of repression or exclusion is necessary for the other. And, though considerable difficulties have always been experienced in maintaining the dominance of the policy-model and organisational style that we find, the basic parameters of discussion about the North-East have been determined by this twin set of assumptions. In emphasising the regional, attention is directed away from the social. The causes of legitimate grievances are displaced from the area of general or societal politics into an area of purely regional politics. An overall assessment of this kind suggests that the real meaning of regionalism lies not in the unfolding of the administrative apparatus of British indicative planning but in the political and organisational handling of sources of possible opposition in British society (for example, Trade Union Organisations, regional Labour authorities).

Notes

[1] For a critique of this kind of analysis see A.G. Frank (1971), *The Sociology of Development and the Underdevelopment of Sociology*, Pluto Press, London; and for practical examples relevant to the North, see NEDC (1972), *The North in the 'Sixties*. Newcastle; and Rowntree Research Unit (1972b), *Some Inconsistencies in Regional Development Policy, The Case of the North-East.*

[2] 'Government and local action are both called into being by the same obvious needs' – remark made by an eminent regional Civil Servant now retired, in the course of a conversation, carried out as one of a large number of interviews with notables in the Northern Region. A report on these interviews is in course of preparation.

[3] Figure 5.1 shows the relationship between the Northern Planning Region and the North-East, in the context of the Planning Regions of England and Wales. Table 5.1 is a statistical comparison of the Northern Region with Great Britain along a number of the major 'axes' of regional developmynt.

[4] For a history of development organizations up to 1946 see M. P. Fogarty (1947). The struggle for influence of different areas and different interests is in itself an interesting reflection on regionalism. The NIG (1946): Notes on Organisation and Methods makes it very clear how industrialists wished to keep their 'own' organisation free of the political influence of local Councils.

Bibliography

Allen, E., Odber, A. and Bowden, P., *Development Area Policy in the North-East*, NEIDA, Newcastle, 1957.

Armstrong College, *An Industrial Survey of the North-East Coast*, Board of Trade, London, 1931.

Armstrong College, *The Industrial Position of the North-East Coast of England*, Newcastle, 1935.

Dennison, S.R., *The Location of Industry and the Depressed Areas*, Oxford University Press, 1939.

Fogarty, M.P., *The Prospects of the Industrial Areas of Great Britain*, Methuen, London 1945.

Fogarty M.P., *Plan Your Own Industries: A History of Local and Regional Development Organizations*, Oxford University Press, 1947.

Frank, A.G., *Sociology of Development or Underdevelopment of Sociology*, Pluto Press, London, 1971.

Hansard, vol. 707, 25 February 1965, pp. 609 ff, HMSO, London, 1965a.

Hansard, vol. 707, 18 February 1965, pp. 1352. HMSO, London, 1965b.

Hansard, vol. 778, 20 February 1969, written replies, HMSO, London, 1969.

McCrone, G, *Regional Policy in Britain*, Allen & Unwin, London, 1968.

McKinney, J.C. and Bouroue, L.B., 'The Changing South', *American Soc. Rev.*, vol. 36, 1971, pp. 399-412.

Ministry of Labour, *Report on Conditions in Certain Depressed Areas*, HMSO, London, 1934

Mumford, L., 'Regionalism and irregionalism', *Soc. Rev.*, vol. 19, 1927, pp. 277-88.

North-East Development Association (NEDA), *Some Notes on Organization and Activities*, Newcastle, 1949.

North-East Development Council, *Annual Reports*, Newcastle, 1960-72.

North-East Development Council, *The North in the 'Sixties*, Newcastle, 1972.

North-East Industrial and Development Association, *Annual Reports*, Newcastle, 1953-61.

Northern Economic Planning Council, *Outline Strategy for the North to 1981*, HMSO, London, 1969.

Northern Industrial Group, *Considerations Affecting Postwar Employment in the North-East*, Newcastle, 1943.

Northern Industral Group, *Objects, Organization and Methods*, Newcastle, 1946.

Northumberland County Council, *County Development Plan*, Newcastle, 1952.

Northumberland County Council, *First Development Plan Review*, Newcastle, 1964.

Pahl, R.E., 'The rural—urban continuum', *Soc. Rur.*, vol. 4, 1966.

Pigou, A.C., *Industrial Fluctuations*, Macmillan, London, 1927.

Rowntree Research Unit, 'Towards a Theoretical Analysis of Regional Policy' (mimeo), Department of Sociology, University of Durham, 1972a.

Rowntree Research Unit, 'Some Inconsistencies in Regional Development Policy' (mimeo), Department of Sociology, University of Durham, 1972b.

Stacey, M., 'The myth of community studies', *B.J.S.*, 1969.

Wirth, L., *Limitations of Regionalism in Cities and Social Life*, Chicago University Press, 1924.

PART III

PROCESSES OF REGIONAL PLANNING

Overview of Part III

This third part of the book is concerned with political and administrative processes of regional planning. Following this brief introduction and overview, the three selected writings are by J. Friend, J. Power and C. Yewlett (1974, Chapter 6), C. Painter (1972, Chapter 7) and Douglas Hart (1976, Chapter 8).

The Friend et al contribution is in many respects the result of a pioneering piece of research into the complexities of the political administration of regional planning in the UK context. Employing a conceptual model of public planning, which emphasises the administrative and managerial dimensions. Friend et al focus attention on a particular issue — a strategic urban expansion scheme in the West Midlands. From this treatment they attempt to extract some implications for the qualitative improvement of regional planning processes. The contribution selected for inclusion in this volume is concerned with the explicit regional dimension of their research programme.

This theme is continued by Painter; the context is again the West Midlands, but the perspective is very much more an assessment of the political and administrative processes of regional planning, rather than the managerial-conceptual dimension. Emphasis is placed on an attempt to estimate the repercussions associated with administrative innovation — in this case the setting-up of the West Midlands Economic Planning Council.

The Friend et al and Painter writings offer insights into the political, administrative and managerial contexts of regional planning. Missing from both is an explicit consideration of the internal processes of planning. This is the perspective of the contribution by Douglas Hart. He is concerned with the substantive procedures of planning, developing an argument for an iterative approach based upon a critical evaluation of the rational-consensus model and its corollary, disjointed incrementalism.

6 Processes of public planning: the regional dimension

Excerpt from J. Friend, J. Power and C. Yewlett, *Public Planning: The Inter-Corporate Dimension* Institute of Operational Research, Tavistock Publications, London 1974.

Evolution in the processes of regional planning

In these pages, we begin to explore some important processes of innovation which have been taking place since the early 1960s in the organisation of regional planning in Britain. Although these processes have often been hesitant and sometimes controversial, we shall argue that the new forms of skill and of organisational relationship which have been emerging at the regional level are of considerable importance for the evolution of public planning in general, and offer some significant opportunities for future experiment.

Throughout most of this examination, we shall employ the perspective of the West Midlands Region of England, which provides the regional context for the planned expansion of Droitwich. Similar processes of change to those that we shall trace have also been developing in other regional divisions of England, though not always in the same way or at the same pace . . . . The events upon which we shall focus most closely took place over the years between 1968 and 1971, before the main priorities of our research shifted from observation to written interpretation. These were years of considerable flux in the organisational arrangements for regional planning in England; but they saw a momentum established which culminated in the formation of more clearly-defined structures during 1972 and 1973. Of necessity, therefore, our emphasis here is on a transitional process, in which the roles and relationships of the actors could change rapidly from one year to the next. However, it is a process which, in our belief, yields some important lessons for the evolution of inter-agency planning in general.

Ministry initiatives in the West Midlands

The processes of regional planning in the West Midlands can be traced from the publication of the original West Midlands Plan in 1948 — as a first attempt to provide a cohesive analytical base for land-planning in the region — up to the public inquiry at Wythall in 1969, which exposed a state of open conflict between Birmingham and two of its adjoining counties over a wide range of strategic issues. This inquiry was to be only the first in a series of such confrontations over the future of Wythall, and later of other sites on the fringe of the West Midlands conurbation. However, it was the first to focus public attention on the complex patterns of relationship between different planning issues within the region, and had a corresponding effect in stimulating pressures for the exploration of such issues through wide-ranging regional planning studies.

A Ministry of Housing and Local Government commitment to the Droitwich expansion proposal emerged from a wider process of review of possible sites for overspill development in the West Midlands, following the inconclusive outcome of the first Wythall inquiry. The political priority given to this process is indicated by the fact that much of the intricate negotiation which followed was conducted in person by the Ministry's Permanent Secretary, Dame Evelyn (later Baroness) Sharp. The search now was for three or four substantial development schemes that could yield quick results, including possibly one or two where the use of New Town powers could be justified. This meant conducting explorations, individually and collectively, with a wider range of Midland planning authorities than had hitherto been involved, extending from Herefordshire in the west to Northamptonshire in the east. It also meant approaching the Treasury over possible financial inducements to ease the path of overspill negotiations, and arguing the merits of alternative New Town sites with other government departments, most notably the Agriculture and Industrial Development Ministries.

Meanwhile anxieties as to what was happening began to built up within the region until, in 1961, the results of the Ministry's explorations were announced, having been given political sanction at Cabinet level. Support was to be given to major overspill schemes then under discussion at Worcester, at Redditch, and at Daventry, just outside the region's eastern boundary in Northamptonshire. A marginal adjustment to the green belt was to be permitted at Wythall, and investigations were to be pursued as a matter of urgency into the designation of a New Town at Dawley in Shropshire.

None of these various outcomes could be seen as irrevocable decisions, but rather as significant increments in political commitment at national level to schemes which, in many cases, would still require painstaking processes of negotiations or challenge at the interfaces with the local interests affected. As it happened, the schemes for the New Town at Dawley and the expansion of Daventry were duly launched in the years that followed. However, the negotiations at Worcester were to remain inconclusive, while in 1963 events at Redditch took a dramatic turn with an announcement by the then Land Planning Minister that he was to seize the initiative by imposing a New Town solution, because of a breakdown over financial questions in negotiating a voluntary town expansion agreement. Such difficulties, accentuated by a continued resistance from Warwickshire and Worcestershire to any further erosion of the proposed green belt boundaries, combined to increase the pressure from Birmingham for short term solutions to its search for sites for municipal housing development, through peripheral expansion on the southern and eastern fringes of the city.

During this period, none of the Ministry's staff concerned with land planning problems were based in the region itself. However, pressures were beginning to mount towards a more explicit regional devolution of central government activities, particularly in response to the chronic problems of economic deprivation in the northern parts of the country. In 1962, the Industrial Development Minister was given the new title of Secretary of State for Industry, Trade and Regional Development, with an immediate assignment to investigate the economic problems of the north-east corner of England, supported by a new regional office of the Ministry in Newcastle, covering both land planning and housing functions.

A further initiative in the direction of more explicit concern with regional planning came in 1964, when the government decided to launch wide-ranging studies of the three regions of England dominated by major conurbations – the South-East, the West Midlands, and the North-West – and assembled special inter-departmental teams of civil servants for this purpose. The study group for the West Midlands proceeded to collate as much relevant information on the problems of the region as could be obtained through the analysis of the data already available to central government on demographic, employment, and other trends, and to supplement this information through a programme of discussions with local planning authorities and other regional interests, thus adding a dimension of more localised appreciation to their search for acceptable regional strategies.

The introduction of an economic planning framework

Shortly before the West Midlands Study Group was due to report its findings, the growing commitment to regional planning activities in Britain was given an additional impetus by the election of a Labour government, publicly committed to policies of more extensive intervention by central government in the management of the economy. One of the first actions of the new government was to set up a new Department of Economic Affairs, which was intended to provide a positive lead in sustaining progress towards faster economic growth, and to act as a counterweight to what were seen as the financial orthodoxies of the Treasury. One of the tasks with which the new Ministry was charged was the formulation of a first 'National Plan', setting broad targets for economic growth which could be interpreted in terms of planned levels of achievement for different sectors of the national economy. Such an exercise could, it was hoped, provide a framework for more realistic planning activities at a regional level, where uncertainty over future rates of economic growth had been identified as one of the inhibiting factors in drawing up realistic capital investments programmes.

In 1965, a more explicitly defined basis for the administration of regional planning was established by the sub-division of England into the eight Economic Planning Regions. In most but not all parts of the country, their boundaries corresponded closely to those of the 'standard regions' which, for some years previously, had been used to provide a common framework for the presentation of departmental statistics. At this time, several government departments already exercised some of their local responsibilities from offices in the regions, but most of the land planning and housing functions of the Ministry of Housing and Local

Government were still exercised from London, except for the two most northerly regions of England. As a step towards fuller coordination between the regional activities of the various ministries concerned in the new economic planning framework, a decision was taken that, in each region, the activities of all the relevant ministries should, wherever possible, be grouped together in a single building. In every case, this new centre should include a regional office of the Ministry of Housing and Local Government, while a central coordinating role was to be taken by a senior official of the new Department of Economic Affairs, who would serve as Chairman of a new Regional Economic Planning Board. This board was to consist of senior civil servants representing all the various ministries concerned in regional affairs, including those responsible for housing and land planning, transport, employment, industry and technology, education, agriculture, and investment in public utility services.

In order to provide a body of informed regional opinion to which the Regional Economic Planning Board could refer, a new Regional Economic Planning Council was appointed for each region by the Secretary of State for Economic Affairs. This Council was to consist of about twenty-five people selected for their knowledge and experience of the region concerned. Although it was stressed that the members of each Council were to be appointed for their individual qualities, rather than as representatives of particular sectional interests, some care was taken to select a set of people for each region who could be seen to reflect a fair balance of territorial interests, and of important sectors of regional influence, such as industry, the trade unions, the universities, agriculture, and local government.

On their formation, the Economic Planning Councils were given the following terms of reference: first, 'to assist in the formulation of regional plans, having regard to the best use of the region's resources'; second, 'to advise on the steps necessary for implementing the regional plans on the basis of information and assessments provided by the economic planning boards'; and, third, 'to advise on the regional implications of national economic policies'. Further, they were encouraged to take an active initiating role in bringing matters to the attention of the Boards where they felt this to be necessary. Given these responsibilities, it was accepted that the proceedings of the Councils would have to be treated as largely confidential. If sensitive information on current issues of central government policy was to be freely discussed, then even a full disclosure of the items covered on the agenda could make the Council members uncomfortably vulnerable to their sectional constituency interests.

The new regional structure drew some immediate criticism from those who had been advocating bolder moves towards the establishment of elected regional assemblies equipped with 'teeth' in the form of specific executive powers. However, even the limited functions envisaged for the Economic Planning Councils and Boards raised some difficult questions of demarcation with existing agencies of planning and co-ordination, not least of which was the then Ministry of Housing and Local Government with its established role in land planning and related fields. It was largely to avoid the appearance of trespassing on the Ministry's statutory responsibilities in such areas — concerned largely with processes of contextual control over the activities of local planning authorities — that the prefix 'Economic' was attached to the new Planning Councils and Boards. However, as we shall see, the relationship of 'physical' planning was to prove at first a difficult one to define, giving rise at times to much uncertainty about the institutional relationships between the Land Planning Ministry and the Department of Economic Affairs. These uncertainties were reduced to some extent when the DEA was disbanded in 1969 after five years of independent existence — largely because of national political pressures and difficulties in defining its role in relation to the all-pervading influence of the Treasury. Significantly, the DEA's small nuclei of economic planning staff in the regions were retained, later to be integrated with the physical and transportation planners in the new Department of the Environment. Gradually, the relationships between these various forms of planning skill began to become more clearly established, in a context of exploratory activities that varied somewhat in their emphasis from region to region, but which we shall now discuss more fully from our perspective of the West Midlands of England.

The growth of regional processes in the West Midlands

The broad discussion, which follows, of the evolution of regional planning in the West Midlands rests largely on information gathered in discussions with civil servants and others who played central roles in the processes of physical and economic planning in the region during the period 1967-71; on a review of documents published by the Economic Planning Council and other relevant agencies; on published discussions of the role and influence of the Council (Cadbury, 1968; Painter, 1972 — included in this volume as Chapter 7); and on our own participation in various activities of the West Midlands branch of the Regional Studies Association.

The most readily visible outputs of the new regional machinery were a series of published planning studies, the first of which, entitled simply 'The West Midlands: a Regional Study', appeared in 1965 under the auspices of the DEA. This reported the work of the inter-departmental team of civil servants which had been commissioned the previous year, shortly before the DEA had been formed or the new regional structure had been established. Much of the information assembled fits the description of 'regional stocktaking' suggested by Cullingworth (1970), in that it brought together various forms of data from the records of different ministries, on the region's demographic, economic, and employment structure, as a background against which to review existing and potential commitments for the future distribution of population and public services.

Like others of its generation, this study can be viewed as reflecting a comparatively early stage in the process of learning about relevant approaches to the appraisal of regional options. The Director of one subsequent regional study team has described much of the work of this period as being conditioned by the traditional administrator's response of focusing on specific topics rather than broader issues, seeking to tackle each exhaustively rather than selectively, and extrapolating from the present to the future without the help of any explicit methodology for coping with uncertainties either internal or external to the region. However, despite the paucity of systematic techniques with which to reach beyond the level of stocktaking and qualitative appraisal, the authors of the 1965 study found themselves inexorably focusing on the still-pervasive issue of Birmingham overspill. The conclusion they reached was that the commitments so far negotiated still left a substantial population increase to be accommodated in new locations, in a manner that — at least in the medium term — would have to take into account constraints in industrial location arising from inter-regional employment policies.

The overall problem was diagnosed as one of striking a balance between the peripheral expansion of the conurbation, the growth of 'satellite' communities within commuter range, and commitments to major new centres of growth further afield. One such centre already existed at the time in the newly designated New Town at Dawley in Shropshire (Salop), and one of the team's more specific recommendations concerned the possibility of locating additional population in this area. If, as then mooted, other centres of expansion were eventually to be established in the neighbouring regions to the north and south — around the Dee and Severn estuaries respectively — then it was argued that an attractive long term strategy could be to establish a new 'axis of national growth' extending along the full length of the border between England and Wales, and serving to relieve much of the pressure from the West Midlands conurbation and its immediate environs.

In a preface to this report, the government expressed itself as yet uncommitted to its findings, and referred it to the newly formed West Midlands Economic Planning Council to provide a considered appraisal, after consultation with local authorities and other relevant agencies. Some eight months later, the Council submitted its first interim reactions. These added support, with varying degrees of qualification, to the specific proposals that the study team had made for further expansion in the Dawley area and elsewhere. However, the view was also expressed that the areas of study for possible longer-term growth should not be confined in an 'arbitrary' way to the north/south axis recommended in the earlier study, and three other alternative axes were suggested for further evaluation.

A year later, a more comprehensive review of the region's problems was published by the Council (*The West Midlands: Patterns of Growth*, West Midlands Economic Planning Council, 1967), with the staff work this time carried out by the civil servants in the new regional office. While still accepting the 1965 study as a source of basic data, some of the group's assumptions were modified in the light of subsequent information, and a revised set of overspill proposals was put forward for meeting the modified estimates of growth over the next fifteen years. One of the Council's main arguments was that the provision of new housing and social services for an expanding population depended on vigorous action to exploit more fully the region's economic potential. To this end, a variety of initiatives were suggested in the fields of further education, industrial training, and research; and it was argued that governmental controls over the movement of industry should in future be applied in a more positive and more flexible way.

When the national government issued its formal reply to the points raised in the report, several of the recommendations were accepted without demur. However, those relating to the more vigorous support of industrial dispersal within the region were rejected, as being incompatible with the national priority attached to reducing the differentials of unemployment between regions. Accordingly, it was argued that — at least in the shorter term — more attention would have to be focused on the promotion of overspill schemes within reasonable commuting distance of the conurbation.

Initiatives by local authorities

While this kind of debate was taking place between the central government and the new Regional Council, the question arose of what part the local authorities in the region should seek to play in the evolving planning process. At this time, relations between particular county and city authorities were continuing to impede progress towards the relief of the problems of congestion within the conurbation. Warwickshire and Worcestershire continued to resist incursions by Birmingham into the proposed green belt - although some private housing development was conceded at Wythall - while progress in the New Town at Dawley was held up by the high cost of infrastructure development.

One interest that the local authorities clearly had in common was that of retaining some capacity to work towards their own solutions, rather than of allowing all initiative to pass to central government and the new Regional Council. With active encouragement from central government, Birmingham and Worcestershire therefore agreed to initiate a joint study of possible locations for peripheral development which could contribute to the city's short term housing problem, on the understanding that other local planning authorities would join in a wider review process of other future locations for expansion within the region. Here, the emphasis would be on schemes that might avoid both the continual erosion of the prospective green belt boundaries, and the heavy investment costs of distant New Town development.

In 1966, those local authorities with a clear concern in this wider review process therefore came together to form a new permanent multi-organisational structure, known as the West Midlands Planning Authorities Conference or, more informally, the 'Standing Conference'. Subsequently, the membership of this was extended to embrace all five Counties and eleven County Boroughs within the Economic Planning Region. In some ways, this Conference was a successor to that established some fifteen years earlier in response to the 1948 Abercrombie and Jackson Plan. Although this earlier Conference had established one piece of permanent coordinating machinery in the form of a 'Technical Committee' of Chief Planning Officers, the meetings of this group had lost much of their significance through being consistently steered away from politically controversial issues.

This time, the local authorities, with encouragement and occasional advice from the regional civil service, agreed to form a joint study team, to be steered through a new 'Technical Officers Panel' on which the delicate question of Chairmanship would be settled through a rotation system. Also, an administrative panel was appointed to take decisions on budgeting and staffing matters. A senior planning officer was seconded from Birmingham to lead the study team, while most of the other posts were also filled by secondment from among the contributing authorities. Consultants were appointed to deal with a number of specialist aspects of the study, and it was agreed that civil servants from the regional office and headquarters would provide skills relating to demographic, social, and economic analysis, either on a full or a part-time basis.

The new study team took its place in an office in Birmingham adjoining that of another joint local authority team which had already been recently established, concerned with transportation planning over the conurbation and adjoining areas. The origins of the transport study were somewhat different, in that it had been initiated as a second phase in an ongoing process of transportation planning, the first phase having already been completed by a team of specialist consultants. The consultants had set out many of the major issues and some tentative conclusions, with the aid of some of the sophisticated processes of mathematical modelling that were then becoming accepted in the transportation planning field; and it was accepted that the next step should be for the local authorities themselves to form a joint team which would be directed more explicitly towards the complex field of executive decision that would be involved. As with the Regional Study Team, the joint transport study team was assisted by central funds and reported formally through a 'technical' committee of relevant officials from the sponsoring local authorities. However, the staff differed in being appointed on a permanent basis, with a view to creating a permanent competence which, after the impending reorganisation of local government, could be handed on to any metropolitan or regional agency of government which might be established within the conurbation area.

Meanwhile, another initiative towards inter-agency planning was crystallising in the east of the region. In Coventry, a review of the City's Development Plan was disclosing the dimensions of a future problem of shortage of housing land after the mid-seventies, at a time when the Land Planning Ministry was beginning to encourage the experimental formation of sub-regional planning teams in a few carefully selected parts of the country. After settling some delicate problems of political balance which have been touched on elsewhere (Friend and Jessop, 1969), it was agreed that a study team should be appointed under the joint auspices of Coventry, Warwickshire, and Solihull, with a limited two-year life.

Also, within the main West Midlands conurbation, another sub-regional planning process was being mobilised at a more informal level. The 1968 Town and Country Planning Act introduced the new concept of the 'Structure Plan' as the primary instrument of strategic land use policy, intended to overcome the procedural and other rigidities of the established development plan system by concentrating on broad statements of policy rather than specified land zonings. More localised options were to be dealt with through a system of 'Local Plans' at the level of districts, including plans for selected local 'Action Areas' of various kinds. Here, planning authorities would have an increased degree of local discretion, leaving the Land Planning Ministry free to concentrate its formal powers of scrutiny at the broader policy level. Among the group of authorities invited to take part in the first wave of structure plan preparation were the seven County Boroughs in the West Midlands conurbation, and an *ad hoc* preparatory group was established with encouragement and technical assistance from the Ministry's regional planning offices.

Thus, a number of joint study teams were established during the late 1960s, working in overlapping but by no means identical territorial boundaries. These boundaries are indicated in Fig. 6.1 in relation to a mapping of the then planning authorities in which spatial relationships are preserved but areas are distorted in order to make them proportional to population. Thus, the map reflects the relative political weightings of different local constituency interests. Also superimposed on this map is the 'political territory' of the West Midlands Metropolitan County as later settled by the 1972 Local Government Act. Another new executive agency referred to in Fig. 6.1 is the West Midlands Passenger Transport Authority (PTA), which was first established in 1969 with an area slightly wider than that covered by the transport study team. This authority represented a further addition to the set of *ad hoc* joint local authority agencies established in the years prior to local government reorganisation, to overcome problems of fragmentation in the planning of specific executive functions. In the case of the PTA, the joint agency was equipped with an explicit statutory role in relation to the provisions of the 1968 Transport Act, and a strong executive arm of its own in the form of a new Passenger Transport Executive (PTE), bringing together the municipal bus undertakings of Birmingham and the County Boroughs within the conurbation.

Activities in the economic planning field

While these developments were taking place in the local government field, the economic planning staff of the government departments within the regional office were also engaged on a somewhat different front, in association with members of the Economic Planning Council. Following publication of the *Patterns of Growth* report in 1967, adverse trends in the national economy threw an increasingly sharp light on the vulnerability of the region's traditional industrial base. The members of the Planning Council therefore resolved to set up a working party from among their numbers to carry out a deeper appraisal of the economic potential of the region, and the actions that might be considered to stimulate further growth. Most of the eleven members of the working party were leading figures in the region's industrial life, who undertook between them to carry out a wide-ranging series of interviews to gather both impressionistic and other information about economic conditions, trends, and perceived conditions for future prosperity in various relevant sectors of

101

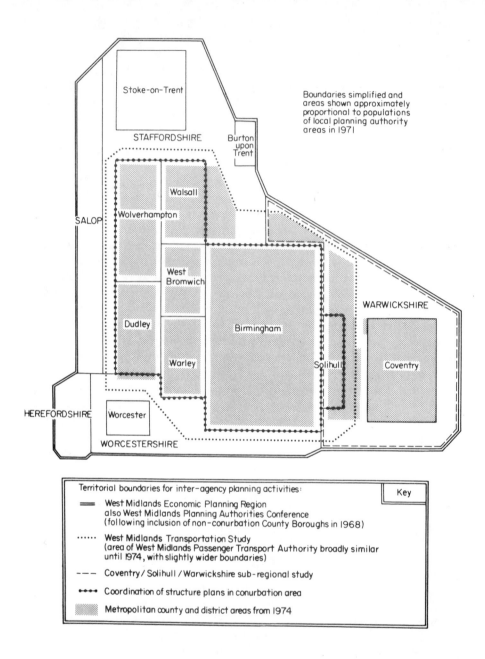

Figure 6.1 Political map of inter-agency planning activities in West Midlands, 1965-73

industry.

The approach adopted was to analyse employment trends both by type of industry and by the territorial sub-divisions of the Employment Ministry, and then to pick out for further exploration by interview methods certain selected types of industry believed to be of special significance either because of a high existing concentration within the region, or because of an apparent deficiency of employment when compared to other regions, or because of future potential in terms of national economic growth. The results of the surveys and interviews carried out were presented in the second full report of the Economic Planning Council, entitled *The West Midlands: an Economic Appraisal* (West Midlands Economic Planning Council, 1971). This set out an ambitious set of proposals for governmental action to stimulate economic growth, with a less pronounced emphasis on spatial distribution within the region than had the proposals of earlier regional studies.

The main argument was for more positive support by government for growth within the region, including relaxation of IDC constraints. It was argued that such growth could serve to produce a 'spin-off' for other regions, as well as to reduce the level of unemployment in the West Midlands, which was now showing itself more sensitive than most other regions to fluctuations in the state of the national economy. At a meeting of the Regional Studies Association in Birmingham, the report was exposed to some criticism on the grounds that it represented a piece of special pleading on behalf of a set of predominantly industrial interests whose members shared the same implicit assumptions about the beneficial effects of continued economic growth (Herson, 1972), and that there was little evidence of any systematic planning process underlying the choice of recommendations advanced (Barbara Smith, 1972). In defence of the approach adopted, a leading member of the working party argued that the exercise had been carried out under intense time pressures, depending heavily on the accumulated expertise of individuals with long experience in the region's industries. Even when seen as a piece of informed regional advocacy, it was argued that the study could only help to improve the background against which central government confronted their major decisions of national economic policy.

Such a view is supported in the article by Painter (1972 — included in this volume as Chapter 7), in which the 'Economic Appraisal' report is seen as setting a seal of regional approval on a more diffuse set of representations by various regional interests, led by Birmingham's City Council and Chamber of Commerce, for modification of government industrial development policy in the West Midlands. Painter suggests that the report was in fact influential in bringing about certain changes in government IDC policy during 1972, which distinguished for the first time between the conditions of the West Midlands and those of the less vulnerable South East. He argues that the formation of the Council and working party helped to institutionalise the existing informal relationships between a variety of commercial, managerial, and trade union groupings in the region, as well as the more influential individual firms, to produce a new and more effective pressure group for effective regional development.

One of the intended functions of the Economic Planning Council was to participate in the strategic planning of public investment, through an annual review of the five-year projections of capital expenditure in the region by the ministries concerned with housing, transport, education, health, and other relevant sectors. In the West Midlands, these projections were scrutinised by a sub-committee of the Regional Council, with regional civil servants acting as technical assessors. They were then coordinated nationally through the Public Expenditure Survey Committee, a new piece of governmental machinery which had been established to increase the effectiveness of national economic management. At first, it proved by no means easy for the Regional Economic Planning Councils to intervene effectively in this national process of adjustment between the interests of different ministries, each with a powerful hierarchical organisation built around the principle of ultimate political accountability to the Minister. In the West Midlands, the opportunities for effective regional influence were especially limited, because of the continuing policy of steering as much as possible of the limited national potential for public investment towards the assisted areas of the North and West.

The new projections of regional expenditure were carried out and evaluated on a confidential basis. Nevertheless, they were found helpful by the regional civil servants in appreciating more clearly the economic dimension of their planning task, and the process of regional scrutiny was felt to work more effectively in the West Midlands than in some other regions. Although Painter (1972) suggests that it may have had no more than a marginal effect on the allocation of public resources, he does attribute one important decision of investment priority to the influence of the Council through its annual review cycle: the early programming of a strategic link between the New Town at Telford and the national motorway system. Although other pressures may well have been involved in this and other similar programming decisions, it would be surprising if the exploratory processes of the Regional Council during this period did not have a much more important influence in terms of mutual adjustment between different decision-making agencies than their publicly visible outputs might suggest. In the West Midlands, as elsewhere, there has been much criticism of the limited practical influence of the Economic Planning Councils, not least from those invited to serve as members during the early years; but, in terms of the gradual evolution of networks of decision-making activity at the regional level, it appears likely that their contribution may have been a comparatively subtle one, with indirect influences at many different points in the total machinery of government.

An evolving pattern of inter-agency explorations

In Figure 6.2, the various regional and sub-regional planning studies described in the last two sections are brought together to present a picture of an evolving pattern of exploratory processes in the West Midlands during the late 1960s and early 1970s — some of them based primarily on coordinative activity among local authorities,

104

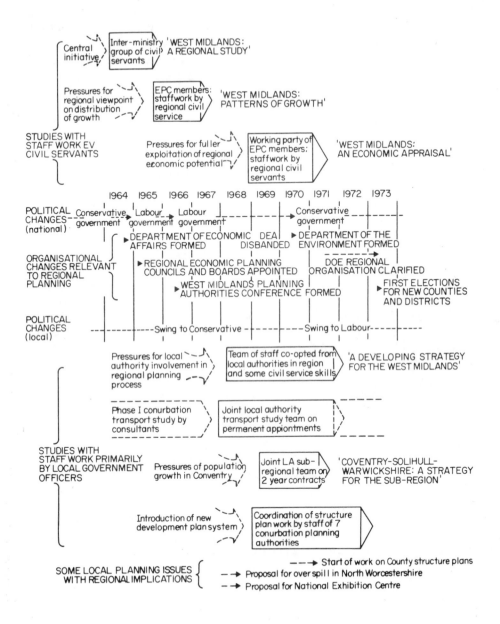

Figure 6.2 Pattern of main regional and sub-regional studies in West Midlands, 1964-73

while others were initiated under central government or Economic Planning Council auspices.

As we have already discussed, each of these exploratory processes was initiated in response to a somewhat different set of pressures — national, regional, or local. Accordingly, they differed in terms of reference, pattern of accountability, management structure, and sources of exploratory skill. As indicated in Fig. 6.2, the arrangements for assignment of staff varied from permanent recruitment to the formation of *ad hoc* working parties, backed by differing levels of financial support from central government. Inevitably, these different organisational settings led to differences of exploratory style, leading the teams concerned towards different planning horizons, different approaches to the gathering of relevant survey information, and different practices of consultation with relevant outside interests.

In the case of the regional study team sponsored by the Planning Authorities Conference, the management of the exploratory process posed some particularly exacting problems. It was launched at a time of rising professional concern to adopt a comprehensive 'systems approach' to regional planning studies, and specialist firms of consultants were retained both to analyse communications aspects and, once the range of locational solutions had been narrowed down to four 'fine options', to carry out a systematic evaluation of these using the Planning Balance Sheet method of cost-benefit analysis. Meanwhile, many specialist officers from the local authorities became involved in working parties for detailed exploration of such topics as population, employment, leisure, and financial resources. The outside consultants themselves related to two influential working parties concerned with communications and with 'strategy', which brought some of the most powerful local officials of the constituent authorities into direct round-the-table confrontation.

Thus, mechanisms were built up to extend the field of exploration beyond that which the study team could hope to cover through its own resources alone. This made the problem of coordination a formidable one for the team's Director and for the Administrative Committee of the Conference, which controlled the flow of resources. Because of the underlying conflicts of interest between the contributing local authorities, there was a lack of clear political guidance to the team, and also a tendency for the authorities continually to reclaim key staff who had been seconded to it, so creating a climate of instability and inhibiting any opportunities for interactive learning within the study team. Because of these difficulties, the team's reporting horizon was repeatedly delayed; and it became clear that the choice of recommendations would be a matter of some delicacy, in which the results of the team's analytical work was likely to be subjected to political challenge from one direction or another, however systematic their exploratory process and however clearly stated their assumptions.

When the report finally appeared, under the title of *A Developing Strategy for the West Midlands* (West Midlands PAC, 1971), it advocated a solution based on a main axis of growth extending north-eastwards and south-westwards from Birmingham, with three new centres of short-term population growth and five centres of new employment on the fringes of the conurbation. These recommendations were immediately subjected to public criticism from the political leadership of Birmingham City Council, on the grounds that they would mean a further erosion in the economic viability of the city. Subsequently, the City Council voted by a narrow margin to revoke its membership of the Conference, withdrawing the Director and other seconded members of the team.

A further criticism of the study, based on its methods rather than the content of its recommendations, came some months later in the publication of an informal letter of comment from the regional planning staff of the Environment Ministry. It was argued that there had been inconsistencies in the logic leading up to the choice of proposals, and that the team had failed to make use of much of the survey material on the region which other people had accumulated over the last few years. This criticism was underlined by the local reaction of the officers of the Development Group at Droitwich, who were able to point out that the modest 'additional' population growth recommended for the town was in fact less than the target to which the partners to the agreement were already committed. Despite these criticisms, The chairman of the Conference — a position at that time held by the Chairman of Worcestershire County Council — was able to argue that the study process was intended to be a developing one, so that the published results could be 'amended to make room for change' by the remaining members of the study team, which had been kept in being for this purpose. By this time, new economic and demographic trends were beginning to reduce quite markedly the size of the expected regional population increase and therefore the size of the political problem involved and, following a change of political control within Birmingham, the city duly re-opened its membership of the Conference. So another crisis in the relations between neighbouring authorities had been successfully overcome, but only at a time when relations between the cities and counties were becoming increasingly overshadowed by the impending reorganisation of local government in 1974.

The influence on decisions in the region

The reports of most other parallel planning studies were received with rather more equanimity within the region. Taken together, the flow of outputs generated by the various exploratory processes provided inputs of information and policy guidance to a variety of other ongoing processes at different levels of governmental organisation, including the modest influences already discussed on the economic planning activities and capital expenditure programmes of central government. Among the other major political concerns in the region at this time were two important planning applications, carrying major strategic implications yet surrounded by urgent pressures for commitment. One of these again concerned a proposal for expansion on the boundaries of Birmingham and Worcestershire. The other application, promoted jointly by Birmingham's City Council and its Chamber of Commerce, was for a National Exhibition Centre strategically sited in the rural belt between Birmingham and Coventry. This proposal, justified essentially through the 'central place' advantages of the West Midlands within England, was fiercely contested by rival interests in the London area and became a major national policy issue. Painter, in his paper on the West Midlands Economic Planning Council (1972), argues that this was an issue where the Council was only marginally involved, because the initiative lay very clearly with what he calls the 'Birmingham lobby' in arguing its case to the central government in London.

Because of the difficulty of synchronising the outputs of the various regional planning processes with the more urgent pressures for taking specific decisions within the region, there were many other local planning issues during this period that had to be confronted in a state of uncertainty about future regional strategies. This applied in particular to the land-use options faced by some of the County Councils in the West Midlands, all of which during 1971 and 1972 were in the process of preparing their first draft Structure Plans. In Warwickshire, the County planners were able to work largely within the framework of the report published in 1971 by the Coventry/Warwickshire/Solihull sub-regional team, which had already been approved at political level. In Worcestershire, however, the planners faced a more open situation, in view of the lack of a similar commitment to the results of the West Midlands Conference Study.

In its initial response to the regional team's report, the County Council asserted firmly its right to exercise its own discretion in deciding the pace and direction of the proposed future growth of Redditch, Droitwich, and any other prospective growth centres within its territory. Later, in their draft Structure Plan, the County planners put forward seven alternative strategies for growth within its area. The preferred alternative advocated, among other measures, an increase from 30,000 to 46,000 in the population target for Droitwich. So, once more, as in the late 1950s, the processes of regional exploration were beginning to impinge directly on the future prospects of Droitwich and other local communities in Worcestershire. Again, however, many further processes of local consultation and central government appraisal lay ahead before such proposals could form the basis of specific local actions. In this instance, the uncertainties appeared likely to be exacerbated by the imminence of local government reorganisation in 1974. Not only could new political groupings be expected to emerge in the West Midlands Metropolitan County and its constituent districts, but also in the new Hereford and Worcester County Council, and in the county district of Wychavon, of which the town of Droitwich would form only one constituent part.

The emergence of regional decision networks

The achievement of some degree of coordination and consistency between these various regional and local activities inevitably became a matter of direct concern to those senior civil servants in the regional office most directly involved in physical and economic planning. Over the years, some complex networks of influence began to evolve, resting largely but by no means entirely on the formal responsibilities that had been created by the developing pattern of institutional relationships within the regional planning framework.

The Economic Planning Board provided an obvious focus for mutual adjustment between senior civil servants from the various ministries operating within the region. However, after its first few full meetings — involving representatives of some ministries that had no more than a marginal interest in regional economic policy issues — the Board met only infrequently in full session. Its place was taken in effect by a smaller 'steering committee' which met every Monday morning and was attended by representatives of the four or five ministries most directly concerned in economic planning matters. At this level, the policy interests originally represented were those of economic planning, industrial development, employment, transport, housing and agriculture.

At a less senior level, the same departments were all represented on a Research Committee, which was set up under the chairmanship of the Principal Planning Officer of the then Ministry of Housing and Local Government. Although, at that time, this officer occupied a crucial position as the main point of contact with the local planning authorities, he was not automatically entitled to representation of the Economic Planning Board, as he was not the most senior officer in the regional organisation of his department. However, his role as Chairman of the regional research committee earned him a place on the Board and, more importantly, on its steering committee. At a time when relations with local authorities were developing rapidly through the various joint study processes, but most local planners preferred to relate to the regional machinery through their own professional channels, linking these to civil service decision networks was clearly important.

As argued by B.C. Smith in his study of regional planning in the South West (1969), the Chairmanship of the Economic Planning Council was another potentially crucial position, as it allowed its occupant to play an active role in establishing communications between the regional planning organisation and other regional interests. As Smith suggests, an energetic Chairman could become a 'natural initiator of a coordinated regional effort'. This point is endorsed by Painter (1972) with particular reference to the role of Mr. Adrian Cadbury, as Chairman of the Economic Council in the West Midlands between 1967 and 1970. In such a position, important linkages could be formed with representatives of industrial and other economic interests in the region, drawing where possible on the knowledge and influence of his fellow members of the Council. For the Chairman, the range of alternative strategies in the mobilisation of regional decision networks could therefore become exceptionally wide, demanding — in our terms — a high order of reticulist judgement.

A third major node in the formation of decision networks was that provided by the senior regional official who acted as Chairman of the Economic Planning Board, and who carried direct accountability to the central government in London for the operation of the overall regional economic planning machinery. We were able to gain some insights into this role, at one stage of its development, through a discussion with the civil servant holding this position in 1971, who had initially been appointed to the regional office as an Under-Secretary in the Department of Economic Affairs. He had retained the role of Chairman of the Board after the disbandment of that Ministry and upon his reassignment to the the Environment Ministry during the following year. At the time of interview, a further step in the development of the regional planning machinery had just brought him to the position of Regional Director within the enlarged Ministry, although he was in fact due to retire a few months later. He likened his new position to one at the centre of an hourglass, as he was now placed more clearly in a position of central responsibility within the regional office of his Ministry, yet remained accountable upwards to some five or six Deputy Secretaries at headquarters, where responsibilities at that time remained organised primarily on functional lines. His own view was that such a position called for quick and confident judgements, often with little opportunity for hesitation, whenever issues arose for which the choice of channels was not clear-cut. In our own terminology, the role could be seen as one calling for a high order of reticulist judgement, especially in the routeing of exploratory processes within the civil service structure itself.

In the following years, further changes in the internal organisations of the Environment Ministry were to bring a more clearly-defined pattern to the management of the regional office. The responsibilities for statutory Development Plan functions, as well as the advisory functions of the Principal Planning Officer, were decentralised to the region under a Regional Controller (Plans and Planning), reporting to the Regional Director alongside parallel Controllers for Housing and Environment and for Roads and Transportation respectively. The primary channel of accountability of the Regional Director now lay through a single Deputy Secretary at headquarters, and it was envisaged that the new structure would endure at least until after the forthcoming report of the Royal Commission on the Constitution, which might conceivably point the way to further proposals for regional devolution of central government powers.

The principal planning officer and his network

During the period we have been discussing, the three main interfaces of the regional planning organisation could be regarded as that with regional industry and related interests, that with the central government, and that with the local planning authorities. We have now seen that the actors occupying the most crucial reticulist roles in relation to each of these interfaces, in the transitional form of the regional planning the Principal Planning Officer of the Land Planning Ministry. The network diagram presented in Fig. 6.3 indicates the broad pattern of the Principal Planning Officer of the Land Planning Ministry. The network diagram presented in Fig. 6.3 indicated the broad pattern of communications in which the Principal Planning Officer became involved over the period from the formation of the regional office in 1965 until his retirement in 1971. This diagram identifies, among his primary points of contact, both the Chairman of the Economic Planning Board and of the

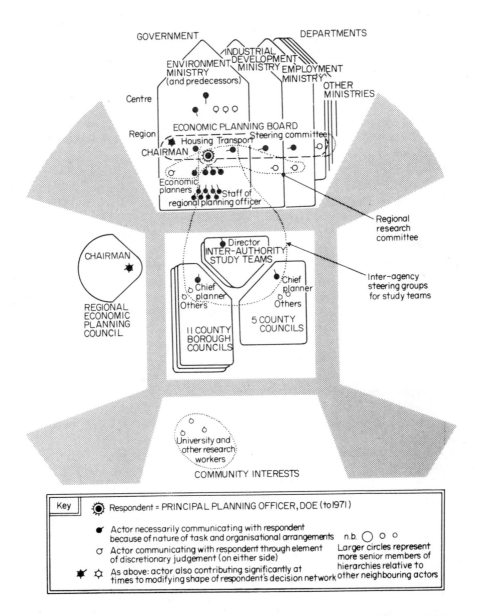

GOVERNMENT   DEPARTMENTS

INDUSTRIAL
DEVELOPMENT
ENVIRONMENT MINISTRY EMPLOYMENT
MINISTRY   MINISTRY
(and predecessors)
OTHER
MINISTRIES

Centre

Region   ECONOMIC PLANNING BOARD
Housing Transport   Steering committee
CHAIRMAN

Economic
planners   Staff of
regional planning officer

Regional
research
committee

Director
INTER-AUTHORITY
STUDY TEAMS

CHAIRMAN

Chief
planner
Others

Chief
planner
Others

Inter-agency
steering groups
for study teams

REGIONAL
ECONOMIC
PLANNING
COUNCIL

II COUNTY
BOROUGH
COUNCILS

5 COUNTY
COUNCILS

University and
other research
workers

COMMUNITY INTERESTS

Key   Respondent = PRINCIPAL PLANNING OFFICER, DOE (to 1971)

Actor necessarily communicating with respondent
because of nature of task and organisational arrangements   n.b.

Larger circles represent
more senior members of
hierarchies relative to
other neighbouring actors

Actor communicating with respondent through element
of discretionary judgement (on either side)

As above: actor also contributing significantly at
times to modifying shape of respondent's decision network

Figure 6.3 Regional planning: network relationships of Principal Planning Officer

111

Economic Planning Council. Indeed, he had first been brought closely into contact with both in the course of the early explorations that had preceded the publication in 1967 of *The West Midlands: Patterns of Growth*, a document that can be regarded as the first major contribution by the new regional organisation to the formation of regional policies.

During this period, the Principal Planning Officer was able to build up a team of some ten planners and research officers, most of whom were in fact recruited from local authorities in the region, and therefore provided ready access to networks of information on local planning issues. Such information could be drawn on extensively when contributing to, or advising upon, strategic planning studies; and it could also provide a regional context against which to advise on 'casework' applications, for instance relating to applications for Industrial Development Certificates. The structure of this regional planning team was so designed as to provide cross-connections between territorial and functional lines of delegation, backed by a small 'strategic group' to provide a broader and more forward-looking exploratory capacity. Although many of the external relationships of the office could be managed by other members of the team, the Principal Planning Officer considered it important to act in person as Chairman of the regional research committee. Also, he was invited to join the technical panel of the West Midlands Regional Study team and the equivalent steering groups of the two other joint planning teams which were operating during that period. In this way, he could act directly as a custodian of his Ministry's interests, speaking with additional authority in so far as there was any contribution of Ministry finance or manpower to the work of the study team concerned.

While such roles in group processes inevitably brought the Principal Planning Officer into contact with a variety of local authority officers and other public servants, his general responsibility for the dissemination of new planning methods and procedures required him to develop more direct individual relationships with the Chief Planning Officers of the local authorities within the region. Among his other significant relationships was that with research workers in outside institutions, as developed through his chairmanship of the Regional Research Committee and his involvement in the activities of the regional branches of the Royal Town Planning Institute and the Regional Studies Association. Indeed, it was through the interests he expressed in the kind of research into planning processes reported here that we were first directed to Droitwich as a potentially fruitful site for our work.

The linkages which the Principal Planning Officer had to maintain with his departmental headquarters in London included the administrators who were formally responsible for statutory planning functions — not at that time delegated to the regional office — and also certain professional scientific colleagues who could provide advice or information on a variety of specialised topics. The Principal Planning Officer in Birmingham therefore found himself in a position of little formal authority, yet potentially of considerable influence at the intersection of several types of exploratory network. As indicated in Fig. 6.3, these included not only the evolving networks of activity within governmental departments, the local authorities, and the Economic Planning Council, but also those within the multi-organisational structures of the overlapping regional study teams and the Economic Planning Board with its steering and research committees. Later, the pattern of communication was to evolve further through the delegation of statutory land planning responsibilities from headquarters, the appointment of the three Regional Controllers under the Regional Director, and the establishment of closer working linkages with the Chief Executives as well as the Chief Planning Officers of the leading local authorities in the region.

Often, in the late 1960s and early 1970s, the argument was put forward that the development of a cohesive regional planning activity in England was being inhibited by the absence of the kind of political authority that might be provided by an elected regional assembly, and also by the pressures arising from the hierarchical structure of government departments, built around the principle of final accountability through a single Minister of the Crown (Mackintosh, 1968). This view was indeed supported by discussions held with the Chairman of the Economic Planning Board in a neighbouring region during 1968, when the regional machinery was still at an early stage of development. The Civil Servant concerned saw his only possible role in terms of attempting to extend the breadth of evaluation applied to proposals for action that had been generated elsewhere. However, the Principal Planning Officer in the West Midlands believed that a considerably more creative role was possible in his own particular set of regional circumstances, even given the constraints of the very limited degree of formal authority which he and his colleagues had at their disposal. Furthermore, he believed that a spirit of genuine cooperation was evolving both among the officials of different government departments within the regional office, and also between regional and central officials within his own departmental establishment.

The region as a centre of innovation

Viewed in the perspective of the various regional activities indicated in Fig. 6.2, and the networks of relationships between actors set out in Fig. 6.3, the regional organisation of government in England, as it was evolving during the late 1960s and early 1970s, emerges as an important focus for processes of mutual adaptation and learning, at least in the case of the West Midlands. In the planning and management of the various regional and sub-regional studies, and also in the search for mutual consistency between those studies, methods of reconciliation had to be discovered between the very different traditions of economic, physical, and transportation planning. The problem of this reconciliation process were brought out by one planner on the staff of the Principal Planning Officer for the West Midlands, in a paper presented to the annual Town and Country Planning Summer School (Bird, 1968). Using the imagery of social anthropology to discuss relations between the two 'tribes' of economic and physical planners, Bird argued that both had now prospered to the extent that they were competing for the same territory, located at the regional level of government where traditional boundaries were ill-defined. The economists, approaching this territory from an established base in central government, brought with them tools and attitudes concerned with the projection of highly aggregated measures of activity on comparatively modest time horizons. On the other hand, the tools and attitudes of the physical planners were rooted in their traditional ties with local planning authorities. Members of this profession had been accustomed to looking towards more distant time horizons, while reviewing choices of a much more localised character where considerations of imaginative design had traditionally taken precedence over those of quantitative evaluation. Bird speculated that the key to a gradual fusion of these very different traditions of planning might lie in the development of new types of systems approach to the planning process, in which the contributions of each type of discipline could ultimately become much more fully integrated.

Meanwhile, new disciplines, ranging from sociology to operational research, were being slowly introduced into the field of regional planning in the West Midlands and elsewhere and the staff of the regional office in Birmingham became actively involved in the encouragement of experimentation with new techniques to assist the formulation and evaluation of alternatives and the handling of uncertainty and flexibility (Coventry/Solihull/Warwickshire, 1971).

In Britain and elsewhere (Alonso, 1971), speculations have been voiced about a trend towards the emergence of new 'meta-disciplines' in the urban and regional fields, through which the barriers of communication between such disciplinary frameworks as those of economics, sociology, and physical and transportation planning can ultimately be broken down. Although such an erosion of professional barriers was clearly discernible in many of the activities we have been reviewing in the West Midlands, our own evaluation suggests that perhaps the most powerful integrative force may be that generated by the pressures to achieve mutual adjustment between a multitude of political forces, each emanating from a different type of local, regional, or national constituency. As we have already indicated, the management of relationships between these various interests calls for highly developed reticulist skills from certain actors who occupy strategic roles in the regional planning structure. They must be able both to penetrate the conceptual frameworks of different types of planning expert, and also to choose their points of intervention at different levels of decision-making with a shrewd awareness of any underlying political implications.

In a broad sense, this tends to make the role of the administrator an increasingly political one, the less routinised and clearly structured his field of responsibility becomes. This is a point which emerges rather more directly at another emergent level of public planning – that of the supranational agency. In the case of the European Community, for instance, the role of the Commissioner is explicitly recognised as being intermediate between that of the politician and the civil servant, with a high degree of responsibility for the initiation of proposals for political action, which must be steered through many complex channels of further exploration and authorisation before they can be translated into specific executive decisions.

Implications for connective planning

In evaluating the lessons of this review, it is clear that the evolving multi-organisational structure of the regional office in the West Midlands emerges as an important interface for interactive learning between central and local governments, and between those contributing diverse skills in such fields as economic, physical, and transportation planning. The structural complexity of the problems faced, compounded by the complexity of political relationships at the regional interface, creates a situation in which the success or otherwise of regional explorations can only be gauged in terms of the degree of influence exercised over incremental commitment at many diverse points of decision. This means that much comes to depend on the reticulist skills of certain actors, occupying crucial positions in regional networks, who operate through processes of mediation that do not often attract much public attention, but can sometimes radically modify the context of the mutual adjustment process.

Despite the low profile of the regional structure in terms of public political debate, we conclude that the processes of innovation and interactive learning which have been developing in Britain in recent years — and which we believe may have their parallels in a number of other countries — are of much potential significance, in terms of the long term challenge of creating processes for effective participatory planning in an increasingly disturbed and unpredictable environment. It is, of course, not only at the regional level of planning that motivations towards connective planning across agency boundaries may be found to dominate the motivation to organise and contain the planning process within the boundaries of a single corporate agency. Nor is it only at the regional level that a tendency can be found towards innovation in patterns of inter-agency relations. However, the regional level of government, at least as it has been developing in England since the mid-sixties, has, in our belief, a special significance which can be further exploited in future. It combines a climate of strong motivation towards the formation of inter-agency decision networks with a scale of operation that supports the formation of an important type of organisational resource, in the shape of inter-disciplinary teams which are oriented specifically towards exploratory rather than executive activity. Within such a setting, experimentation becomes possible with new forms of evaluative and exploratory techniques, through which those concerned in the shaping of inter-agency networks can be assisted to adapt more consciously to the changing problem situations they confront.

Bibliography

Alonso, W., 'Beyond the Inter-disciplinary Approach to Planning', *American Institue of Planners Journal*, vol. 27, 1971, p.169.

Bird, R.A., 'The Relationship of Economic and Physical Planning', Paper presented at Town and Country Planning Summer School, University oof Manchester, 1968.

Cadbury, G.A.H., 'The Objectives and Manner of Working of the Regional Economic Planning Council', Paper presented at the Conference of the West Midlands Branch of the Regional Studies Association, October, 1968, London Regional Studies Association.

Coventry City Council, Solihull County Borough Council, and Warwickshire County Council, *Coventry-Solihull-Warwickshire: a Strategy for the Sub-region: the Report on the Sub-Regional Planning Study*, Coventry, 1971.

Cullingworth, J.B., *Town and Country Planning in England and Wales: the Changing Scene.* (3rd ed.), Allen and Unwin, London, 1970.

Friend, J.K. and Jessop, W.M., *Local Government and Strategic Choice: an Operational Research Approach to the Processes of Public Planning*, Tavistock Publications, London, 1969.

Herson, J., 'The West Midlands — an Economic Appraisal', A discussion paper produced for the West Midlands Branch of the Regional Studies Association, January, 1972. Regional Studies Association, London.

Painter, C., 'The Repercussions of Administrative Innovation: the West Midlands Economic Planning Council', *Public Administration,* vol. 50, 1972, p.467. (Included in this volume as Chapter 7.)

Smith, B.C., *Advising Ministers,* Routledge & Kegan Paul, London, 1969.

Smith, B.M.D., 'Appraising the Appraisal: some Discursive Comments on reading the West Midlands Economic Planning Council's *The West Midlands: an Economic Appraisal*', A discussion paper for the Regional Studies Association, London, 1972.

7 The repercussions of administrative innovation

C. Painter, 'The Repercussions of Administrative Innovation: The West Midlands Economic Planning Council', *Public Administration,* vol. 50, Winter 1972, pp. 467-84.

Reaction to the creation of the new regional machinery in 1965, consisting of advisory councils and inter-departmental boards, was characterised in rapid succession by euphoria and disillusionment. Administrative innovation in this country is, however, rarely revolutionary, usually emerging gradually from experiment and precedent. But this does not mean that it remains without consequences.

It is the purpose of this paper to consider the repercussions of the Economic Planning Council/Board in the West Midlands [1] in the first seven years after their inauguration, a period long enough for the ripple effects to have spread outwards. As such, it is not so much a study of the intricacies of the internal workings of the regional machinery, but rather one of the impact on decisions, the extent of the interplay and interaction with other groups and forces in the West Midlands, and an attempt to determine whether the interaction has been consensus or conflict-orientated.

Nevertheless, it will be illuminating to present certain data on the regional machinery in the West Midlands, particularly in relation to the membership and composition of the Regional Economic Planning Council.

The West Midlands Regional Economic Planning Council

There has been little published material on the evolution of the membership of the economic planning councils which traces such phenomena as the changing emphasis in composition and the rate of turnover. To chart a moving picture of this kind in the West Midlands, three base lines for purposes of comparison will be used: the initial membership of the Planning Council in 1965, its membership in 1968 after the end of the members' first three-year contract, and finally the membership in July 1971.

This categorisation is in danger of gross over-simplification and cannot reflect the full range of members' connections. It should also be borne in mind that members sit as individuals and not as delegates. But the figures do not reveal a broad picture of the changing composition of the Economic Planning Council.

Table 7.1 Composition of the WMPEC (by broad category)

	1965	1968 (July)	1971 (July)
Local councillors/officials	9	10	12
Industrialists	5	5	6
Trade unionists	4	5	4
University	4	4	3
Nationalised industries	—	—	1
Miscellaneous	4	1	1
Total	26	25	27

Three significant features emerge from the break-down. Firstly, the growth in the size of the local authority contingent is apparent. The geographical composition of this group can be ascertained from the following:

	1965	1971
County Boroughs	5 (B'ham 2, Stoke, Dudley, Coventry)	4 (B'ham 2, Stoke, Dudley)
County Councils	3 (Salop, Worcs., Staffs.)	7 (Salop, Worcs. 2, Staffs., Herefords. 2, Warks)
Urban/Rural Districts	1 (Willenhall RDC)	1 (Leek UDC)

The heavily populated sub-regions were the most comprehensively represented in 1965 (the Birmingham conurbation, the Coventry sub-region, and the North Staffordshire sub-region). In 1971, unlike 1965, all the five administrative counties in the West Midlands were represented and the emphasis of the local authority component on the Planning Council had moved conspicuously in this direction.

Secondly, the agricultural interest is not directly reflected in the membership. The desire on the part of some of the county organisations of the National Farmers Union (e.g. Worcestershire) to have a nominee on the Planning Council was not acceded to. The poor representation in this respect is surprising, considering that agriculture is such a vital component in land-use thinking, although two of the local authority representatives appointed to the Planning Council by 1971 also had farming connections.

Thirdly, the sparsity of members from the nationalised industries is another feature of the composition of the Planning Council, with the proviso that from 1968 a local authority member, who has since resigned, had links with British Rail, and the Chairman of the West Midlands Gas Board sat on it by 1971. The long-standing weakness of representation of this sector probably reflects the fact that no single nationalised industry stands out as being uniquely vital to the economy of the West Midlands, in the same manner as the coal industry is for the East Midlands for example (i.e. in the East Midlands there are very close links, including membership, between the Planning Council and the Midland Region of the National Coal Board). Generally, however, nationalised industries do pass on any relevant information to the regional planning boards and to the chairmen of the planning councils. They are also represented through the relevant government department on the regional boards.

Table 7.2 Rate of turn-over in membership of the WMEPC

	Total members	Members since 1965	Members since 1968
1965	26	—	—
1968	25	10	—
1971	27	4	10

From the above table it can be seen that sixteen members of the original twenty-six left between 1965 and 1968, representing a considerable turnover. In 1968, only forty-five members had left the eight English planning councils as a whole[2] so that the proportion leaving the West Midlands Planning Council in this period was certainly well above the national average. A contributory factor to this rate of turn-over may have been the unfulfilled expectations at the largely negative reply of the Government in January 1968 to the Planning Council's document, *Patterns of Growth*.[3] Yet the turnover in the second three-year period was still high (i.e. only ten of the twenty-five who were members in 1968 remained), and in 1971 there were only four of the original twenty-six members of 1965 left. In spite of this rate of turnover, the Office of the Economic Planning Board claimed that there had been far more nominations to the Minister than there had been vacancies on the Planning Council in the West Midlands.

Overlapping membership

The membership of the West Midlands Planning Council has had a multitude of links with organisations in the region. Firstly, there have been those links with groups corresponding to the local governmental structures (e.g. Mr. Stedeford, an industrial member of the Council, was also a member of the Birmingham Chamber of Commerce, an organisation that has been consulted on nominations to the Planning Council). Secondly, and more noticeably, links with the organisational sub-divisions of national economic groups such as the Regional Advisory Committee of the TUC (most of the trade union members of the Planning Council have belonged to it) and the Midland Region CBI (in 1970 three members of the Regional Council of the Confederation of British Industry sat on the Planning Council) have existed. The prominence of the connections with the TUC and the CBI is to a substantial extent derived from the influential role of these bodies in consultation with ministers over nominations. It exemplifies how membership of the Planning Council is in many respects an indirect extension of the established web of central government. The above mentioned organisations themselves make use of such connections — the Regional CBI has raised the question of the effects of the restrictionist Industrial Development Certificate policy, via its members on the Planning Council, for example.

In addition to overlapping membership, all the permutations of which have not been stated above, other devices have been used to create an intermeshing between the Planning Council and groups in the region, the most significant of which is the meeting of delegations. To enlist two examples, in the early days of its functioning, the Planning Council in the West Midlands had a meeting with MPs of the region, while in 1968 a delegation from the county organisations of the National Farmers Union was received.

The Chairman of the Economic Planning Council

The West Midlands Economic Planning Council has had three chairmen, all of whom have been industrialists. After the resignation of Adrian Cadbury in March 1970, there was a long period with just an acting chairman, the only Planning Council in England in that dubious position at the time. A number of people were approached to take on the task, but they all turned down the invitation. Eventually Mr. Quinton Hazell had to be brought in from outside the Council, in September 1971. The gap of eighteen months had a debilitating effect from the point of view of leadership, a view shared by the Council members at the time. As B. Smith has suggested, the chairman is the 'natural initiator of a coordinated regional effort.'[4] Mr. Cadbury had played a vital role in publicising the views and activities of the Planning Council, especially through speaking tours in the region, through the writing of articles in the local press, and at press conferences after each monthly Planning Council meeting. After his resignation the sense of awareness of the existence of the Council, together with the number of statements emanating from it, diminished. Also, meetings of the Planning Council took place less frequently than once a month in the first half of 1971. There was, however, a revival in its activities in June 1971, following from the publication of an *Economic Appraisal* of the West Midlands[5] a study carried out by a working party of the Council, which Mr.Cadbury had agreed to continue to lead after his resignation as Chairman.

From their side, the Government claimed that the procrastination in the appointment of a new chairman in no way reflected the deliberate running down of the work of the Economic Planning Council. Peter Walker, the Minister responsible, subsequently stated in Parliament that he could easily have got rid of such bodies, but he had believed: 'that they could provide a very useful manner of gathering together leading people . . . to give a broad view on what they considered were important factors in the future development of their regions.'[6]

Relations with the Economic Planning Board

The deficiencies of the economic planning boards are by now well documented. The regional officials have suffered from a lack of delegation from Whitehall, with

Industrial Development Certificate applications for large industrial projects having to be referred to the appropriate Minister, for example. The Chairman of the Planning Board, although with the senior rank of under-secretary in the West Midlands, has only had a persuasive influence over departmental regional officials, compared with the undivided authority of the area chief in a prefectoral system. This derives from the predominantly functional organisation in English government.

These weaknesses were fully recognised in the evidence of the West Midlands Planning Council to the Commission on the Constitution, where it called for greater decentralisation within the structure of government and regional ministers, views summarised in its statement that: 'The Council would like to see regional policy regarded as of equal importance to functional policy.'[7] The Economic Planning Board and its Chairman could only hope to instil into department officials in the West Midlands the wider regional view, so that it might be transmitted back to the parent departments in Whitehall. To this end, the Chairmen of the Planning Board and Planning Council have worked together closely.

Nevertheless, there have been a number of improvements in the delegation of responsibility to the regions and in the promotion of regional coordination. In October 1971 it was announced that some of Whitehall's planning powers were to be handed down to the regional officials of the Department of Environment, Improved departmental coordination, in the field of physical planning and the environment, was effected in the West Midlands through the amalgamation of the Office of the Economic Planning Board's Chairman, the Divisional Road Engineers and the Regional Office of the former Ministry of Housing, to form the DOE Regional Office.[8] Further changes in regional departmental organisation have come into being as a result of the new industrial and regional policies of the Conservative Government, announced in March 1972. A Minister for Industrial Development was appointed, under the broad direction of the Secretary of State for Trade and Industry, taking charge of an Industrial Development Executive. This Executive assumed responsibility for the Department's regional offices and a strong regional organisation was to be an essential part of its machinery, with 'a new positive role in promoting industrial expansion and modernisation, and in stimulating centres of growth. It will have an important degree of devolved authority.'[9] There are to be close relations with the regional offices of the Department of Environment. The links between the economic planning councils/boards and the regional offices of the Department of Trade and Industry are also to be improved, to coordinate industrial and physical planning. The emphasis of this strengthened organisation, though, is to be in the assisted areas, where regional industrial directors and advisory regional industrial development boards are to be part of the structure.

The other main question that has been frequently raised in relation to the planning boards is the danger of their overwhelming the planning councils. In the West Midlands the latter has been serviced only by a small secretariat of two, the members of which belong to the Department of Environment. Also, only two research officers, in the Office of the Planning Board, have been at its disposal.

121

These have carried out their work less inhibited by the policies of the individual departments on the Planning Board, being outside this departmental structure. But they have still been circumscribed by the central civil service career structure, and the Office of the Planning Board has now been amalgamated into the DOE's Regional Office. That there are only two of them means that the Planning Board normally accepts the views of the individual departments anyway, views carried forward into the meetings of the Planning Council itself, as those departments most closely involved in regional planning attend all its meetings.

The West Midlands Planning Council has not, however, advocated having its own independent staff within the existing regional institutional structure, and has seen considerable advantage in having the Planning Board and departments at its disposal, especially in having departments prepare papers for its meetings. The Planning Council has also been reinforced by outside research, including a study at Birmingham University into the mobility and location of industry in the West Midlands.[10] In its *Economic Appraisal* it called widely on the assistance of industry and commerce in the region, in addition to the research papers contributed by the research section of the Planning Board and the Department of Trade and Industry. Thus, for example, although the Planning Board has constantly fed the Council with statistics suggesting that the West Midlands has secured its fair share of Industrial Development Certificates, the Council still came out strongly against the workings of the system in the region.

Repercussions of the regional machinery on decisions

In looking at the impact on decisions of the regional machinery in the West Midlands, there are two considerations of a general nature that have affected this. Firstly, the institutional framework of October 1964 in Whitehall, revolving around the Department of Economic Affairs, which was in part based upon the determination to augment the micro-economic content of policy (and a region is a micro-economic problem), was gradually superseded after July 1966. The Treasury again assumed the mantle of overriding economic power, returning the emphasis to macro-economic demand management. Economic planning, in the sense of long term quantitative commitments, was abandoned. This meant regional economic planning was rendered somewhat anomalous, with confusion over its objectives. This was cushioned by the fact that the West Midlands Planning Council at that point was nowhere near producing a regional plan that was related to the figures in the National Plan in an operational form. Even its 1967 document was conceived in terms of analysing problems and developing a very broad strategic framework for decisions. There has, however, been no redefinition of the terms of reference of the planning councils or any new formal guidelines from Whitehall to meet the changing circumstances.

Some of the fragments of the DEA micro-economic approach were eventually brought closer together departmentally in October 1969, when Mr.Crosland became responsible for the regions and local government. This process was completed when the Department of Environment was formed in 1970. But there remains the problem of the inter-relation of regional with industrial policy (the Department of Trade and Industry), and there are no integral links with the Treasury, responsible of course for broad economic policy and public expenditure.

The second general factor determining the influence of the West Midlands Planning Council has been that the needs of the region required the formulation of demands which were contrary to the policy commitments of the former Labour Administration, that is its commitment of concentrating discriminatory policies and aid towards the needs of the 'unemployment' regions — the desire to 'rectify the imbalance' between the regions. This has made it difficult for the Planning Council in the West Midlands to influence the inter-regional allocation of resources. This was compounded by the Exchequer's reluctance to increase the total of regional financial concessions, as seen in the fact that when the Intermediate Areas were established, this entailed the diversion of some resources from the Development Areas. Furthermore, a situation where all the contenders for policy influence are institutionalised, that is where the same regional structure exists in each region, is likely to favour the regions which have more successfully mobilised a regional interest in the past, such as the North East (for example, the North East Development Association).

The above constraints have contributed to the failure of the West Midlands Planning Council to elicit decisions from central government which it has considered to be necessary for the well-being of the region. The Government rejected the essentials of the strategy embodied in *Patterns of Growth*, especially the need for incentives for industry to move to overspill areas if the more effective correlation of industry and population was to be achieved in those areas. It was a scheme that had, in fact, been with the Minister from 1965. As the members of the Planning Council recognised in the above document: 'their suggestions are for a substantial adjustment of policy'.[11] This is just what the Planning Council has not been able to achieve. It was convinced that in the absence of this the Government was condemning the regional strategy of dispersal from the Birmingham conurbation to failure.[12] The strategy was accordingly modified in its *Economic Appraisal* in 1971 to one where the conurbation was to play an equal part with the overspill areas in housing the growth in population [13] (although the problem has become somewhat less acute with population growth constantly falling below the forecast figures).

The failure of industry to move out of the conurbation on a sufficient scale has meant a repeat of the search for avenues of peripheral development, culminating in a furore over Birmingham's application for commuter settlements in the provisional Green Belt of North Worcestershire. *Patterns of Growth* had suggested there could be small expansions of existing towns and villages in the area outside but around the Green Belt, and the long-term strategy tentatively suggested by the Planning Council was that dispersal from the conurbation should gradually take place along 'corridors of growth', but nowhere was an expansion of the conurbation by means of peripheral development suggested. The whole strategy was based on its containment. The proposed development in North Worcestershire was a hasty reaction to the problem of meeting Birmingham's immediate land needs, a problem accentuated by the slow progress of overspill schemes. The very expedients regional planning was initiated to prevent were being reverted to.

To compound the feeling of a lack of a regional framework, immediately prior to the beginning of the public inquiry into the matter in September 1969 the 'Griffin document' (a document circulated by the Leader of the controlling Conservative Group of Birmingham Corporation) suggested that Birmingham should adopt as its policy further peripheral development to retain its industry and people, to be made possible by future local government reorganisation. This proposition aroused the violent opposition of Worcestershire County Council.[14] From the point of view of regional planning, the whole process ultimately indicated the tendency of local authorities to promote their own interests. The failure of the Planning Council to secure satisfactory decisions from the Government allowed the centrifugal forces of the local governmental process within the West Midlands again to assert themselves. Mr.Phelps, Deputy Clerk of Worcestershire County Council, chose to pose the problem in the following manner: 'In the circumstances which have arisen locally in the last few months, a decision to allow Birmingham to have their way entirely would introduce a new element of *anarchy* into the West Midlands.'[15]

Although eventually only half the land asked for was granted by the Minister, a decision aimed at preserving as much of the Green Belt as possible, P.Heywood has indicated the need for powerful regional planning to prevent large cities from promoting short term solutions to their problems and seeking to retain their influence by peripheral development.[16] The above events would certainly confirm this.

The administrative machinery of the Planning Council/Board, therefore, has not been able to influence decisions substantially enough to promote a coherent regional strategy. Yet, the West Midlands Planning Council has had a recognisable role in decision making. The relation of available data to strategic thinking in terms of policy proposals has been conducive to more sensible decision making. There is a greater understanding of the background against which individual decisions are made. For example, the allocation of road-building funds within the region can be such that communications priorities can promote regional growth and dispersal policies. Telford's success as a new town was threatened by its poor communications with the Birmingham conurbation, and the Planning Council played a prominent role in eliciting the decision to link Telford to the M.6 by 1975-6. Such influence follows in a large degree from the Planning Council's authorised perusal of departmental regional resource allocations, within their functional delineations. This enables it to identify inconsistencies. The West Midlands Planning Council appoints a sub-committee to review public expenditure in this way every twelve months. Accordingly, the informative role of the Planning Council gives it a certain authority, albeit only in securing marginal changes in policy.

Similarly, through this informative role, a small modification in Industrial Development Certificate policy was obtained, so that it was not so stringent in its effects on new towns, again recording a slight shift in decision making rather than a change in Development Area policy. Here the advantage of a regional department to speak up for regional interests was also visible. Liaison between Mr.Benn (at the Ministry of Technology) and Mr.Crosland, in the last Labour Administration, was instrumental in achieving this greater flexibility. Mr.Benn, in relation to the difficulty of overspill areas obtaining industry, stated that:

> The I.D.C. control will of course continue to be operated so as to give first priorities to the Development Areas and the new Intermediate Areas. But I have already made some limited exceptions, after consultations with the Secretary of State for Local Government and Regional Planning, to take account of the needs of the new overspill towns experiencing such difficulties.
>
> For example, save in exceptional circumstances, I.D.C's are at present available to all firms moving to Telford New Town from the West Midlands conurbation and to existing firms wishing to expand there, and I am glad to say that the prospects for keeping employment in balance with housing at Telford have improved.[17]

In the two cases above, that of communications and movement of industry, one cannot calculate the exact weight of the Planning Council alongside other pressure groups (e.g. the new town corporations), but they are issues on which the Council has been active and persistent. But, to reiterate, the effects of the Planning Council on policy, to which one should add generally its ability to give advice at the formative stage of policy making, were only of a marginal nature. The Chairman of the Planning Council has direct access to ministers (after the rejection of incentives for overspill industry representatives of the Council also went to see the Minister) and there are regular meetings of the Planning Council Chairmen attended by ministers. There are also periodic visits of ministers to the West Midlands Planning Council. In the period since November 1969, there have been such visits from Mr. Crosland, Mr. Peter Walker, Mr. Graham Page, and even Mr. Heath in September 1971. Even so, the limitations on the influence of the West Midlands Planning Council have caused much disquiet. Although there have been no resignations by the Chairmen of the Council on the basis of an open clash with the Government in the region, Mr.Cadbury, the previous Chairman, did constantly complain of the lack of responsiveness of the centre to the regions.[18] When Mr.Crosland visited the Council in 1969 there were complaints about the lack of action on plans for the region.[19]

The West Midlands Planning Council and the region

The impact of the West Midlands Planning Council next needs to be traced in terms

125

of its relationship and interplay with other forces in the region.

Relations with local authorities

The position of local government *vis-à-vis* the Planning Council has generally been one of conflict, the former fearing the regional machinery would trespass on its planning functions. An example of this hostility manifested itself in 1968 when the controlling Conservative Group on Birmingham City Council refused to nominate one of their members to the Planning Council, although they eventually acceded. On the other hand the mere existence of the Planning Council has begun the process of creating a regional interest in local government, for in this respect the regional machinery in the West Midlands has acted as a catalyst, leading to the establishment of the Standing Conference of Local Authorities in 1966. This was formed by local authorities out of a fear of being superseded. The Standing Conference set to work on a regional strategy, helped by technical staff seconded from local authorities. An initiative by Mr.Crosland in 1970 brought the Planning Council and the Standing Conference into closer accord,[20] agreeing on the need for the closest exchange of information (the Planning Board now makes its research available to the Standing Conference). The strategy of the Standing Conference was to be presented to the Planning Council for comments before being handed to the Government. This closer collaboration was in line with the DEA memorandum put out in 1968 explaining the need for this very relationship.[21]

The Standing Conference strategy appeared in September 1971.[22] Following this, the Planning Council, the Standing Conference and the Government were to sit down together to agree on a final strategy for the region. Prior to the tripartite discussions, the Planning Council embarked on a series of meetings with individual local authorities. During the first half of 1972 there were meetings with Birmingham City Council, together with the county councils of Shropshire, Worcestershire, Warwickshire, Staffordshire and Herefordshire. Meanwhile, in a parliamentary debate in April 1972, Mr.Walker claimed that the Government intended to pursue a positive regional planning strategy, hoping later in the year to be able to complete a strategy for the Midlands.[23]

The above developments reflect a growing cooperation between the regional machinery and local authorities. The increase in the size of the local authority contingent on the Planning Council has been promoted very much with these clear attachments in mind. In spite of the growing role of the Standing Conference in the regional field, the work of the Planning Council has been a vital stage in the evolution of such regional thinking. It is doubtful whether the local authority regional process would have advanced this far as quickly without the administrative innovations of 1965. It should be emphasised, too, that the real power in the Standing Conference remains with the constituent local authorities, whose diverse demands are still more   conspicuous than any common ground, as seen in the North Worcestershire example.

In other ways the Planning Council's identification of problems, or confirmation of their existence, is producing signs of an emerging regional interest in the West Midlands. In this respect its recent *Economic Appraisal* is important, for elsewhere in England the awareness of a unifying economic problem has proved to be crucial to regional mobilisation. There has been a growing fear in the West Midlands that it will become the 'Lancashire of the 21st Century',[24] if IDC policy continues to divert technological industry from the region and to break up its integrated industrial complex. There has been periodic campaigning on these points by various interests (led by Birmingham Corporation/Chamber of Commerce), reaching a crescendo in 1971 as regional unemployment moved above the national average. The Planning Council's *Economic Appraisal* put an official seal on this awareness of a growing regional economic problem, identifying a number of underlying structural defects, particularly the over-concentration on a few industries in the West Midlands. Accordingly, this document recommended a new set of criteria for the granting of IDC's in the region in order to halt the underlying deterioration in the long term, looking for changes in the Government's policy more radical than any small adjustments achieved in the past. The request for financial incentives for industry to move to overspill areas in the West Midlands was repeated. The *Economic Appraisal* also developed the idea of the function of the region in relation to the national economy, that of a generator of industry for the rest of the country, thereby attempting to place the proposals in the context of the national interest. In all, it was asserted that neither national nor regional policy had been constructive in relation to the West Midlands.

The significance of the Working Party of the Planning Council that produced the above document was the extent to which it institutionalised relations with economic interests in the region. On the committee were formal representatives of the Birmingham Chamber of Commerce, the Midland Region CBI and British Leyland. The TUC Midland Regional Advisory Committee was represented by permanent members of the Planning Council. In this example, the West Midlands Planning Council moulded together economic interests in an attempt to incorporate them into a regional interest — to envelop the previous sectional claims of such bodies as the Birmingham Chamber of Commerce in a well identified wider interest. It is an indication of how, since its inauguration, the Planning Council has developed its roots in the life of the region in an attempt to promote a regional consensus. The extent to which the Government responded to the above recommendations promised to be a crucial test of the potential efficacy of the present regional administrative arrangements,[25] and the Planning Council appointed a committee to follow through and promote the implementation of the report.

Significantly, a relaxation of IDC policy was announced as part of the Government's new regional and industrial policies in March 1972. Under these proposals, an IDC was no longer required for a project under 15,000 sq. ft. in the

West Midlands, compared with the previous figure of 5,000 sq. ft. There was to be a more flexible approach altogether, particularly where an IDC was required for modernisation,[26] a point of emphasis which appeared to reflect very much the arguments put forward by the *Economic Appraising*. As Mr. Davies stated in the Commons: 'many representations had been made that the control inhibits modernization.'[27] When the Government formally set out its response to the *Economic Appraising* in June 1972, it largely, therefore, took the form of a resumé of measures adopted in the previous twelve months by the Government. But it also raised the possibility of transferring government offices to the West Midlands in view of the repeated call for a diversification of the economic structure of the region. Equally significant was the distinction now drawn between the West Midlands and the South East (the IDC limit in the latter had only been raised to 10,000 sq. ft.). During the 1960s the problems of the two regions had been closely equated. The Government's reply was welcomed by the Chairman of the West Midlands Planning Council, Mr.Hazell, particularly the Government's 'agreement with the view that there should be a positive policy of economic growth in the region'.[28]

Lastly, the *Economic Appraisal* signified the development of the economic component in regional planning,[29] for previously the Planning Council's attention had been on the physical aspect. It is now fully recognised that economic analysis is a vital part of the consideration of the advantages and practicality of any given physical strategy, especially in the West Midlands where it is felt that the integrated industrial structure of the conurbation makes it difficult for many industries to alter their location. The development of this component is also producing a division of labour between the Planning Council (economic/industrial analysis) and the Standing Conference (regional physical land-use) in advancing regional planning.

Relations with regional MPs

The tenuous nature of the cross-fertilisation between the regional machinery and regional MPs is very conspicuous in the West Midlands. The Chairman of the West Midland Group of Labour MPs, Mr.Peter Archer, could recall only one meeting of the Group with the Planning Council since 1965, although a meeting had been arranged to discuss the *Economic Appraisal*. This problem in part relates to the lack of regional committees in the House of Commons for English regions. It has been recommended that such all-party regional committees should be created,[30] and that their tasks should include the debating of economic planning councils' studies. The present regional sub-committees of the parliamentary parties are by no means adequate. The Labour West Midland Group has only a small attendance at its meetings (seven or eight MPs on average), which indicates the lack of importance Labour MPs in the region attach to it.

The National Exhibition Centre lobby

The purpose of this final section is to use a recent successful lobby in the West

128

Midlands to exemplify the prerequisites of successful influence and to illuminate further the handicaps under which the West Midlands Planning Council has laboured. It will also illustrate the extent to which an *ad hoc* lobby involved the regional machinery. A brief chronology and analysis of the influence and tactics of the National Exhibition Centre lobby is called for.

At the end of 1968 a joint liaison committee between Birmingham Corporation and Birmingham Chamber of Commerce was formed, initially to direct itself to the problem of the effect on the area of the Government's IDC policy. Subsequently attention switched to the possibility of a National Exhibition Centre being located near to Birmingham. After receiving confirmation of government interest a fully worked out plan was formulated. The Committee proceeded to lobby and negotiate at departmental level to persuade the Government of the scheme's merit, concentrating on the Board of Trade, but also approaching Mr.Crosland when he took over regional affairs after October 1969. The lobby was offering to manage the development of the Centre, but their plan also included a financial provision of £3m. from the Corporation. These terms were combined with an effort to keep the negotiations confidential on the part of the lobby, so that they were virtually complete by the time the plans became public. The overall picture was of a carefully manipulated favourable combination of factors. Mr.Mason at the Board of Trade became convinced of Birmingham's advantage for the location. He won Cabinet approval for the scheme at a time when, because of the lobby's head-start, it was the only concrete one before him. These considerations, combined with the fact that the Government felt the time had arrived for action on such a project, clinched the matter. At the favourable decision Alderman Griffin of Birmingham Corporation remarked: 'It is the first time a major national project of this kind has been taken from the capital and put in the regions.'[31] The scheme would undoubtedly prove to be advantageous to the West Midlands, both in the generation of vital service industry employment, and in the whole economic development of the region through the injection of a large number of British and foreign visitors that the holding of large-scale exhibitions would bring.

In spite of the decision of January 1970, the London lobby, including powerful industrial interests such as the Confederation of British Industry, gathered momentum in an effort to change the decision in favour of a London siting. This was very evident after the accession to power of the Conservative Administration in June 1970. A scheme for an exhibition site at Northolt was hastily drawn up, and the Greater London Council directed powerful pressure on the Board of Trade. By this time, however, the Birmingham lobby had made various financial commitments, including the inauguration of a company to operate the Centre. It was felt that the point of no return had been reached, but more important it exemplified the rapidity with which the Birmingham scheme would become operative. A revived Birmingham lobby advanced these further considerations, bringing them to the attention of both the Prime Minister and Mr.Noble at the Board of Trade. They were formidable enough to warrant a re-affirmation of the earlier decision.[32]

129

For analytic purposes the prominent feature of the Birmingham lobby was the degree to which it was able to utilise the deference of a Government towards a pressure group that can meet its needs. In this case the Labour Government wanted to effect a decision on the National Exhibition Centre, after more than ten years' stalling from the London interests. One component of the lobby, Birmingham Corporation, being an executive tier of government, was able to deal with planning considerations and willing to contribute to the financial cost, while its coalition partner, the Chamber of Commerce, offered the necessary business expertise. This unofficial *ad hoc* grouping, therefore, presented the Government with the means of achieving a desired aim in much the same way as a government needs to rely to a large extent on trade unions to enforce an incomes policy for example. In our example there was a clear commitment from powerful interests who were willing to deliver the goods. It was possible because of the natural alignment of interests, capable of being mobilised and involved in the local governmental process.[33] This very strength is in turn indicative of the fundamental weakness of the West Midland Planning Council. It has no executive powers to give effect to any proposals. It has also faced the considerable difficulty of effecting a regional alignment of interests comparable to that at local level, a dilemma that only showed signs of being resolved through the events associated with the *Economic Appraisal* in the unfamiliar conditions of economic malaise in the West Midlands. Furthermore, the members of the Planning Council do not sit as delegates and are unable to commit interests to any particular action. Again, the existence of executive power and responsibility behind the Birmingham lobby enabled a concrete, well planned and costed project to be presented to the Government, whereas the West Midlands Planning Council, without such power, has not costed its plans in terms of practical implementation. The air of unreality about the latter's proposals is not helpful to Government which has to think in terms of definite financial commitments.

Another factor facilitating the success of the Birmingham lobby was its clearly defined and limited objective of achieving a location near to Birmingham for the National Exhibition Centre, entailing no reversal of any government policy.[34] This again is in contrast to the West Midlands Planning Council, whose objectives have been unclear since the demise of the National Plan, while the implementation of any strategy for a region requires decisions on a wide range of policies, many of which involve a reversal or change of government policies (i.e. the Labour Government had a regional development policy which was felt to be detrimental to the West Midlands). Where the Planning Council's advice is more limited, as in its views on the implications for the region of individual ministerial decisions, it is often unable to mobilise any regional backing, for such advice has to remain confidential to its members, falling within the screen of the Official Secrets Act.

The Birmingham lobby was also helped by Mr.Crosland's appointment as Secretary of State for Regional Planning and Local Government in October 1969, for it was able to win his support. Yet, there was no question of it being in competition with the Development Areas for resources, the only competitor being the London lobby. In terms of this comparison the West Midlands had superiority from the point of view of regional planning, while initially even the competition from the GLC was excluded by the confidentiality of the negotiations, enabling the conflict to be further confined. This compares with the earlier allusion to the fact that the regional structure of the planning councils/boards is in effect an institutionalisation of conflict, with the West Midlands having been less successful in mobilising a regional interest than the traditional 'unemployment' regions and consequently unfavourably placed in such conflicts. Once again it illustrates the contrast between the advantages of the Birmingham lobby and the disadvantages of the West Midlands Planning Council.

The Birmingham lobby, in putting their case directly to the government departments where the power to make the decision resided, won vital strategic support in the decision-making structure from Mr.Mason and Mr.Noble, both of whom played major roles in securing departmental coordination and Cabinet approval for a Birmingham location for the Exhibition Centre. The increasingly vociferous London lobby had also provoked something of a West Midlands regional lobby to back the Birmingham scheme. The West Midlands Group of Conservative MPs was particularly conspicuous in its support,[35] including the lobbying of the Conservative leadership to prevent the reversal of the decision in the event of the Conservative Party winning the imminent election.[36] When, in June 1972, the Government called in question the Birmingham scheme, as a result of proposed changes by Birmingham Corporation in the financing of the project, strong opposition to the Government's equivocation was again apparent in the West Midlands. There was a great amount of activity behind the scenes on the part of the region's MPs, together with support for Birmingham from neighbouring local authorities. As a result, the Government restored its full approval, a response to the intensity of the outcry in Birmingham and the West Midlands.[37] A local coalition, then, presented an issue which created a regional interest. Yet, ironically, on this matter the West Midlands Planning Council was not approached by the Birmingham lobby; nor was it consulted by the Board of Trade, although regional policy considerations entered into the decision. The project was first discussed in the Planning Council after the decision.

Hence, in relation to this important lobby in the region, the West Midlands Planning Council certainly did not act as a focal point in the projection of a regional consensus or interest. In a sense the National Exhibition Centre decision was the Stansted of the West Midlands Planning Council because of lack of consultation.[38] Admittedly it did not raise any objections and subsequently, in its *Economic Appraisal*, came out strongly in favour of the scheme's potential for generating vital service industries. But its non-participation in this decision may also be seen as a reflection on its influence, for as Truman has stated in relation to the institutional factor in pressure-group activity: 'Interest groups tend to concentrate about any locus of power able to affect *appreciably* the objectives that the groups seek to achieve.'[39]

In an article written not long after the administrative innovations that created

131

the new regional machinery, A.W.Peterson suggested that the experience of the present system would provide an indication of the need for more radical structural change.[40] The West Midlands Planning Council, in its evidence to the Commission on the Constitution and in its *Economic Appraisal*, has called for this more radical change. It may well be that the developments beginning to unfold in terms of influence on policy and the development of regional interests need regional executive government and greater decentralisation of the present central government structure to increase the momentum of the growth of the regional dimension in decision making. This will enable more decisions to be taken in the regions, and by creating a regional governmental process will encourage the growth of stronger regional interests and a strengthened regional alignment to exert a more effective influence on those decisions that must remain at the centre. The strength of bargaining power is important in a pluralistic political system, for there are a large number of components involved in the governmental process which have mutually to modify their claims in order to come to agreement. The stronger an individual component is, the more able it is to ensure that its claims are not modified to the extent of being emasculated, and it is widely agreed that the regional component in decision making must be strengthened to overcome the problems of the increasing demand on economic and physical resources.

For all the weaknesses of the regional administrative innovations of 1965, however, the repercussions have not been inconsiderable in the widest context, in spite of some of the pessimistic assumptions about the impact of this machinery after the first bout of optimism subsided. It may yet prove to have been a vital stage in the evolution of thinking and institutional organisation at the regional level.

Notes

[1] Consists of the five administrative counties of Worcestershire, Warwickshire, Herefordshire, Staffordshire and Shropshire for regional economic planning purposes.
[2] This information is derived from an oral answer in Parliament by Mr. Shore, H.C. Deb., 23 May 1968, 765, c. 846.
[3] HMSO, 1967 – this was the first strategic policy document of the Planning Council.
[4] *Advising Ministers*, Routledge and Kegan Paul, 1969, p.57.
[5] HMSO, 1971.
[6] H.C. Deb., 13 April 1972, 834, c. 1537.
[7] Press Notice, summarising the evidence of the Council to the Commission, 18 February 1970, CCI Birmingham.
[8] *The Times*, 25 October 1971, and the *Birmingham Post*, 26 October 1971.
[9] *Industrial and Regional Development*, Cmnd. 4942, HMSO, p.6.
[10] Some of the findings of the study can be found in B.Smith, 'Industrial Overspill in Theory and Practice', *Urban Studies*, June 1970.

[11] Op. cit., p.27.

[12] 'Overspill Towns Plea', *The Times*, 15 April 1970.

[13] Op. cit., p.69.

[14] *Birmingham Post*, 13 and 16 September 1969, and 'Test Case: Can Green Belts Beat the Cities?', *Sunday Times*, 12 October 1969

[15] Overspill Enquiry Report, *Birmingham Post*, 14 November 1969.

[16] 'Regional Planning in the Netherlands and England and Wales', *Journal of the Town Planning Institute*, December 1970.

[17] *The Times*, Commons Report, 'Steering Industry to Overspill Towns', 11 March 1970.

[18] 'Regional Policy Attacked', *The Times*, 15 January 1970.

[19] 'Help New Towns Councils Told', *Birmingham Post*, 25 November 1969.

[20] 'Suspicions Over Crosland Talks With "Rival" Planning Bodies', *Birmingham Post*, 6 March 1970.

[21] 'Regional E.P.C.s and Local Authorities', DEA, June 1968.

[22] *A Developing Strategy for the West Midlands*, West Midlands Regional Study 1971.

[23] H C. Deb., 27 April 1972, 835, c. 1800.

[24] A phrase coined by a local official.

[25] Five regional development associations from the North, Scotland and Wales quickly urged the Government to reject the recommendations: 'G.L.C. Office Space Plan Contested', *The Times*, 11 June 1971.

[26] *Industral and Regional Development*, HMSO, op. cit., pp. 6-7.

[27] H.C. Deb., 22 March 1972, 833, c. 1544.

[28] H.C. Deb., 20 June 1972, Written Answers, c. 82.

[29] Academic research had already been carried out in this direction – see G.M.Lomas and P;A.Wood, *Employment Location in Regional Economic Planning*, F.Cass 1970.

[30] C.H.Jones, B.C.Smith and H.V.Wiseman, 'Regionalism and Parliament', *Parliament Quarterly*, October-December 1967.

[31] Quoted in the *Birmingham Post*, 29 January 1970, along with other material on how the Birmingham lobby secured the decision.

[32] For these events consult 'Show Centre: P.M's Blessing Sought', *Birmingham Post*, 24 June 1970, and the headline report of 14 July 1970.

[33] Intimate connection between local pressures and local government is not, however, common. D.M.Hill's *Participating in Local Affairs* (Penguin 1970) discusses the concept of 'undifferentiated public opinion' at local level (p. 51).

[34] The failure of the Joint Committee in its original task of securing from the Government a relaxation of the policy indicates the importance of the factor of a clash with government policy.

[35] *Birmingham Post*, 4 February 1970.

[36] The election that took place in June 1970.

[37] *Birmingham Post*, 30 June 1972.

[38] Here the South East Planning Council was not consulted over the proposed plan of the Government to site London's third airport at Stansted.

[39] D.B. Truman, 'The Governmental Process', New York: Alfred A.Knopf, p.398.

[40] 'Machinery for Economic Planning: Regional Economic Planning Councils and Boards', *Public Administration*, Spring 1966.

8 Planning as an iterative process

D. Hart, Planning as an Iterative Process', *Local Government Studies*, vol. 2, no. 3, July 1976, pp. 27-42.

Ordering change

Establishing an effective relationship between order and change is at once planning's reason for existence and one of its most difficult problems. From a planning perspective both order and change are relative rather than absolute terms. Both levels of order and degree of change are each partly reflected in, and a partial reflection of, the other. The level of order sought, for example, may be nothing more specific than the establishment of a broad developmental framework, or nothing more comprehensive than the design of a single project, but the conscious intent of the planner remains essentially the same: to encourage what is perceived to be benign development, and reduce the type of disbenefits normally associated with random change. Since planning must therefore both induce and incorporate change its commitment to the uncertain future often exhibits certain apparently paradoxical elements.

Although planning is concerned with predicting and attempting to control the future, some critics have asserted that the one thing which we know about the future with any degree of certainty is that it will not be like the past; yet, the past is the source of our knowledge about the future and it consequently provides the basis for our attempts at prediction and control.[1] Taking this argument one step further, other critics feel that broad-scale, long term planning is not possible precisely because of the current rate of change.[2] More commonly however, even those who acknowledge the extreme difficulty of planning for a broad area over time take the position that change indicates rather than obviates the need for long term planning. Although plans change the environment, the environment changes both individual plans and the inter-related set of concepts underlying the whole of the planning process.[3] From this perspective, planning is something more than a simple projection of the present, and the future is something less than a completely novel and inherently unknowable set of impending conditions.

One key reason for the growth of interest in various types of planning has been the growth of uncertainty about the future.[4] Change is no longer considered to be tantamount to progress, and natural growth has a number of increasingly evident unfortunate third-party disbenefits. As the rate of social and economic change continues to increase, more rather than less planning is being attempted both as an

135

antidote for uncertainty, and as a positive control device. Planning acts to reduce the 'impending' element in the future and make the future not only more understandable. but more acceptable as well.[5] Daniel Bell has remarked about this trend that, 'Men will now seek to anticipate change, measure the course of its direction and its impact, control it, and even shape it for predetermined ends'.[6]

Historically, at least in terms of town planning, the attempt to control change has been equated with an attempt to impose a harmonic set of relationships on the area being dealt with. This often rather holistical view has played a major part in planning thought for a good part of this century. Patrick Abercrombie remarked in 1933, 'The touchstone of what constitutes a planning scheme is this matter of relationship, the accommodation of several units to make a complete but harmonious whole'.[7] In a memorandum concerning the first regional plan for Greater London, published in 1929, the chief planner for the project, Raymond Unwin, wrote:

> The making of a plan for a great city region is a somewhat daunting project because two considerations which claim attention are as clearly true as they seem to be mutually paralysing. On the one hand the task as a whole is so complex that it can be comprehended only if attention be concentrated on one subject at a time; on the other hand the various aspects of the problem are so interdependent that they cannot safely be studied or handled separately; for the main purpose of the plan is to establish harmonious relations among them.[8]

Forty years later the production of the first *Greater London Development Plan* (1969)[9] indicated that the attempt to achieve a harmonious relationship between the various parts of the plan and the whole still occupied a position of crucial importance.[10] During the four decades which had elapsed between 1929 and 1969 however, both physical London and many of the concepts underlying the planning process as a whole had undergone a series of important changes.

One of the most important differences between the 1929 and 1969 plans was the explicit recognition in the latter that the planning subject being dealt with was not only complex and interdependent but dynamic as well. Harmonic order had, at least in part, given way to a more dynamic conception of control, and a new synthesis between the two was beginning to emerge. The *Report of Studies* accompanying the *Greater London Development Plan* (GLDP) remarks,

> Since the war social and demographic change has been rapid in large cities. The pace of such changes will undoubtedly continue and may well increase, and the planning process must take account of these trends if physical and social development are to proceed in harmony.[11]

One manifestation of this new interest was a broadening of planning's scope of concern.[12] The state of constant flux also indicated that earlier plans were often cumbersome and unresponsive. The inability to accommodate change, as exemplified by the lengthy amending and modification process, threatened to

136

overload the whole intricate planning structure.[13]

A significant body of opinion began to crystallise, during the 1960s, around the belief that planning, to remain effective, should operate as a reciprocal system: at the first level plans would continue to guide and control development as they had always done; but at a new second level plans were now also expected to continuously *reflect* change derived from monitoring new environmental circumstances. Probably the single most important exposition of this view was that of the Planning Advisory Group in their report, *The Future of Development Plans*.[14] The Planning Advisory Group (PAG) was initially appointed in 1964 to assist the Ministries of Housing and Local Government and Transport, and the Scottish Development Department, in the attempt to devise a more responsive planning system. It was felt an attempt had to be made to strike a balance between predetermined controlled change, and the ability to adapt to, and learn from, its increasingly uncertain environment.[15]

To resolve the difficulty of synthesising flexibility and commitment the PAG suggested that plans were to be treated as strategic decision documents rather than as detailed maps, with local plans being produced at a later stage in the planning process. The documents would concern themselves with a range of activities occurring within a particular geographical area at the strategic level.[16] The approach at this level, it was felt, would help to free planning from the detailed proceduralism and excessive formalism which were often associated in the public mind with the operation of the existing machinery. By beginning at the policy formulation level, it was hoped that the plans would have a built-in measure of flexibility. The plans were to provide conceptual 'developmental frameworks' which could be altered as proposals were made steadily more specific over time, until they at last emerged as functional programmes and operational projects. Two things are significant about the PAG recommendations: (a) the recognition of the continuous incompleteness of any given plan; and (b) partly because of this, the continuous need for up-to-date information about the environment.[17] Government plans had long been concerned with control of directed change but only since the PAG Report have they been deliberately thought of from the outset as policy vehicles, continuously involved in a process of self-modification.

The attempt to achieve flexibility in planning is by no means new, however, and it has been suggested by at least one observer that it has been occurring — in practice if not in theory — for some time. Writing about planning for the London area, Foley differentiates between the earlier unitary approach to planning and the later adaptive approach which was beginning to take shape during the 1960s.[18] The unitary approach was essentially design oriented and is typified by two of the Abercrombie Plans for London produced during the Second World War. 'The Greater London Plan and the County of London Plan provide almost classic examples of the overwhelmingly unitary approach to planning', Foley asserts. The adaptive approach, on the other hand, is concerned with social interrelationships and the way in which the community develops over time. It is essentially evolutionary rather than deterministic and it recognises the importance of political

137

and economic decisions as factors in the planning process.

Foley illustrates this point clearly. He remarks regarding the Greater London Plan (1944) that 'despite its initial architectural-planner, unitary-character [it] came to be absorbed into a political and administrative process within central government that, by its very nature, was essentially adaptive in character.'[19]

It is thus possible to convert a predominantly unitary plan into a predominantly adaptive plan through the activity of the organisational structure surrounding the planning process. As Britton Harris suggests, this type of adaptation occurs at more than one level since planning must: (a) modify the imperfections of the initial perception of the set of circumstances surrounding the problem being dealt with: and (b) evolve as the planning problems and the society within which they occur continue to change.[20]

Iterative planning

The increasing consciousness of the need for adaptive planning — deliberately conceived to be so from the outset of the plan-making process rather than as an unintentional administrative effect — was finally made law through the passage of the Town and Country Planning Act 1968.[21] Planning was forced, reflecting the new view of the city which it modelled, to become more of a broad flow and less of an intermittent series of discrete acts. Plan-making as a project, in Raymond Unwin's sense of the term mentioned above,[22] was increasingly viewed as one important phase in — rather than the whole of — a complex process. At least in terms of the intent of the Act, planned change no longer meant an attempt to achieve a kind of static order.[23] The planning for an area such as Greater London could be neither complete nor certain, because: (a) its subject — the city region — had no finite end; and (b) perfect prediction could only be achieved through perfect knowledge or complete control. Because both of these conditions did not obtain and because speed in the modification process was essential if the public's confidence in planning was to be maintained, planning had to be made more flexible in conception and more efficient in operation. Planning became less concerned with producing and maintaining 'the plan' and more interested in facilitating a wider planning process which could be used to both incorporate new information and utilise previous experience.[24] Or so, at any rate, the framers of the 1968 Act hoped — but, because of the relative newness of the Act, it is only now becoming possible to make an analysis of its effects.

In a sense, the Town and Country Planning Acts of 1947, 1962 and 1968 have all been attempts to reduce the inflexibility caused by the increasing administrative precision with which each preceding Act had been applied. The governmental process which Foley saw as inherently adaptive often had the effect of steadily narrowing — through increasing specificity — the channels through which change was designed to flow. Adaptation became steadily slower as the channels of change began to narrow and the process of planning change became steadily more rigidly institutionalised itself.[25] In the *Explanatory Memorandum* accompanying the 1947 Act it was stated that one of the principal defects with the planning system set up under the 1932 Town and Country Planning Act was that, 'It is static. A planning scheme has the force of law, and can be altered only by a long and cumbersome procedure.'[26] In order to avoid this difficulty, the 1947 Act proposed both that plans be broader and less detailed and that they be reviewed at five-yearly intervals after their approval by the Minister of Town and Country Planning so that they could be periodically up-dated. Unfortunately, as the new system began to function neither the intended breadth nor the quinquennial reviews were capable of preventing them,[27] in the fact of accelerating change, from losing their impetus and tending, if not to inertia, at least to a kind of determined equilibrium. At least in the field of planning dynamics the interesting thing about the 1947 *Explanatory Memorandum*, and the 1964 *Future of Development Plans*, is the similarity of their condemnation of the systems which they replaced.

The 1968 Act differs from earlier Acts in a number of important ways. It seeks to unite land use and transportation considerations; it stresses the policy aspect of planning; and, it emphasises that the planning process is both continuous and, at least in conceptual terms, capable of continuous correction.[28] Although the present idea of a fluid planning operation which is constantly capable of redirecting itself has won widespread approval in governmental and professional circles, there are few examples of how such a process could be made operational.[29] On the basis of what is known about organisational theory — particularly governmental organisations — law, and the recent history of the planning process, there is good reason to believe that the shift to this type of 'second generation' planning will be extremely difficult. There is also reason to believe, in view of the lack of effective guidelines, that the process of incorporating change cannot be defined but must be worked through as a kind of continuous experiment.

The Greater London Development Plan (1969) is an example of a large-scale urban plan which reflects this period of conceptual transition. 'Planning on a broad scale', states the GLDP's Report of Studies, 'is now clearly seen as a continuous process, providing a strategic framework to guide further decisions'.[30] The Plan, its authors feel,

> states a set of principles for the future development of Greater London which will have to undergo a process of validation extending perhaps over several years. For the planning of London to be effective, there will have to be a sustained effort of partnership between the Council and the London Boroughs in which concepts are put forward, tested, amended, re-tested, and so on in what is commonly known these days as an 'iterative process'.[31]

The concept of process in planning

The complexity of planning for an area such as Greater London necessitates that some type of coherent perspective be employed which would allow the analysis to proceed as directly and as economically as possible. Ideally, what is required is a paradigm of the planning process, but a review of the existing literature indicates that the attempt to relate planning to its environment in a systematic or diagrammatic fashion has rarely been attempted in actual field studies. There has been relatively little attention devoted to conceptually demonstrating in what sense planning is a process, and how, in fact, the process operates. While admitting the difficulties inherent in the attempt to undertake an activity of this kind its justification will have to be based on its ability to illuminate and suggest sets of relationships which help to explain why particular goals have been served in particular ways, and the consequences of serving these goals in the ways indicated, on the process of planning itself.

The concept of process plays an important, and largely unquestioned, part in planning as well as in a number of other related fields of social activity.[32] Public planning, for example, takes place within a much wider network of intersecting technical, organisational and political processes.[33] Three recent works on public planning, *The City Planning Process*, by Alan Altshuler,[34] *City Politics and Planning*, by Francine Rabinovitz,[35] and *Poverty, Planning and Politics*, by Stephen Thernstrom,[36] have all been concerned with various aspects of the planning process. It is evident however, that process in the context of these studies has more than one meaning, and that the meaning being employed at a particular time is only rarely defined in spite of its apparent importance. Normally it appears to mean[37] the historical process of plan-making and the focal point of interest is therefore on the events leading up to the adoption (or rejection) of an essentially end-state, unitary projection. The process is a finite one and there is a fairly clear division between producing the plan and causing it to be implemented. Possibly because form follows function, this projection, either a Master Plan or a plan for a particular sub-area has tended to be rather static in terms of policy and design.[38] In one influential planning text which is representative of this viewpoint, *The Urban General Plan*, by T.J. Kent, the author states simply, 'To me therefore, there can be no such thing as a flexible policy in relation to physical development. A so-called "flexible plan" is no plan at all'.[39]

In all of the studies the visible, plastic element is much more the political and administrative process rather than the plan itself, in spite of the fact that the books demonstrate that a plan — and a planning process — which is not capable of responding to changing interpretations of social and physical problems and alternative perceptions of the public interest must by the very nature of the complex system in which it is embedded become inoperative and ultimately irrelevant. What each of the studies does indicate is that in order for plans to succeed there must be a high degree of correspondence between: (a) the planning process and the subject system; and (b) the planning process and the system's own control devices. Planning must concern itself not only with physical reality, but if it is to have an effective impact, with the means whereby reality changes. The operating control devices, most notably the political process, are continually changing and a non-flexible plan which is not capable of accommodating these sequential shifts, is not a plan at all but an artifact from the moment of its creation. In a situation of limited control and manifest uncertainty such as this, the planning process, as Blackman has suggested, must — if it is to effectively mesh with the wider processes surrounding it — approximate the following form:

> Planning initiates a course of action which produces events experienced by the agent, in the light of which he modifies the plan; so that in a sequence of phases, the plan is continuously initiating action or being modified by the results of action; and this modification is not merely a more efficacious employment of means to an originally intended end (a continuous adjustment on the feedback principle), but also a modification of the end in view, a revision of intention . . . a development in understanding.[40]

Implicit in this definition of the planning process are two points which will now be developed and related to the paradigm: (a) that the planning process continues to occur after the initial acceptance of the strategy to be employed, and is changed because of its employment: and (b) that the traditional means-ends dichotomy, for the process as a whole, is a false one.

If this view of planning is tentatively accepted, even at the conceptual level, a problem immediately arises: if planning is conceived of as an agent-initiated, continuously iterative process, in what sense does it remain planning, as the word is traditionally employed? If the planning process operates not merely through error-controlled feedback but also through a much more fundamental, successive recasting of intent, what is left of the assertion that what is taking place is in fact planning at all? To answer these questions it is essential that at least some of the assumptions upon which urban planning rests should be briefly sketched.

The concept of planning appears to concern itself, at a minimum, with the following types of implicit assumptions:

(a) Planning presents, with varying degrees of specificity, an organisational perspective of a series of events or activities which have not, by definition, as yet occurred.

(b) The components of the perspective, presented in statement form, numerically, or by illustration, may be either: (i) predictive, or (ii) prescriptive in character; normally however they are a combination of the two.

(c) The predictive statements tend to take the form: if P^1, the initially perceived problem — which 'is in fact a cluster of interlocked problems with interdependent solutions'[41] — continues to occur and nothing is done (i.e. nothing is purposively done), we can expect that by time T^n, unfavourable condition D will result.

141

(d) The manipulative statements tend to take the form: if we wish to avoid condition D and the disadvantageous effects which it will bring in its train, we must prevent P^1 from growing steadily more unacceptable by pursuing strategy S^1, a selected line of approach or set of approaches, beginning as quickly as possible at time T^1.

(e) If S^1 is adopted at T^1 not only will the disbenefits of D be avoided but a more acceptable state of affairs, condition A, will be created and maintained in a way which would not have occurred either through the operation of random chance or through the employment of any of the other strategies (S^2-S^n) considered at T^1.

(f) ,The manipulative strategy, S^1, proposed on the plan must, to be effective be capable of actually being implemented through the deliberate activity of some effectuating body by means of a series of operating programmes (OP^1-OP^n) derived from S^1.

(g) Since the selection of a strategy relies heavily on (then) current organisational judgements of fact or value which will be shown, during the process of operating programme implementation, to be incorrect, many projected facts or values will be either modified or falsified by subsequent events or activities — even when these events or activities are direct outgrowths of the continuing implementation of the accepted plan.

(i) Since both the perceived initial problem, P^1, and the manipulative strategy employed to resolve it, S^1, are functions of a particular period of time and since the relationship between P^1 and S^1 is a reciprocally changing one, operating through the elimination of observed error, EE, the more effective the operating elements of a plan are the less likely that precisely the same problem will be dealt with over a given span of time because the same problem, in precisely the same perceptual or factual terms, no longer exists.

(j) Continuous planning would therefore more closely resemble a procedural spiral rather than the traditional closed circle.[42] From this point of view, planning would resemble a layered horizontal scanning process, with previous lines affecting the formation of each of the subsequent ones. Each scan of this process planning activity would thus help to both direct and constrain its successive iterations.

Since, we hinted earlier, error-elimination consists not only of marginally or fundamentally modifying the successive tentative solutions attempted, but in iteratively reshaping the problem perception itself. In fact this activity by a single organisation is very rarely carried out in isolation. In most planning situations a core organisation exists which is part of a cluster of interlinked authorities with interdependent operating procedures. Fig. 8.1 [43] serves as a useful point of departure for analysis but inter-authority considerations require that a broader focus of attention also be employed.

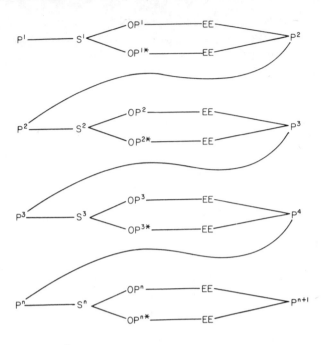

Fig 8.1 Planning as an iterative process

The import of the numbered assumptions mentioned above when considered collectively is that violence is not done to any of the traditional definitional components of planning — such as rationality-bias, policy-coordination, future-orientation, or breadth of focus — by maintaining that something resembling learning takes place through sequential iterations; that these iterations are an integral part of the planning process and that the crux of the process is the interrelationship between future anticipation and experiential adaptation.

The planning spiral is composed of two, often very closely intertwined, principal strands: commitment-anticipation and information-adaptation. The first strand is based upon a historical expectancy linked with some level of control, regarding a planned segment of the future. The second strand is composed of on-going knowledge of the recent past which will have a hitherto unexpected or unknown effect on the unfolding present and will, therefore, modify the conceptual future. Planning occurs at the inter-face between the two, continuously combining previous commitment with present knowledge by synthesising the two. The traditional future anticipation component of the planning process is a necessary part of that process — but it is not, in and of itself, a sufficient condition for effective implementation. Future anticipation at the plan formulation level can easily lend itself to deterministic planning of the architectonic kind, but this type of control is difficult to sustain for the process as a whole since there are few absolute goals in public planning.[44] Even when these goals can be ranked either cardinally or ordinally it is difficult to translate them into operating programmes without changing either their ordering or their content as implementation proceeds. A plan is a statement of conditional intent and it remains valid only as long as the conditions upon which it is based continue to maintain their projected values.

In addition, although there are many determinant elements in planning, the process in its entirety is intrinsically indeterminant [45] because: (a) of the increasing level of uncertainty — the funnel of doubt effect — as projection recedes into the distant future; and (b) because of the plasticity of the external control devices upon which intent relies for effect. In general, the level of determinancy for a particular part of a plan is a function of the extent to which commitment has been implemented. The continually spiralling planning process however has no concretely realisable final end. It is, more realistically, a series of means transformations extended through time. Means are converted into finite ends which are in turn fed back into the process at a new level upon their completion and become part of the means process for the realisation of more temporally distant ends. In many ways planning is a search procedure which derives its value not solely through problem resolution attempts, but also through its concern with both the impact of unexpected external events and with the ramifications of its own resolution attempts.[46] Planning is probable rather than certain because everything affects everything else and because the intricacy of the interconnections is such that they often must be experienced to determine their nature and extent. Prediction no less than reaction is based upon historical and therefore singular change.[47] The closed circle conception of planning indicating repetitive underlying change patterns is an appealing belief, but it is essentially an organic concept [48] which is neither an apt illustration nor an applicable ideal for something as complex, multi-directional and dynamic as a city such as London. This is a point which will be examined in more detail as this study proceeds.

Iterative planning and disjointed incrementalism

Because uncertainty in public policy-making, with regard to both clientele demand and actual proposal impact, is a continuing constraint on the finality of any decision, some theorists have asserted that the type of inclusive rationality which a good deal of modern planning is still nominally based upon[49] is simply not possible. They maintain instead that policy is, in fact, formulated on the basis of marginally shifting the *status quo* by utilising limited existing knowledge to solve problems as they arise. As Etzioni observes, 'Rather than attempting to foresee all of the consequences of various alternative routes, one route is tried and the unforeseen consequences are left to be discovered and treated by subsequent increments'.[50] The incrementalists regard the sin of information omission to be preferable to the sin of confusion and inaction.

One of the leading figures involved in this type of approach is the economist Charles Lindblom, who calls his alternative to the classical rational-deductive method of policy making 'disjointed incrementalism'.[51] In an article entitled, 'The Science of "Muddling Through"', Lindblom suggests that some of the advantages of this type of 'successively limited comparisons' are that they: (a) reduce the amount of information required; (b) reduce reliance upon theory; and (c) reduce the need to distinctly clarify objectives and then deduce from them empirical strategies which can be judged on the basis of the extent to which they achieve these objectives.[52] It is asserted that not only is incrementalism more economical in its use of scarce resources but it is also more effective and more likely to be employed in practice.[53] While this approach carries the concept of discrete experiential adaptation to its logical limits it is fundamentally anti-planning in terms of its basic intent since no attempt at all is made to anticipate a more desirable future which could be approached through a roughly consistent set of operating programmes.

Disjointed incrementalism's fatal flaw from the self-correcting, continuous planning standpoint is that its method of operation is also its ultimate goal. It seeks nothing less than marginal change but it also seeks nothing more. Incrementalism is, under the best possible conditions, consequential and fragmented in operation, while planning is, under the same conditions, coherent and purposeful. Incrementalism's modesty of purpose is bred of general satisfaction with the present, while planning seeks advantageous change because it is possible to imagine at least one better possible future. Incrementalism has no imagination, because imagination requires future-oriented abstraction and this type of abstraction is simply not necessary when the sole focus of concern is the present.

Continuously iterative planning differs from disjointed incrementalism in several fundamental ways: (1) it discriminately creates change in addition to merely responding to it; (2) it concerns itself with the interactional third-party effects as well as the transactional two-party effects of the change 'ripples' thus created; (3) it seeks to achieve a more desirable set of future states by tending asymptotically toward optimality; and finally, (4) it anticipates the future and on the basis of that anticipation and its on-going knowledge of the recent past coordinates the relevant components of the present to achieve it.[54] In spite of the often rather black and white, Manichean character of the theoretical universe inhabited by both planners and their critics,[55] it is possible to reject both the fluid approach implicit in disjointed incrementalism and the cast-iron approach symbolised by the unitary Master Plan, and assert that there is at least one other way in which it would be possible to conceive of planning as policy making. The third logically possible mode of planning — which has been briefly suggested in the previous few pages - views iterative planning as a spiral which seeks to serially and reciprocally relate image to reality within a context of induced, anticipated and unexpected change. Plans are necessarily probablistic from this viewpoint because they have limited actual control over their environments and also because they are chronically short of reliable information. Even the best plans are not error-free and it is important to acknowledge from the outset that errors are inevitable and 'that incorrect predictions are not accidents but are as much a part of the Predicting System as the correct predictions themselves'.[56] Iterative learning makes it theoretically possible to identify and correct these errors rather than allowing them to be perpetuated as the process proceeds.[57]

Notes

[1]   See Edmund Leach, 'Planning and Evolution', *Journal of the Town Planning Institute*, vol. 55, no. 1, January 1969, pp. 5-6.

[2]   See, for example, Edward C. Banfield, 'The Uses and Limitations of Metropolitan Planning in Massachusetts', in H. Wentworth Eldredge (ed.), *Taming Megalopolis* vol. II, Doubleday, 1967, p. 712; and Constantine Doxiadis' statement regarding the need to slow change, *Ekistics*, Hutchinson, 1968, p. 493.

[3]   On this, see also the comments of Sir Geoffrey Vickers and Colin Buchanan, *Journal of the Town Planning Institute*, vol. 55, no. 1, January 1969, pp. 9-10.

[4]   On this generally see J.K. Friend and W.N. Jessop, *Local Government and Strategic Choice*, Tavistock, 1969.

[5]   As samples of the increasing rate of change in society and its expression in public planning see Alvin Toffler, *Future Shock*, Bodley Head, 1970, pp. 397-8; and Donald Schon, *Beyond the Stable State*, Temple Smith, 1971, pp. 23-4.

[6]   Quoted by Lloyd Rodwin, in *Nations and Cities*, Houghton Mifflin, 1970, p. 286.

[7]   Patrick Abercrombie, *Town and Country Planning*, 2nd ed., Oxford University Press, 1943, p. 11. For an even earlier example of this type of thought see a lecture given by Patrick Geddes — a botanist and another of the major figures in the planning movement — at the New School for Social Research in New York City in 1923 and incorporated in the second edition of his 1915 work, *Cities in Evolution*, Williams and Norgate Ltd, 1949 (reprinted by Ernest Benn, 1968).

[8]   Memorandum No. 1, *First Report of the Greater London Regional Planning Committee*, Knapp, Drewitt and Sons Ltd, December 1929, p. 8.

[9]   Greater London Council, *GLDP Statement*, 1969.

[10] See for example GLC, *Tomorrow's London*, 1969, p. 44.

[11] *Report* (1969), p. 15.

[12] As Peter Self suggests, this broad concern was, in itself, nothing new. Town planning has always had socio-economic objectives. What is different about planning is the open-endedness of its future commitments. Peter J. Self, *Metropolitan Planning*, Weidenfeld and Nicolson, 1971, p. 3.

[13] See, for example, an early attempt to increase administrative flexibility

between land and trunk road development and cut down the amount of time involved. Circular No. 82, 'Town and Country Planning (General Development)', issued by the Ministry of Town and Country Planning, 6 March 1950, para. 7. See also the diagnosis put forward in the 1967 White Paper, *Town and Country Planning*, HMSO, paras. 4-5.

[14] HMSO, 1965.
[15] PAG (1965), paras. 2.36 and 2.37; and *Town and Country Planning,* paras. 11 and 19; see, for a professional view, J. Brian McLoughlin, 'The PAG Report: Background and Prospects', *Journal of the Town Planning Institute*, vol. 52, no. 6, July 1965, p. 255; and D. M. Riley, 'The Future of Development Plans', *Town and Country Planning*, vol. 34, no. 3, March 1966, p. 145.
[16] PAG (1965), paras. 1.46 and 7.11; and see also for a broad-scale American view, Harvey S. Perloff and Lowdon Wingo Jr, 'Planning and Development in Metropolitan Affairs', *Journal of the American Institute of Planners*, vol. 28, no. 2, May 1962, pp. 70-1.
[17] J. Brian McLoughlin, *Urban and Regional Planning*, Faber, 1969, pp. 87-9.
[18] Donald L. Foley, *Controlling London's Growth*, University of California Press, 1963; for a more recent view along very similar lines see Cherry's distinction between static and adaptive planning, Gordon E. Cherry, *Town Planning in its Social Context*, Leonard Hill, 1970, p. 60; and see also for an operational research perspective, Stafford Beer, 'Planning as a Process of Adaptation', in John Lawrence, (ed.), *OR 69*, Tavistock, 1970, p. 31.
[19] Foley (1963) p. 173.
[20] Britton Harris, 'Generating Projects for Urban Research', *Environment and Planning*, vol. 2, no. 1, 1970, p. 2.
[21] For a parallel development in the US, in thought if not in law, see Doris B. Holleb, *Social and Economic Information for Urban Planning*, Centre for Urban Studies of the University of Chicago, 1969, p. 12.
[22] See note [8].
[23] See, for example, the comment made by Desmond Heap in *An Outline of Planning Law*, 5th ed., Sweet and Maxwell, 1969 p. 33.
[24] See also *Development Plans: A Manual on Form and Content*, Ministry of Housing and Local Government/Welsh Office, HMSO, 1970.
[25] See, on the relationship between the institutionalised change and the urban crisis, Albert Gorvine and Samuel L. Marguilies, 'The Urban Crisis: An Alternative Perspective', *Urban Affairs Quarterly*, vol. 6, no. 3, March 1971, p. 264.
[26] *Explanatory Memorandum*, Town and Country Planning Bill, Ministry of Town and Country Planning, Cmd. 7006, paras. 8-9, HMSO, January 1947.
[27] See, for the review provision, for instance, Town and Country Planning Act, 1947.
[28] See Cullingworth's comment on the impact of the PAG proposals, J. B. Cullingworth, *Town and Country Planning in England and Wales* (2nd ed.),

Simon Shand, 1967, p. 297.

[29] On this see Anthony Downs, 'The Coming Revolution in City Planning', in Edward Banfield (ed.), *Urban Government*, Glencoe: The Free Press, 1969 (revised edition), p. 597. See also, Constance Perrin, 'A Noiseless Secession from the Comprehensive Plan', *Journal of the American Institute of Planners*, vol. 33, no. 5, September 1967, p. 340.

[30] *Report*, p. 1, and see also, *Statement*, p. 9. For an example of the process in action see the explanatory leaflet, 'This Way to London - A Summary of the Greater London Development Plan', which has been revised twice and still contains an addendum. (published by GLC in September 1969 and revised in February 1970 and February 1971).

[31] *Statement* p. 9, and *Tomorrow's London*, p. 49.

[32] See for a general discussion of this problem from a wide perspective, Paul F. Kress, *Social Science and the Idea of Process*, University of Chicago Press, 1970.

[33] On this subject see J. K. Friend, J. M. Power and C. J. L. Yewlett, *Public Planning : The Inter-Corporate Dimension*, Tavistock, 1974.

[34] Cornell University Press, 1965.

[35] Atherton Press, 1969.

[36] Basic Books, 1969; see especially pp. 129-62.

[37] Altshuler provides a good illustration; in *The City Planning Process*, there are eleven references to 'city planning' in the index to the book, but there are no no references at all to 'process'.

[38] Henry Fagin has characterised the early attempts at this kind of architectonic control as the 'one-sheet, one-shot approach'; Henry Fagin, 'The Evolving Philosophy of Urban Planning', in Leo F. Schnore and Henry Fagin (eds), *Urban Research and Policy Planning*, vol. 1, Sage Publications, 1968, p. 318.

[39] Chandler Publishing, 1964, p. 20. Kent does, however, later concede that the plan should be reviewed from time to time, but it is a bit difficult to reconcile these two very different views.

[40] Quoted by John Dyckman in 'Planning and Decision Theory', *Journal of the American Institute of Planners*, vol. 17, November 1961, p. 342.

[41] David Braybrooke and Charles E. Lindblom, *A Strategy of Decision*, New York: The Free Press, 1963, p. 54.

[42] See for examples of the traditional view: a diagram of the planning process in Milton Keynes, Jonathan Welfare, 'Programme Budgeting: The Experience in Milton Keynes', *Journal of the Royal Town Planning Institute*, vol. 57, no. 8, Sept./Oct. 1971, p. 362; see also Melvin Branch's illustration, *Planning: Aspects and Applications*, John Wiley, 1966, p. 305.

[43] Compare, for example, with Karl Popper's example of the way in which organisms solve problems. 'Of Clouds and Clocks', The Compton Memorial Lecture, presented at Washington University, St. Louis, 1966, p. 24.

[44] Melvin Branch, 'Goals and Objectives of Comprehensive Planning', in John Lawrence (ed.), *OR 69*, Tavistock, 1970, p. 62.

[45] Indeterminancy should not be confused with nondeterminancy. *Indeterminant* in the sense in which it is used here simply means not strictly limited to fixed values. *Nondeterminant*, on the other hand, means random, without continuity or purpose.

[46] Compare with Rabinovitz, 'Even decisions presumably within the planner's control can create unexpected problems' (note [35]), p. 79.

[47] Karl Popper, *The Poverty of Historicism* (2nd ed.), Routledge & Kegan Paul, 1960. Although Popper stresses the tentativeness of hypotheses and the uni-directionality of change, he seems to place a good deal of faith in the relative permanence of the present.

[48] See Robert Nisbet, *Social Change and History*, Oxford University Press, 1969, pp. 211-23.

[49] See for examples of this type of rational thinking, Donald N. Rothblatt, 'Rational Planning Re-examined', *Journal of the American Institute of Planners*, vol. 37, no. 1, January 1971, pp. 26-37; and Susan and Norman Fainstein, 'City Planning and Political Values', *Urban Affairs Quarterly*, vol. 6, no. 3, March 1971, pp. 341-62.

[50] Amaitai Etzioni, *The Active Society*, New York: The Free Press, 1968, p. 271.

[51] Braybrooke and Lindblom (1963), pp. 81-110; and more recently, Charles E. Lindblom, *The Intelligence of Democracy*, New York: The Free Press, 1965, pp. 143-51.

[52] Charles E. Lindblom, *Public Administration Review*, vol. 19, no. 2, Spring 1959, p. 81.

[53] Lindblom (1959), p. 88.

[54] For rather different criticisms of Lindblom's thesis, see, Yehezkial Dror, 'Muddling Through - "Science" or Inertia?', *Public Administration Review*, vol. 24, no. 3, September 1964, pp. 153-7; and see also Etzioni (1968), pp. 288-90. Both authors also put forward alternatives to the Lindblom model.

[55] These types of either-or propositions are not limited to planning mode. Dichotomous functions within the mode also play an important part. See Britton Harris' examination of model dimensions, 'Quantitative Models of Urban Development', in Harvey S. Perloff and Lowdon Wingo (eds.), *Issues in Urban Economics*, Johns Hopkins Press, 1968, p. 367.

[56] Irwin, D.J. Bross, *Design for Decision*, Collier-Macmillan, 1966.

[57] For a development of this concept see, D. A. Hart, *Strategic Planning in London*, Oxford: Pergamon Press, 1976.

149

PART IV

PRESCRIPTIONS FOR REGIONAL PLANNING

Overview of Part IV

This fourth and final part of the book is an attempt to bring together some dominant themes suggestive of ways in which current regional planning practice might evolve and be recast, if not transformed.

Three selected writings follow this brief introduction and overview, John Friedmann (1972, Chapter 9), the North West Joint Planning Team (1974, Chapter 10) and Felix Wedgwood-Oppenheim, Douglas Hart and Brian Cobley (1975, Chapter 11).

The paper by John Friedmann is a particularly cogent, wide-ranging and synthetic treatment indicating directions which regional planning could take. This contribution is also important because of the emphasis it places on the role of regional planning as implementation and the associated — though underplayed — themes which stress that public planning should be as much, if not more, concerned with the consequences of actions as with the arguably simpler task of promoting change.

The second contribution, it can be contended, has its roots in that long line of regional planning exercises which reach back to Patrick Abercrombie's *Greater London Plan 1944* — which represents in many ways an approach to regional planning which has not been surpassed in the United Kingdom to date. For underpinning the 1944 plan, as well as the earlier 1943 *County of London Plan* and its forerunners, are the foundations of an interventionist philosophy of regional planning which are strongly linked to the themes dominating the writings of Benton MacKaye. An examination of Abercrombie's influence whilst a member of the Barlow Commission provides further evidence to support the idea of this emerging philosophy. The contention here is that those with an interest in or commitment to regional planning as a form of public intervention may learn not so much from the application of Abercrombie's ideas but rather from the development of the ideas themselves, especially their derivation and subsequent incorporation into more contemporary planning exercises.

The ideas which most closely approximate to the Abercrombie model — in terms of intellectual qualities as well as proposals for the 'internal' recasting of contemporary regional planning — are those emanating from the North West Joint Planning Team, and in particular their report — the *Strategic Plan for the North West*, published in 1974. For the first time since Abercrombie a planning team promoted proposals for changing the very 'internal' processes of regional planning with which they had been concerned — both administratively and conceptually. The contribution included here is taken from the penultimate chapter to that report.

The final contribution is part of a Department of the Environment-sponsored research programme which emanated from one of the prescriptions which the

NorthWest Joint Planning Team proposed in their report. This concerned the problem of what the Team called 'the need for continuous planning'. As a result of their deliberations they proposed that the prospects for a monitoring-cum-review unit be investigated, to be set up within the region to continuously review the progress of the implementation of the policies contained in the *Strategic Plan*. The results of this investigation, published in 1976 by Wedgwood-Oppenheim et al, proposed that a performance-evaluation and policy-review unit should become an accepted feature of current regional planning practice. Indeed, from a prescriptive point of view they argue the case that regional planning is in essence the continuous interaction and constant iteration between performance-evaluation and policy-review.

9 Implementation and regional planning

J. Friedmann, 'Implementation', *International Social Development Review*, no. 4, 1972, pp. 95-105.

To plan for development is to practise the art of the improbable. Although much progress has been made in the ability to prescribe policies for regional development, there is now need to consider the specific methods of implementation. The relevant experience is discussed under four major principles:

(1) Planning must be joined to effective power for implementation;
(2) Political commitment to a policy must be sustained;
(3) The use of instruments for regional development must be concerted;
(4) A national balance in interregional development must be maintained.

Failure to observe these principles in practice increases the likelihood that regional planning will remain ineffective, following the most probable, not necessarily the most desirable, course.

Joining planning to effective power

In most countries, planning for specific sectors of the public economy, such as transport, housing, education, electric power or agriculture, is considerably more successful than either coordinated intersectoral or regional planning at the national level. The reason is that sectoral planning is done by the very agencies that are in charge of making the programmed investments. For instance, a department of transportation plans for the use of its own resources, including its regulatory powers, to achieve intended, if usually quite limited, effects. A rural housing agency does likewise; the allocator of its investments is not the 'unseen hand' of a competitive market but an explicit decision process in which technical factors are weighed along with other considerations. Planning in these cases is used to guide the daily work of the agency. It provides the necessary information and analysis, produces future projections, furnishes evaluations of costs and benefits, and in a multiplicity of other ways is tied into the formulation of policies, programme development and project design.

Planning can be called effective in this sense because it is intimately joined to the exercise of power, that is, to control over the legal and monetary resources to carry out intended actions. Where planning is so integrated with organised actions, it must operate under a set of realistic constraints that make its contributions immediately relevant to the managers of power. Plans are usually formulated in terms of the available instruments for implementing programmes; questions posed by the potential use of these instruments are the problems to which planning will usually respond.[1] Sectoral planning has, therefore, a close fit with the available instruments of power.

At the national level, both intersectoral and regional (or spatial) planning are further removed from the management of effective power than is sectoral planning. In most countries, the role of national planners is to advise on policy. Yet, being divorced from the instruments of action, national planners have no specific means for getting their advice accepted. Indeed, their advice is often judged irrelevant to the immediate needs of resource managers. This point is made, time and again, in the new literature on regional planning.[2] Planners' advice, separated from the uses of effective power, accomplishes little. Concluding his lengthy study of regional policy in the United Kingdom of Great Britain and Northern Ireland, McCrone writes: 'Regional planning cannot be said to have had much impact on the regional problem so far and in many respects it has still to find its role. Much depends on whether the regional bodies are to remain advisory or are to be given some executive power.'[3]

Regional development authorities, having a corporate structure, are the leading exception to this condition of relative impotence. Established as semi-autonomous agencies of the national Government, they operate within the confines of a specific geographical area and usually, control resources sufficient to carry out a variety of closely coordinated investment programmes. The prototype of all these agencies is the Tennessee Valley Authority (United States of America), established in 1933. The Guayana Corporation of Venezuela, the Cauca Valley Corporation in Colombia, and the Superintendency for the Development of the North-east (SUDENE) in Brazil are more recent and equally well-known examples. At the urban scale, the Foundation for the Development of Brasilia, the New York Port Authority, and the proposed Metropolitan Development Corporation for Valparaiso (Chile) embody the same principle of fusing planning with effective power.[4] In all these cases, planning focuses attention on the short run future and is likely to be more concerned with strategies, programmes, projects and even operational details than with long-range plans that endeavour to portray an image of the finished work.

The corporate approach to regional development has yielded impressive results whenever the powers of the development agency were commensurate with its mission. But these results have had to be bought at a cost. The authority of a regional agency extends over a defined geographical area that is only a small part of the national territory. Since few industrialising countries have adequate financial and technical resources to undertake more than one or two concerted efforts of this kind at the same time, use of the corporate approach has meant, in practice, that certain regions were favoured at the expens of other areas.[5] The justification for such a policy of imbalanced development has nearly always been based on arguments that stressed the overriding national importance of the regional scheme. Even so, the demonstration effect of a successful regional enterprise is often difficult to control. Regions that consider themselves neglected frequently bring pressure on the Government to mount similar efforts in their own areas. Although strenuously resisted by national planners who fear a geographical dispersion of resources and, more generally, a gradual attrition of their own powers to guide the overall course of national development, these pressures may lead to a multiplication of regional agencies and, consequently, to a dilution of resources for promoting development in any one area. Returning to the example of South America, both Venezuela and Colombia have six regional development agencies in operation, each with some resources of its own; Peru has blanketed the entire country with a series of Departmental Development Corporations; and Brazil has established, in addition to the powerful SUDENE, three regional superintendencies, the Foundation for the Development of Brasilia and several other intensive programmes of regional development.[6]

The apprehensions of national planners appear to be well founded. Development authorities are potent institutions. Being regionally based, they often succeed in obtaining the support of local populations and so become increasingly immune to central control and direction.[7] The technical staffs attracted to these agencies – not least because of the higher salaries and the *élan* of their mission – often provide it with technical talents superior to those available to central authorities. In a sense, one might say that where planning is closely linked to effective power, the true danger lies in its becoming excessively effective. Regional authorities, for example, are extraordinarily skilled in mobilising external resources. They become the pampered clients of international lending agencies and star exhibits of national progress. They may even begin to act as quasi-governments for their own regions, replacing central authorities in important respects. This behaviour may raise not only questions of political representation and accountability, but the grave issue of regional separatism. National Governments are jealous of their prerogatives. The drive of regional authorities for territorial supremacy is therefore likely to be checked before it can pose a threat to national unity. On the other hand, once they are institutionally entrenched, regional development agencies are difficult to eliminate and become more or less permanent features of planning administration.

Sustaining political commitment

Rudimentary patterns of urbanisation and regional social structure, established quite early in a country's history, tend to maintain themselves over long periods of time. Subsequent flows of controlling decisions, innovation diffusion, migration and economic location will tend to reinforce this pattern. The most probable future pattern will therefore resemble that of the past. Planned changes may require decades and even generations of counter-intuitive effort to alter this structural pattern in a significant way.

By way of illustration, the data given in Table 9.1 may be cited. Despite a century of technological change and population growth, the relative proportions of major regions in the United States of America have changed by only a few percentage points; and these changes reflect primarily the opening for settlement of the new areas west of the Mississippi River.

Table 9.1 United States of America: geographical distribution of population, 1850–1960 (%)

Year	North	South	West	Total country
	\multicolumn{4}{c}{Area of country}			
1850	57.0	34.5	8.5	100.0
1900	62.0	32.0	6.0	100.0
1920	60.0	31.0	9.0	100.0
1940	57.5	31.5	11.0	100.0
1960	54.0	30.5	15.5	100.0

Source: Jerome P. Pickard, *Trends and Projections of Future Population Growth in the United States, with Special Data on Large Urban Regions and Major Metropolitan Areas, for the Period 1970-2000.* Technical paper No. 4 (Washington, D.C., United States Department of Housing and Urban Development, 1969).

Numerous other examples might be adduced, such as the relative stability in the rank-size order of cities down to approximately the tenth rank.[8] In any event, this built-in tendency of any spatial pattern to maintain itself can be counteracted not only by controlling the basic rates of flow through the system and by changing their direction in ways that are highly improbable. These improbable rates of change must themselves be maintained over long periods of time. They require sustained public intervention.

This point can be illustrated simply. Suppose that the capital city of a country has established primacy over all other cities by a factor of 5:1, so that the largest city has five times the population of the next three largest cities combined. This is the case for Lima, Peru. In the foreseeable future, the most probable pattern of population migration will be one that will tend to maintain this ratio in the distribution of urban population.[9] If, for some reason, the national Government should decide to reduce the primacy of the capital to a ratio of, say, 3:1, it would have to adopt policies for accelerating migration towards provincial cities while decreasing the flow of population to the national capital. This change in the direction of migration would represent a significant departure from the normal, system-maintaining pattern. In order to accomplish its objective, the Government would have to sustain its commitment to this policy over a period of several decades. Furthermore, the policy change would have to be sufficiently bold in conception to ensure that non-planned, random events, such as changes in industrial technology, should not cancel any possible gains achieved through application of the policy.[10]

157

Spain, for instance, has adopted a kind of 'infant' industry policy for encouraging the industrial development of four growth-pole centres. The location subsidy is paid to private firms for a maximum period of seven years, after which it is to be withdrawn. Commenting on this feature of the policy, Richardson asks some pertinent questions:

> What will be the long-run consequences of a short benefit period strategy? What happens when the designation period for the four new poles expires? Will a new set of poles be created for another five or six years, and then another set, and so on? In this case, the long-run effect would be that a large number of centres would have experienced modest expansions, and that either Spain would have a hierarchical distribution similar (relatively if not absolutely) to that which exists at present . . . . [11]

In other words, Richardson is implicitly arguing for a sustained policy of giving favoured treatment to selected areas having a high potential for industrial expansion. Frequent shifts in the objects of this policy may not lead to any system change whatever.

The practical difficulties of sustaining major policy commitments should not be underestimated. If the period of desirable commitment should last for several decades, it will have to cut across several periods of governmental change, becoming a suprapolitical policy capable of receiving endorsement from more than one political regime. Few policies are ever likely to enjoy such support. Above all, they must serve important long-term national requirements of development. Although this functional relationship is not always easy to prove, it must at least be widely believed to exist. In addition, experience suggests that such policies must conform to a number of pragmatic criteria.

The first criterion is that the policy must be simple in concept and dramatic in its implications. So conceived, a policy will stimulate the popular imagination and will tend to be elevated to a national commitment. Examples come readily to mind: the conquest of the desert in Israel; the harnessing of major river basin resources in Egypt and Ghana; the building of new towns in the United Kingdom; the building of new national capitals in Brazil, Pakistan and Turkey; the reclamation of new land from the sea in the Netherlands; the construction of a transcontinental transport system in the United States of America; the establishment of a major industrial growth centre in Venezuela.

These historical examples have at least one important characteristic in common: they refer to projects whose primary impact is physical. Their appeal derives from man's emotional attachment to the land and from his pride in physical construction. If the projects are sufficiently large to become national in scope and to project an image of man pitting himself against the insensate forces of nature (deserts, rivers, the sea), or, alternately, undertaking the monumental task of building a new capital city, they stand a good chance of mobilising national support.

Irrational motives are powerful incentives to action. Support for building the new capital of Brazil was mobilised, in part, because of the 'almost mystical feeling that the city-bred Brazilian has for the interior; a feeling that the great wealth of the country is locked up there, far away from the coastal region where ninety per cent of the people live'.[12]

A 'mystical' belief of a different order was the inspiration of Islamabad, the new capital of Pakistan. 'The capital of a country is the focus and centre of the people's ambitions and desires', wrote the former President of Pakistan. 'It is wrong to put them in an existing city. The city must have a colour of its own and character of its own. And that character is the sum total of the aspirations, the life and the ambitions of people of the whole of Pakistan. With the two provinces of Pakistan, separated as they are from each other, you want to bring the people on a common platform. The thing to do was to take them to a new place altogether.'[13]

Yet another epic theme — that man should dominate nature — lies at the root of much regional planning in the Union of Soviet Socialist Republics, where it has been used for more than a generation as a basis for sustaining policy commitments. In a textbook for children published by the Government in 1929, truly poetic feelings are expressed that reach far beyond a purely rational examination of costs and benefits:

> We must discover and conquer the country in which we live. It is a tremendous country, but not yet entirely ours. Our steppe will truly become ours only when we come with columns of tractors and plows to break the thousand-year-old virgin soil. On a far-flung front we must wage war. We must burrow into the earth, break rocks, dig mines, construct houses. We must take from the earth. . . [14]

This appeal to protean feelings, however, is not without its hidden costs. For the ultimate objective is not a physical artifact (a flowering desert, a new capital city, a transcontinental railway, the conquest of the steppe), but ome specific improvement in the national 'welfare', as expressed in relevant social and economic terms, such as an increase in production, improved social conditions or national integration. The physical project, although intended as a means towards these ends, often replaces the ultimate objective and assumes the character of an end in its own right. The desert *must* be irrigated, the dam *must* be built, the land *must* be reclaimed, the highway *must* be built, the steppe *must* be made fertile — regardless of the costs imposed or even the ultimate (and sometimes doubtful) benefits. The project — like the moon shot — becomes a national obsession. A man must be placed on the moon; he will be placed. Alternatives to the man on the moon are not explored; alternative uses for the resources are not studied or seriously contemplated. The irrationality of the original appeal (which, in this author's opinion, ensures a sustained national commitment to the undertaking) may also lead to a perversion of the ultimate objectives of the project expressed in welfare terms, as the unforeseen consequences of the project spill over to affect other areas of national life. Projects of this kind can be the ruin of a country.

The very fact of national commitment suggests that the project will not be abandoned even if negative consequences should materialise. The project is undertaken, as it were, on trust in the 'principle of the hiding hand' that any problems which might arise in the course of its implementation will somehow produce an adequate, creative response to deal with them.[15] Impending ruin, joined to the promise of great benefits (however vague), may call forth extraordinary efforts to avoid it. Only a fraction of the power available from the Aswan Dam in Egypt is currently being used. The fact that the facilities are now available, but wasted, is leading to a redoubled effort to increase the country's industrial capacity, particularly of heavy power users. The destruction of fisheries in the Nile delta, due to changes wrought in the physical ecology of the delta by the construction of the dam, is adding impetus to the development of new fisheries in Lake Nasser. The change-over from periodic flooding to artificial fertilisation in Upper Egypt is seriously disturbing an ecological balance that has been maintained successfully over thousands of years. It is also inducing a major effort to bring about structural changes in the organisation of agriculture that promise to bring the population of the region into the twentieth century within the span of a few years.

The second criterion is that a policy, in order to enjoy long term political commitment, must be embodied in new institutions capable of outlasting periodic changes in the Government. Three forms of institutionalisation may be tried. The first is legal and may be illustrated by the provision in the Brazilian Constitution of a fixed percentage of national revenues that must be applied each year to the development of particular regions.[16] This provision is mandatory on all governments (so long as it remains a part of the Constitution); it has the disadvantage of being excessively rigid and unrelated to the actual cost of realistic opportunities for investment. The total amount thus set aside may be either too small or too large and can easily lead to a serious misallocation of national resources.

The second form of institutionalisation is administrative. This may be illustrated by the proposed regionalisation of public administration and development efforts in France.[17] To the extent that regionalisation is successful, shifting the gravity of decision-making power away from the Paris region, this re-organisation of the French administrative apparatus would be difficult to reverse. The obstacles to regionalisation have, however, proved to be formidable. Institutionalisation by administrative decree may be too weak an instrument to bring about substantial changes in the probable distribution of development benefits among the different parts of a country.

The third form of institutionalisation is corporate. An example would be the creation of the Guayana Corporation of Venezuela.[18] This corporate authority has ample financial resources; it has gradually built a political basis of support in the region of its primary impact, and it has managed to draw to it superior technical skills and leadership abilities. Its principal drawback has been the acquisition of too much power, a problem that already has been discussed. There is no question, however, about the effectiveness of this type of institutional arrangement. By now, the Guayana Corporation has become the largest single enterprise in Venezuela. In

160

the future, its powers may be restricted; but its existence is reasonably ensured for a long time to come.

Lastly, long term policy commitments require that the policy in question quickly produces visible results. A policy is most vulnerable during the first few years of its application. If results are not timely, those opposing it may be more successful in their efforts to persuade the Government to abandon it in favour of their preferred alternative. Yet, frequent changes in policy for spatial development are counterproductive. They usually involve changes in objectives as well. Where this happens, the results of one policy will be counteracted by the results of alternate policies and so will tend to cancel each other. The requirement of quick and visible results argues, once again, for works of physical construction. A dam is visible; the building of a new capital city is visible; a new subway is visible. The social and economic effects of works of physical construction, such as increased employment, higher incomes, more efficient administration and more efficient mass transit, are not visible in the same way. They are captured only in statistics and, in many cases, are difficult to attribute to a given policy. Indeed, quite aside from the possibility of their measurement, there is a deeply-seated folk prejudice (not entirely unwarranted) against relying exclusively on statistical measurements for justifying the continuation of public policies. As nearly everyone knows, statistical results can be deceptive. Moreover, the effects of a given policy may take years to produce results that are statistically significant. The instruments of measurement are frequently insensitive to minor, but significant, variations in the phenomena observed. When a programme of physical construction is a feasible alternative to a people-oriented programme that will have intangible results, the physical project is likely to be chosen.

A land redistribution scheme, for instance, which leads to the quick reallocation of property to a landless peasantry, is likely to be more popular with politicians than a policy seeking to encourage cooperatives, expand production credit and set up new marketing arrangements as elements of a general land reform programme. The latter policy would almost certainly be slower in its impact, and the total amount of land passing to the peasants would be smaller. Politicians, no less than the public, are primarily interested in the symbolic gesture. Although willing to allocate millions of dollars for a quick scheme of land redistribution, they may be reluctant to support a more elaborate and complex programme of reform whose results would be more gradual and, in any event, less visible and dramatic.

The sunken costs in the original investment may make the policy, once initiated, irreversible. The former President of Brazil insisted on accelerating the building of Brasilia so that succeeding governments might find it impossible to back off from the original decision. A tremendous effort was therefore launched to complete the physical infrastructure of the city under his administration. The potential monstrosity of having a brand-new ghost capital sit unoccupied would force subsequent governments to make the city work. Adversity would thus call forth its own solutions.

Concerting the use of instruments for political development

The measures that have been applied to carry out specific regional policies are extraordinarily varied. Some order may be imposed on this jumbled profusion by classifying the principal policy measures in the following categories; physical land-use controls; directed migration; public investments; and financial location incentives. Following a brief discussion of these measures, it is argued that none of them can be relied upon to produce significant results unless a set of complementary measures is brought to bear in a coordinated and focused way on a limited geographical area.

Descriptive surveys, such as the study recently published by the Organisation for Economic Cooperation and Development, are of little help to policy-makers who are interested in knowing the relative effectiveness of particular measures in a variety of contexts.[19] Rodwin's excellent review of national policies for urban and regional development does attempt to arrive at a balanced judgement concerning their success; but his evidence is, for the most part, impressionistic and only incidentally related to the instruments of implementation currently available.[20] What is needed, and is not available, is a theoretical scheme for evaluating different methods for implementing regional policies in a variety of socio-economic settings. This ambitious task is outside the scope of this article, and the comments here are directed to the question of inherent limits in a number of widely used practices. The larger issue of their relative effectiveness requires a more systematic study.

Physical controls of land use

Land-use zoning applied to regions on a national scale has been tried in a number of European countries, but not, to this author's knowledge, in any of the newly industrialising countries. A typical example is the Danish Zoning Plan, which uses a four-part division of the country: urban and industrial development areas; areas potentially attractive for urban and industrial development; landscapes of recreational and cultural values; and agricultural areas.[21] A more elaborate classification emerges from the further subdivision of these categories and from stipulation of patterns of spatial juxtaposition.

Conceptually, the zoning plan in Denmark appears to be a useful device for focusing public attention on critical problem areas. Its principal use is as a technical document for guiding public decisions. But, unless positive incentives exist for ensuring a desired pattern of location, the essentially negative controls of a zoning map are unlikely to be very effective. Urban experience in the United States of America suggests that land-use zoning is, at best, a procedure for slowing down the processes of changing land occupance.[22] Essentially a negative instrument intended to prevent certain undesirable actions from occurring, it generates no positive action of its own.

Despite these obvious short-comings, a simple zoning plan that is easy to administer (through a system of licensing, for example) may be a useful complement to other more positive measures, especially in areas of relatively dense settlement. For the capital region of Chile, it has been proposed to designate agro-industrial corridors and tourist zones for the purpose of excluding manufacturing activities from those areas, and a suggestion has also been made to set up an environmental protection district to control urban pollution.[23] These measures, however, have not been enacted. Given the agenda of priorities in the newly industrialising countries, the political appeal of regional zoning legislation is likely to remain low.

Directed migration

Direct controls over migration have been attempted in several centrally planned economies.[24] Before a person can acquire legal residence in certain cities, he must be able to produce an official work-permit or, at least, show evidence of having found a job and housing. This allows the planning authority to restrict migration to large cities and to facilitate a policy of industrial decentralisation by assuring an adequate supply of labour in the smaller centres.

As with other controlling devices, this system of direct migration controls is basically a preventive measure. Even so, it is difficult to stop the flow of urban migrants altogether, and to hold the population of major cities to the limits ideally desired by the planners.

In a number of western European countries, directed migration has taken the form of extending financial incentives to workers, without restricting labour mobility as such. Sweden has carried this concept of an active migration policy furthest. Allowances are given to workers who leave depressed areas, as well as to those who move to growth centres within them. Since 1963, around 10,000 workers from the northern part of the country have obtained special transfer grants each year to take up jobs in the central and southern areas. At the same time, over 6,000 workers per annum have obtained such grants for moving from the southern and central regions to jobs in growth centres within the northern areas.[25]

Incentive programmes such as that in Sweden would, in principle, appear to be more suited for fully industrialised countries than for newly industrialising countries where migration to cities from rural areas occurs at a pace in excess of the capacity of the urban economy to absorb new workers. For these countries, direct migration control as applied in some centrally planned economies would appear to be more appropriate. The enormous task of managing such controls must, however be recognised. The policy would also raise the inevitable question of whether individual mobility ought, in principle, to be restricted at all. The whole issue deserves more careful study than it has received.

Lastly, the provision of housing and social amenities in selected urban areas may be mentioned as a possible instrument for attracting opulation to them. This policy has been applied in Israel and in the United Kingdom as one of the principal inducements for population to move into new towns where job opportunities have tended to follow rather than precede an expansion of the labour force.[26] Occasionally, it has also been argued that the improvement of living conditions in rural areas might contribute to stemming the massive transfer of population to cities. This belief, however, has not been borne out in practice. As a rule, it is the most 'urbanised' part of the rural labour force that shows the highest propensity to migrate to cities. The closer the omnibus services and the greater the extension of mass media into rural areas, among other means — the more people can be expected to leave their villages to seek their fortune in the cities.[27]

Direct public investment

Direct public investment is the most widely used method for implementing regional development policies. The underlying notion is that the provision of critical facilities in designated districts, such as generating plants for electric power, transport facilities, housing and other social services, or large manufacturing plants in basic industries, will help establish conditions favourable to private investors and so set in motion a self-sustaining process of regional growth.[28] Such investments are best carried out in coordinated fashion according to a carefully worked out programme of development. Isolated efforts, such as construction of an electric generating plant, are not likely to produce significant changes in the attractiveness of a region for private investors without supporting investments in other facilities. This consideration argues strongly for the corporate approach to regional development planning. Even a tightly coordinated approach, however, offers no guarantee that a cumulative growth cycle will be initiated. For instance, the potential growth centre of Concepción in Chile has proved incapable of attracting private investments on a scale sufficient to allow this important provincial city to compete with Santiago as the country's principal centre of manufacturing, and this despite the general excellence of the facilities at Concepción, including a leading private university. The remoteness of the city from national markets, its relatively high cost of living, the absence of a diversified structure of private services to industry and the extreme centralisation of decision-making power in the capital of the country combine to militate against the self-supporting economic growth of the region. Further overhead investments or even the enlargement of the government steel plant in the area would do little to encourage private investors unless additional conditions preventing spontaneous growth were to change. The situation may be radically transformed under the current (1972) Popular Unity Government of Chile as a result of both the increased public ownership of industry and a general restructuring of the final output of manufacturing towards a greater emphasis on capital goods and working-class consumer products.

Examples of the failure of public investment programmes to induce economic growth are probably more numerous, on balance, than the successful cases. Though public infrastructure may be necessary for regional development, it is by no means a sufficient condition. Additional incentives, especially of a financial nature, may have to be offered to bring the private calculus of costs and benefits into a harmony

164

with policy designs. The social response of local communities to government incentives is also relevant. Similar economic programmes may not elicit similar responses on the part of the community. In some cases, a programme may lead to its mobilisation around the objective of economic growth, while, in others, it will meet with apathy or even passive resistance. This ability of the local community to organise itself for economic growth and development must be considered an important variable in the implementation of development policies.

Almost no empirical studies have been carried out to substantiate this point, and the evidence that does exist is chiefly based on personal impressions.[29] Nevertheless, it would seem that the social structures of communities do differ with respect to their ability to generate and absorb changes conducive to economic growth. Some towns ary essentially 'open' and dynamic systems, welcoming change and capable of rapidly adapting to new conditions of life; other towns are highly controlled by traditional élites and are much less receptive. The question deserves a great deal more study than it has received.[30]

Financial location incentives

Financial location incentives are among the most popular devices for promoting the development of designated areas in private or mixed enterprise economies. Principally, they include tax incentives, import tariff reductions, location subsidies and investment credits. These measures are applied to individual firms in the hope of inducing them to invest their capital in the development areas. Experience has provided contradictory evidence concerning their effectiveness. Four major problems may be identified:

(1) It is politically difficult to restrict the geographical incidence of financial inducements to only a few areas. Yet, the multiplication of areas eligible for favoured treatment will encourage an excessive spread of industrial locations, dissipating the potential effectiveness of the incentives. An interesting proposal for a regionally differentiated pay-roll tax has recently been made in the United Kingdom by Colin Clark. This plan would involve varying rates which, at one extreme, would penalise most heavily locations at London; and, at the other, give enormous benefits to firms operating in the Hebrides.[31]

(2) Unless financial subsidies make up a substantial proportion of total variable costs in production dependent upon location, they may not lead the industry to locate in areas that, in other respects, are lacking in decisive economic advantage. The subsidy must be at least sufficient to compensate the producer for higher costs of transport of raw materials and/or finished products, as well as for other costs he may incur by locating outside existing core regions. Yet, the provision of an adequate level of subsidy may place an excessive burden on the public treasury and decelerate the over-all process of national economic growth.

(3) Financial incentives may encourage industry in locations that are inefficient from the standpoint of private cost-accounting and thus reduce the overall competitive position of national industry in foreign markets. Additional export

165

subsidies may therefore be required. This, however, would further raise the costs of regional development to the country.

(4) Withdrawal of financial incentives after the initial starting-up period may lead to a shift of industries out of the region and back to the core areas of the country. Should this happen, and the mere threat to do so could be sufficient, a policy of permanent subsidisation might be required, resulting in a structural distortion of the resource allocation pattern that would be difficult to reverse.

The most celebrated instance of the use of financial incentives is the development programme for the north-eastern region of Brazil.[32] Some 600 industrial projects resulted from this programme between 1960 and 1968.[33] Even so, the provision of new jobs has apparently been unable to keep pace with population growth in the region, and unemployment is reported to be increasing. Moreover, the various financial incentives, such as the 50 per cent relief in corporate income-tax for an equivalent amount of investment in the region, have had, on balance, a regressive effect on the distribution of income.

The above-mentioned development effort in Brazil is notable in that it combines a number of the 'success' elements which have been discussed. It is focused on a single region; it has acquired an institutional form in the Superintendency for the Development of the North-east; it has survived several changes of government by acquiring a strong political base in the region; and it has achieved a remarkable degree of coordination in the use of development instruments.

An insightful critique of this programme has been made by Stöhr in his comprehensive survey of regional development policies in Latin America. His conclusions are worth citing at some length, because they demonstrate that even the very best programmes may only partially succeed in what they set out to accomplish:

> The conviction that a direct strengthening of the economy and the improvement of social welfare levels was essential for obtaining a lasting effect led to the creation of SUDENE. Some 600 industrial projects were the result between 1960 and 1968. A road and communications system was established, a modern educational system was introduced, versatile professional opportunities were newly opened in the region, and a change in the style of regional politics and decision-making was initiated along with the opportunity for the states to participate in program formulation for the allocation of federal funds in the region. Of the original strategy components of SUDENE — intensification of industrial development, reorganization of agriculture, and relocation of population surpluses — only the first one was achieved to a major extent. Since the main incentives were for capital inputs, most of the new industries turned out to be highly capital-intensive, using modern technology; their contribution to the creation of regional income and the expansion of regional markets however, was relatively small. In effect, these new industries remained modern enclaves within a large and backward area. They received their capital and technology from the outside, mainly

from the South-East, and shipped an increasing amount of their products to South-Eastern markets. The hoped for impact on the rural areas by absorbing manpower and creating additional income for rural population was not realised. Due to the lack of regional market expansion, these new industries created yet another problem for the nation: subsidized competition from the North-East emerged for some of the industries in the South-East, and in some sectors idle capacity arose due to the limited absorption possibilities of the national market.

A great part of the income created by this new industrialization flows back to the South-East. In addition, an instability has recently been created by pressure on the Government to liberate the sale of newly established enterprises by their original tax-favoured owners. This would indicate an inclination of investors in the South-East to withdraw their capital from the North-East as soon as they have secured their initial tax benefit.

The rural sector has been relatively little changed, first because practically all of the private capital under the tax savings legislation went into industrial rather than agricultural investment, and second, because the relocation of surplus agricultural labor as well as agricultural reform proceeded very slowly. Both have recently been de-emphasized even more because of fear that they would aggravate the unemployment problem still further.

In summary, three key problems have arisen in connection with the program for the North-East. The first lies in a failure to create a self-sustained process of regional growth with decreasing dependency on extra-regional inputs. To a large extent, this may be ascribed to the lack of a sufficient multiplier effect under which growth would increasingly be based on regional savings, and regional markets would be enlarged. The second problem results from a failure of the development process to diffuse from the few industrial enclaves to the rest of the region. The third problem is the insufficient compatibility between the development of the North-East and national development criteria.[34]

Maintaining a national balance

Discussion of the preceding three principles has, in various ways, stressed the importance of an approach focused on specific development requirements of a given region. It is now necessary to back off from this emphasis to attain a wider national perspective. A country can be divided into major development areas, each of which will present a different problem constellation to the planner. Regional development strategies must reflect these differences, but they must also strive to achieve a balance of all programmes throughout the country, in what may be called a 'balanced' approach. A balanced approach is required, first, because the development issues of different spatial subsystems are interrelated among themselves; and, secondly, because the highest level of policy integration must be the country. A regional development programme conceived and carried out without concern for its impact on the rest of the country is likely to be harmful from a national point of view. The successful implementation of a regional policy, therefore, depends upon the ability of planners to relate it in functional ways to the development of the country as a whole. Whereas the focused approach clearly favours some areas over others, the balanced approach requires a mechanism not only for adequately differentiating among strategies for regional development, but for assuring the consistency of these strategies (and the programmes through which they are implemented) with the over-all development policy for the country. In other words, all areas of the country will receive at least some separate attention; a few areas will receive concentrated attention; and the policies and programmes for all areas will be coordinated at the national level through sectoral and intersectoral policies, programmes and budgets. Because this arrangement is fairly complicated, a diagram may help to clarify it further.

In Fig. 9.1, three levels are distinguished; level 1 is essentially political and brings together the Council of Ministers, as well as other political decision-makers of national stature; level II includes primarily the technical skills of the central guidance system (national planning, budget office, treasury, central bank and technical officials from the ministries and other specialised agencies); level III joins political and technical functions in the several regions and cities of the country.

Effective power in this system refers to the management of budgetary resources. Policy-making, planning and investment programming are closely linked in the diagram with effective power. For ease of communication, it is advisable that planning and budgetary functions be closely related or even joined within a single agency or planning ministry. In addition to the financial budget, a separate accounting for manpower and resources is suggested. Few countries have thus far extended their management systems to include the budgeting of critical skills and scarce physical resources, but it is desirable that they do so.

Spatial planning-budgeting is shown to relate closely to both the sectoral and the intersectoral planning-budgeting process. This relation suggests that spatial planning represents a new level of synthesis which attempts to coordinate both sectoral and intersectoral programmes according to the requirements of regional policy; while, at the same time, assuring the consistency of these policies with the overall development policy for the country.

To make this possible, level III becomes a necessary component of the planning-budgeting system. Specialised planning offices must be established in each of the country's development areas (including the major cities), replicating organisations at the national level. In those regions which are undergoing intensive development, the regional (or metropolitan) development authority replaces the planning office as the focus for planning and coordination. In contrast to the ordinary planning office which commands no investment budget of its own, the regional authority has a corporate form and its own source of funds for carrying out its work.

An intricate web of communication brings these several elements into a related system. The administrative arrangements can get rather complicated and must, in every case, be adapted to local circumstances. A number of variants of this basic scheme are possible, depending upon whether the country concerned is a federal or unitary State and the extent to which participation in policy planning is practised by different groups and organised interests.

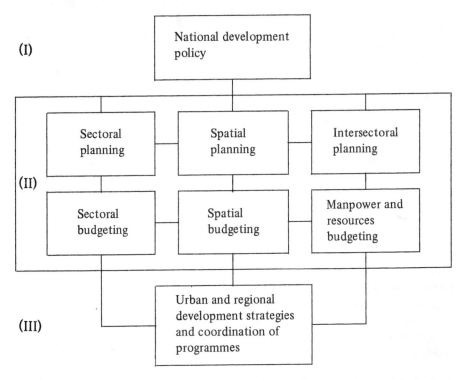

Fig. 9.1 Comprehensive system for National Planning Programming and Budgeting

This model for a comprehensive system of planning for regional development is based on a prototype evolved in Chile between 1964 and 1969.[35] Similar arrangements have been put into practice in France[36] and Turkey[37]. Although no country has yet succeeded in perfecting a system of regional programme budgeting, considerable progress has been made in Chile, where an interregional econometric model is used for achieving consistency between regional and national growth targets.[38] Each year, the National Planning Office provides regional offices with a current statement of policy, programme guidelines and budgetary ceilings, which are used to detail the components of the annual investment programme in close collaboration with the representatives of the functional agencies in the area. A draft of this programme is sent back to the national office for revision and for coordination with other regional programmes, with overall national economic policies, with the Budget Directorate of the Ministry of Finance and with the Council of Ministers. The original draft submitted by the regional office is thus subjected to several revisions with the active collaboration of the regional office until a satisfactory allocation of investment funds has been made. The regional (or spatial) budget for the country as a whole is then submitted, through the Minister of Finance, to the President for his approval. It is not, however, submitted to the Congress for legislative action, but remains an administrative document. Since representation in the Congress is on a territorial basis, explicit discussion of regional allocations would lead to needless controversy and would undoubtedly produce so many changes in the budget as to render the entire budgetary process meaningless.

Even as an internal, administrative document, however, the regionalised national budget has many uses. It results in a good deal of intersectoral consultation; it helps to focus attention on the regional consistency of sectoral programmes; it serves to highlight the requirements of certain projects that are of national importance; it heightens awareness of the systemic character of interregional balance in the programming of national investments. The regionalised national budget certainly does not lower the efficiency of resource use; quite possibly, it succeeds in raising it. All in all, it is a hopeful beginning.

Conclusion

Regional development planning, as a component of national planning, is a very recent innovation. Its extraordinary appeal is reflected in the frequent international conferences on the subject, the growing number of scholarly publications, and, most importantly, in the acceptances of this new technique by an increasing number of national Governments. No one would deny that many problems of a conceptual and practical nature remain to be solved. But the base already exists for any country, wishing to achieve the maximum beneficial effects from its development programmes, to undertake a regionalisation of the development effort. An adequate body of theory exists; major policy issues for regional development have been identified; good analytical techniques can be applied to furnish a factual basis for spatial planning; there is a wide array of implementing tools; sufficient experience has been gathered to distil from it a number of principles for the implementation of regional policies; and the necessary technical expertise – thanks to the efforts of the United Nations and a number of development institutes in different parts of the world – is becoming available. Although the gap between intent and realisation remains a large one, progress is visible on all fronts.

Notes

[1] This process is clearly demonstrated in city planning, which, traditionally, has had to rely on zoning as its principal instrument of effectuation. The master

plan for a city is chiefly a two-dimensional map of desirable land uses that can be easily translated into a zoning map for purposes of control. Lacking direct influence over municipal investments, city planners have done little so far to advance the art of capital budgeting for urban development. Their planning expresses primarily the instruments of control available to them.

[2] Gavin McCrone, *Regional Policy in Britain* (London, George Allen & Unwin, 1969); Niles M. Hansen, *French Regional Planning* (Bloomington, Indiana; and London, Indiana University Press, 1968); Niles M. Hansen, *Rural Poverty and the Urban Crisis: A Strategy for Regional Development* (Bloomington, Indiana; and London, Indiana University Press, 1970); Lloyd Rodwin et al, *Planning Urban Growth and Regional Development: The Experience of the Guayana Program of Venezuela* (Cambridge, Massachusetts Institute of Technology Press, 1969); Lloyd Rodwin, *Nations and Cities: A Comparison of Strategies of Urban Growth* (Boston, Houghton Mifflin & Co., 1970); Malcolm D. Rivkin, *Area Development for National Growth: The Turkish Precedent* (New York, Frederick A. Praeger, 1965); John Friedmann, *Urban and Regional Development in Chile: A Case Study of Innovative Planning* (Santiago, Ford Foundation, 1969); Walter Stöhr, *Materials on Regional Development in Latin America: Experience and Prospects* (Hamilton, Ontario, McMaster's University, 1970); United States of America, Department of Commerce, *Area Redevelopment Policies in Britain and the Countries of the Common Market* (Washington D.C., Government Printing Office, 1965); and H.W. Richardson, 'Regional development policy in Spain', *Urban Studies* (Edinburgh), vol. VIII, no. 1 (1971), pp. 39-54.

[3] McCrone, op. cit., p. 276.

[4] John Friedmann and Andrés Necochea, 'Some problems of urbanization policy in the capital region of Chile', August 1970 (mimeographed).

[5] The poverty of administrative skills is a more serious impediment to successful development planners than is normally realised. A brief but insightful assessment of the Brazilian situation is given in Jean Claude Garcia-Zamor, *An Ecological Approach to Administration Reform: the Brazilian Case*, Offprint series no. 98 (Austin, University of Texas, Institute of Latin American Studies, 1969). An extended, more systematic treatment of the topic is found in Fred W. Riggs, *Administration in Developing Countries: The Theory of Prismatic Society* (Boston, Houghton Mifflin, 1964).

[6] See Stöhr, op. cit., table 1.

[7] Philip Selznick, *TVA and the Grass Roots* (Berkeley, University of California Press, 1949).

[8] On the stability of the rank-size order of cities, see John Friedmann, *Regional Development Policy: A Case Study of Venezuela* (Cambridge, Massachusetts Institute of Technology Press, 1966).

[9] Kingsley Davis has constructed a four-city index of primacy covering the period 1950-70 for a total of 38 countries. During those 20 years, only

171

Mexico showed a marked decline in the index, from 2.44 to 1.22. All other countries changed their index in either direction by less than a single order of magnitude, and most countries displayed remarkable stability in the over all pattern of population distribution. Stability was greatest for countries that had a low rate of rural to urban migration. See Kingsley Davis, *World Urbanization 1950-1970*; Vol. 1: *Basic Data for Cities, Countries, and Regions*. Population monograph series, no. 4 (Berkeley, University of California Press, 1969), table G.

[10] The probability of success of such a policy would also depend upon the overall growth of population, the extent of prior urbanisation and the rate of migration from rural to urban areas. See D.H.K. Amiran and A. Shachar, *Development Towns in Israel* (Jerusalem, Hebrew University, 1969).

[11] Richardson, op. cit., p. 50.

[12] Glenn V. Stephenson, 'Two newly-created capitals: Islamabad and Brasilia', *Town Planning Review* (Liverpool, vol. XLI, no. 4 (1970), p. 321.

[13] Ayub Khan, quoted in Stephenson, op. cit., p. 323.

[14] M. Ilin, *Velikii Plan*. cited in Albert E. Burke, 'Influence of man upon nature — the Russian view : A case study', in William L. Thomas, Jr (ed), *Man's Role in Changing the Face of the Earth* (Chicago, University of Chicago Press, 1956), p.1048.

[15] The 'principle of the hiding hand' is discussed in Albert O. Hirschman, *Development Projects Observed* (Washington, D.C., The Brookings Institution, 1967), chap. I.

[16] Antonio Cerqueira Antunes, 'La política de industrialización del nordeste Brazileño', Santiago, Latin American Institute for Economic and Social Planning, November 1966 (mimeographed).

[17] Rodwin, *Nations and Cities*; see also Hansen, *French Regional Planning*.

[18] Lloyd Rodwin et al., op. cit.

[19] Organisation for Economic Cooperation and Development, *The Regional Factor in Economic Development: Policies in Fifteen Industrialised OECD Countries* (Paris, 1970). See also Europaeische Wirtschaftsgemeinschaft, *Massnahimen der Regionalpolitik in den Mitgliedstaaten der EWG* (Brussels, 1964).

[20] Rodwin, *Nations and Cities*.

[21] Denmark, *Zoneplan 1962 for Denmark* (Copenhagen, Landsplanuvalget, 1962). In the United States of America, Hawaii, Oregon and Maine have adopted state-wide zoning controls, and Colorado is currently studying such legislation.

[22] R.F. Babcock, *The Zoning Game: Municipal Practices and Policies* (Madison, University of Wisconsin Press, 1966).

[23] Friedmann and Necochea, op. cit.

[24] See, for example, the account for Bulgaria in Philippe Bernard, *Growth Poles and Growth Centres as Instruments of Regional Development and Modernisation, With Special Reference to Bulgaria and France*; Vol. III of

Growth Poles and Growth Centres in Regional Development (Geneva, United Nations Research Institute for Social Development, 1970; UNRISD/70/C.25); and Kosta Mihailović, *Regional Development in Eastern Europe: Experiences and Prospects* (Geneva, United Nations Research Institute for Social Development, 1970; UNRISD/70/C.49), pp. 93-101.

[25] Organisation for Economic Cooperation and Development, op. cit., p. 79.

[26] 'Population movements and the distribution of social services', *International Social Development Review, No. 1; Urbanization: Development Policies and Planning* (United Nations publication, Sales No.: E.68.IV.1), pp. 89-95.

[27] The evidence is widely scattered, but nearly all studies that have looked into this issue agree on this basic point. See, for instance, Joan Nelson. 'The urban poor: disruption or political integration in Third World cities?', *World Politics* (Princeton, N.J.), vol. 23, no. 3 (1970), pp. 393-414.

[28] For a discussion of the role of overhead investments in the urbanization process, see Lowdon Wingo, Jr 'Latin American urbanization: plan or process?', in Bernard J. Frieden and William W. Nash, Jr (eds.,) *Shaping an Urban Future: Essays in Memory of Catherine Bauer Wurster* (Cambridge, Massachusetts Institute of Technology Press, 1969), pp. 62-4. A more exhaustive treatment is given in A.J. Youngson, *Overhead Capital: A Study in Development Economics* (Edinburgh, University Press, 1967).

[29] The social response of communities to the challenge of economic development is discussed extensively in John Friedmann. 'The future of urbanization in Latin America', Vol. V, *Studies in Comparative International Development* (St. Louis, Mo., Washington University, 1969-70), pp. 179-97.

[30] Chung-tong Wu is currently preparing a doctoral dissertation on 'the social conditions of economic progress in Hong Kong', in the Urban Planning Program of the University of California at Los Angeles. This study is expected to shed some light on the critical social variables in regional economic development.

[31] McCrone, op. cit., pp. 187-8. He argues strongly in favour of the regionalisation of fiscal policies. Unfortunately, there is not as yet any experience on which to base a reasonable assessment of such policies.

[32] Cerqueira Antunes, op. cit.

[33] Stöhr, op. cit., p. 62.

[34] Ibid., pp. 62-3.

[35] John Friedmann and Walter Stöhr, 'The uses of regional science: policy planning in Chile', Vol. XVII, *Papers of the Regional Science Association* (Philadelphia, 1967), pp. 207-22. A more detailed evaluation has been made by Mariano Valle, 'Planning regional development in Chile: achievements and perspectives', paper prepared under the Special Program on Urban and Regional Development, Cambridge, Massachusetts Institute of Technology, 1969.

[36] Hansen, *French Regional Planning*.

[37] Rodwin, *Nations and Cities*. Additional information may be found in Turan

Esroy, 'Financing of housing and urban development in Turkey', monograph No. 17 submitted to the Interregional Seminar on Financing of Housing and Urban Development, Copenhagen, 25 May to 10 June 1970.

[38] Chile, National Planning Office, 'A model of interregional programming and compatibility', Santiago, 1968. This model, in turn, is based on concepts developed in L. B. M. Mennes, Jan Tinbergen and J. George Waardenburg, *The Element of Space in Development Planning* (Amsterdam, North Holland Publishing Co., 1969). Mr. Mennes served for a time as consultant to the National Planning Office of Chile.

10 The need for continuous planning

Excerpt from North West Joint Planning Team, *Strategic Plan for the North West*, HMSO, London 1974.

© 1974, HMSO.

Continuous planning

Our terms of reference require us to make 'recommendations about the form of a continuous planning process for the region after completion of the study'. This requirement (which we welcome) lies behind our whole approach to the preparation of the strategic plan: that it is not a once-for-all blueprint for the future. The idea of evolution, in response to changing circumstances, has been accepted for structure planning. This concept must be equally valid for regional planning. The need for continuity in the process is well illustrated by the fact that, during the short time in which this report has been actually written, important government policy statements and changes have been made covering housing and green belts; housing action areas; urban transport; and local government finance. Legislation on the reorganisation of water supply and water pollution measures and on compensation in relation to new highways has also been enacted during this period in the Water Act 1973 and the Land Compensation Act 1973 respectively.

Thus, while we consider that the report gives a firm basis for strategic planning in the North West, it indicates a number of subjects to be further pursued as part of the continuous planning we advocate for the region. In addition there are other items of regional significance still to be examined. Some of the assumptions in the plan may well turn out to be wrong. Decisions and policy formulation will have to take the new circumstances into account. We therefore endorse the need for continuous planning – including the monitoring of progress on the plan; assembly of new or revised data; and regular reviews of the plan itself. The following paragraphs analyse the form it should take.

A Regional Planning Unit

We favour the setting up of a permanent 'Regional Planning Unit', which would have the following purposes: (a) to continue the process of plan and policy formulation and revision; (b) to formulate policy advice on specific issues that arise in the region; and (c) to react to emerging policies and proposals of regional significance.

Since no single regional agency exists to implement the strategy as a whole a Regional Planning Unit could at present only be advisory – it could not institute

175

change, but it should have the means of influencing decisions and policies. To do this the Unit must have access both to information and to the decision-making machinery on issues of regional importance. The arrangements for steering and controlling the work of such a Unit, and its place in relation to central and local government machinery, would therefore be just as important as what the Unit should do. We return to this later. First we need to look at the main activities the proposed Regional Planning Unit would undertake.

Activities of a Regional Planning Unit

The Unit would be mainly concerned with advice and recommendations on modifications and additions to the regional strategy and changes in regional policies. This would entail research into regional problems; and the monitoring both of trends and of progress towards achieving the aims of the strategy. Thus it would not be sufficient for the Unit merely to determine whether the proposals in the plan were being implemented. It would also need to investigate whether they were still relevant, and if so whether additional policies or different emphases were needed to ensure implementation; whether any amendments should be made to the assumptions behind the proposals; and whether the original objectives of the plan were still valid. Figure 10.1 shows the inter-relationships between these various activities.

The Unit would produce a regular flow of information and reports, assessing progress, pointing out where changes were needed, carrying out new research and making new policy recommendations. Its output might include: (a) periodic reports, in accordance with a work programme, analysing in depth key issues of regional significance; (b) occasional reports advising on matters of regional importance when they occur; (c) annual 'state-of-the-region' and 'state-of-the-strategy' reports, up-dating statistics and reviewing policy changes; (d) less frequent but regular (perhaps 5 yearly) reviews of the strategy — i.e. deeper and more fundamental examinations of the relationship between intentions and actions.

Monitoring

The monitoring activity itself would be concerned with watching the progress of the present strategy as it evolved over time — and noting, with relevant advice, if it appeared to be veering away from the intended course. It would be concerned with: (a) monitoring of trends in areas where specific policies or objectives had not been stated but where a regional issue existed and where problems might arise in the future (a good example is the 'growth' question); (b) monitoring progress towards the achievement of stated and approved objectives and assessing the impact and effectiveness of policies and programmes; (c) monitoring reactions to the plan — both official and unofficial.

This is not the place to examine in detail all the items of data and information which monitoring should cover. The process should concentrate on those items which are significant at the time and should avoid being swamped by irrelevant

176

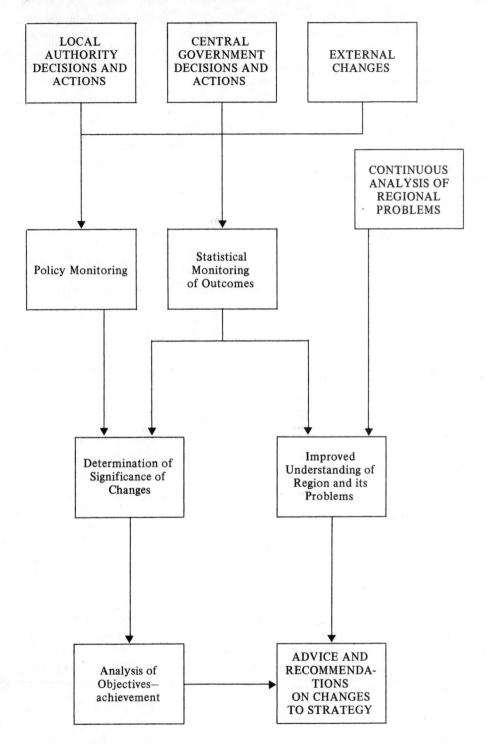

Fig 10.1 Continuous planning interactions of activities

177

data. An important distinction should be drawn between statistical monitoring — collecting factual data on trends and performance indicators which can be compared with the assumptions, forecasts and targets specified in the strategy — and policy monitoring — watching the evolution of both central and local government policies; assessing the effect of policy changes upon the objectives and proposals of the plan; and giving early warning of failure to implement the policies on which the plan depends. For instance, the second cycle of evaluation indicated a need to watch the effects of current development and intermediate area policies.

There might well be difficulties in deciding whether changes were in fact departing from or undermining the plan in a serious way, especially in cases where our proposals are general rather than specific, and long term rather than short term. Some warning system — which would indicate when differences between the actual and the predicted were reaching such critical thresholds that intervention or modification of the plan was required — might be feasible where we have set targets for achievement (e.g. pollution). But for other aspects of the strategy (e.g. the spatial pattern) the system we are dealing with is so complex that such precision would be impossible and monitoring would need to keep track of a wide range of variables. Difficulties might arise in distinguishing changes arising specifically from the impact of policy and those arising from other causes.

Sources of data and their improvement, relation of the data to the region and frequency of up-dating are critical matters which would need to be considered early in the life of the Regional Planning Unit, and which would partly determine the timing and frequency of its reports. One of its first tasks would be to up-date the strategy in the light of the 1971 Census. Some of the data will be the same as those we have used in preparing the plan and will appear regularly in published or unpublished form, but special arrangements might have to be made to ensure a regular flow of others. Considerations would also have to be given to the inter-relationships between the monitoring of the regional plan and that of structure plans, with suitable arrangements for a two-way flow of information, both between structure plan units and the regional unit, and between central and local government data sources. In many critical areas data are inadequate or non-existent. There is a particular need for the region to be recognised as a valid statistical unit in many items of data production and collection, notably on the resources and expenditure side.

Continuing work on regional problems

It became clear soon after the start of the present study that we should have to be selective in the choice of topics to be covered and in the depth to which the topics selected could be analysed in a first report. We are conscious that practically all our work could have been improved by more time and better data — especially up-to-date data. Our understanding of the region is still at best partial and can only be improved if work continues.

Revising the plan

The purpose of continuous monitoring and further research is to keep the objectives and policies of the strategy, and progress towards their attainment, under constant review. If things are shown to be significantly off-course, two inter-related courses of action would be open: (a) to demonstrate the acceptability of the emerging course in its own right and identify what implications this would have for alteration of the original policies and objectives of the plan; (b) to indicate necessary action required, by adjusting policies or introducing new ones, to put the system back on course, stating the advantages and disadvantages of doing so.

But to be completely effective it would be important for the unit not just to react to events but to be able to influence them. This means that it must be given the opportunity to comment upon important regional issues and to influence impending decisions. Machinery would need to be set up to ensure that all matters relevant to the regional strategy were brought to the notice of the unit and that its advice was taken into account in making decisions. The success of the unit would be partly determined by the extent to which those with executive and policy responsibilities for the region chose to use the unit's research and advisory capability and partly by the unit's own ability to engender confidence in its role. To develop this confidence the unit would have to demonstrate that the advice it gave was useful, relevant and responsible.

Organisation

In the absence of a single decision-making body at regional level, where should a Regional Planning Unit be placed, how should it be staffed, and to whom should it be responsible? At the time of writing, two uncertainties make it difficult to propose a form of organisation which would best fit future circumstances. First and foremost, we do not know what the Kilbrandon Commission on the Constitution may recommend by way of changes to government machinery at regional level. Secondly, we do not know, in advance of the hand-over to the new local authorities, what form of collaboration there might be among local planning authorities at the regional level.

In the light of the existing situation we can however state certain requirements for the operation of a Regional Planning Unit — requirements not likely to be invalidated whatever the consequences of the Kilbrandon Commission and of local government reorganisation. There needs to be a means of looking at the region as a whole which: (a) could examine and be involved in matters of interest to both central and local government without duplication and misunderstanding; (b) would be capable of influencing the policy and decision-making of central and local government and acceptable to them in this role; and (c) would retain sufficient independence of both sides to guarantee the objectivity of its work and recommendations and thus retain the confidence of each.

The organisational requirement of this appears to be a single body, backed and 'steered' jointly by central and local government at policy-making level (i.e. at elected member level in the case of local government); adequately staffed (i.e. having the right disciplines, quality and reasonable continuity) and adequately equipped; and with access to such other financial resources as are necessary to enable effective work to be done. Access to data is also important -- especially, in the case of both central and local government and other sources, where problems of confidentiality may need to be overcome.

The decision about such a unit will be for central and local government to make at a political level. We recognise that our requirements point to a unit whose joint control, financing and staffing would be comparable to the arrangements which apply to the present team - and this is precisely our conclusion. We also recognise that on a continuing basis this would be a new feature of regional life. Nonetheless we believe that this is required if regional planning is to be seen and to develop as a meaningful activity by central and local government.

We therefore recommend that a joint team as proposed be established to operate from 1 April 1974, preserving continuity of the work as best may be; and that further details should be worked out between central government, the Economic Planning Council and the new local authorities.

11 Performance evaluation and policy review

Excerpts from F. Wedgwood-Oppenheim, D. Hart and B. Cobley, *An Exploratory Study in Strategic Monitoring*, Progress in Planning Series, Pergamon Press, Oxford 1976.

© 1976, Pergamon Press

From traditional to strategic monitoring

Monitoring has to be considered as part of the planning and control system in which it is embedded. It appears that some of the confusion surrounding the concept of monitoring relates to lack of clarity about the planning and control model which it is supposed to serve, and in fact many of the beliefs about monitoring relate to planning and control models that are only to a limited extent applicable to the regional and strategic situation.

It is useful to categorise planning and control into three levels referred to by Anthony,[1] in relation to business activities as operational control, management control and strategic planning. The three approaches to monitoring which serve these levels might be described as (a) *implementation monitoring*, (b) *impact monitoring*, annd (c) *strategic monitoring* respectively. In these pages we will outline briefly these three levels as they apply to public planning, relating the final level to the regional situation before outlining our recommendations for what we have labelled performance evaluation and policy review (PEPR). In the second half we will highlight some of the characteristics of strategic monitoring by examining some of the limitations of lower level monitoring models.

Implementation monitoring

The model of monitoring used here relates to the assumption of a stable environment which is well understood and where there is a high degree of control over the situation planned. It is appropriate where there is a task to be completed and where little account need be taken of changes external to that task. This model was held implicitly, though not always appropriately, by the early physical planners particularly in relation to new towns. The role of monitoring here is to see that implementation takes place according to plan.

Impact monitoring

Impact monitoring is associated with the 'managerial control' level and is the model widely held by those concerned with monitoring.

The assumptions here are that there is a fairly high level of control of the issues planned for, and that, as in the previous model, the plan relates to a clearly demarcated field of interest. However, even where the plan is being successfully implemented the outcomes may not be as intended, and the plan therefore allows for a variety of resource allocation choices. Impacts are monitored and if these deviate from planned targets where there is sufficient understanding of the situation for resources to be re-allocated — within pre-set limits - to bring the system back into line. Adjustments can also be made if the operational control system cannot ensure implementation as planned. Monitoring may also be concerned with checking the accuracy of forecasts on which the planned outcomes are dependent. In the ideal situation, mathematical models of the planned system exist which not only determine the information to be collected, but can be used to inform, or even determine, the response.

In the public sector this form of control is appropriate to National Economic Management, at least in more settled times than these.

Strategic monitoring

In strategic planning and control we are concerned with coping with a dynamic, imperfectly understood, and imperfectly controlled environment, encompassing an unlimited number of potential fields of interest. We are concerned here with the situation where 'management control' is no longer sufficient because the actual contingencies are not allowed for and because the unintended consequences require new policies. We are concerned with dealing with problems and opportunities, actual or predicted, arising out of existing plans, or creating the need for new ones.

The need at this level is for a continuing planning activity, anticipating possible future developments, responding to current situations by developing new policies and reviewing past policies to establish their impact on the current and possible future situations. The information requirements for this task are unlimited. There is not only a need to be concerned with information relevant to past policies but also with information relevant to possible new policies. If this is to be adequately carried out there will have to be a process of information selection which is efficient in terms of the task. The approach we are recommending may be described as mixed-scanning and is related to the mixed-scanning approach proposed by Etzioni.[2] Mixed-scanning involves collecting specific information with high resolution of detail about issues that we know to be of regional importance and analysing them in depth. This will include reviewing the performance of current policies. At the same time this approach involves taking a very wide, low resolution scan of all matters that could potentially affect the region, and 'zooming in' on those matters which in the judgement of those involved are of regional importance. For this intensive analysis, information will need to be collected with specific reference to the problem and detailed quantification will be important. In the broad scan we want to be able to increase our awareness of as wide a range of information as possible. Depth will give way to breadth, and in seeking to absorb large quantities we will look for it in condensed forms, such as articles, written reports, etc., rather than as raw data.

Performance evaluation and policy review

What we have said so far relevant to regional monitoring has in fact taken us away from the common use of that word. Similarly many of the common connotations of the word 'planning' bear little relationship to the strategic planning process that we have outlined. We will be concerning ourselves further with scanning, with evaluating past performance and reviewing the need for policy change, and we will be talking about the use of influence to affect change. Performance evaluation and policy review (PEPR) are at the heart of this function, and we propose to give this name to the Unit that we are recommending.

Some problems of traditional approaches to monitoring

Monitoring has become a popular word amongst those concerned with planning, but there is a great deal of discussion about what monitoring should imply in practice. It appears to us that much of what has been written and discussed is based on the impact monitoring model that we referred to in the previous section. This model clearly applies to a wide range of planning situations, where there is a limited number of clear objectives, and a reasonably well understood and demarcated subject area. It is appropriate for the monitoring policies on smoke control or the reclamation of derelict land by a local authority, or the control of river pollution by a water authority. However, when considering plans that are more strategic and regional — implying a concern with wide-ranging consequences, taking into account long term considerations and involving a wide range of organisations in implementation — this model becomes insufficient. It is worth examining some of the assumptions of the model, if only to indicate some of its weaknesses for strategic planning and thus to highlight some of the requirements of a strategic regional planning and monitoring system that we have attempted to meet in our proposed PEPR Unit. These assumptions relate to:

(a) the use of objectives and targets;
(b) the monitoring of planning assumptions;
(c) the relationship between planning and action;
(d) the role of the plan in defining information needs.

The rest of this section will be devoted to examining these assumptions.

The use of objectives and targets

It is widely held that monitoring reveals problems or issues for consideration by identifying gaps between planned outcomes (targets) and reality. We have come to the conclusion that for a number of reasons relatively few problems are actually

183

revealed in this way in Strategic Planning situations.

First, if gaps between actual and planned outcomes are to be recognised, targets (sometimes referred to as achievement or performance standards) must be expressed in operational terms; that is, they must be precise statements of what is expected. The achievement of these targets is instrumental in fulfilling higher level objectives, usually providing a general sense of direction, without being operational themselves. However, in many physical plans, operationally specified targets are few, and where they do exist, it is often difficult to establish the relationships between the stated objectives and the targets specified.

The widespread belief that setting operational targets is necessary for good planning is in marked contrast to planning practice, and leads us to doubt whether in fact target setting is appropriate for strategic plans covering many years ahead in a situation where there is little control or where control is widely dispersed.

Where targets do not exist it becomes immediately less clear what information it is crucial to monitor and it becomes much more a matter of judgement what can be regarded as being 'off course'.

We can take as an example in the *Strategic Plan for the North West (SPNW)* the section on Public Expenditure Priorities. In Chapter 5, the *SPNW* report gives general support for the government's objective on river pollution control 'to make the widest possible use of all Britain's water space, not only for water supply, sewerage and drainage but as a recreational asset'.[3] While accepting this aim, this is not treated as an absolute imperative, and in fact the report recommends that river pollution should rank third in priority after smoke and derelict land when considering public expenditure priorities in these three sectors of environmental pollution. The report does show forecasts of river conditions in 1980 made by the old River Authorities in the North West,[4] but although these might be regarded as targets for the new Water Authority, the report points out that it is unlikely that the capital expenditure available will be sufficient. It does not however suggest more modest targets of its own.

This example relates to the second problem in the use of targets. It highlights the ambiguity experienced in strategic planning, particularly where planners depend on other institutions for implementation, between forecasts of independent factors, targets and mere hopes. This ambiguity is made more acute because a simple causal relationship does not exist between planned actions and their outcomes. Factors such as population levels can be seen either as variables that affect the outcomes of our activity (independent variables) and thus need to be forecast, or as a consequence of our plans (dependent variables) and for which it is appropriate to set targets.

Our third reason for doubting the general usefulness of monitoring the gap between reality and target is based on the experience of the Notts/Derbys Monitoring and Advisory Unit.[5] The finding of the unit was that significant deviations from the strategy were rarely detected by the monitoring unit *before they were pointed out by one of the local authorities in the sub-region.* Where there were divergencies the determination of whether these were significant was never a technical activity. Rather the determination of significance depended on judgement and varied according to the viewpoint.[6]

What is more, in spite of having performance indicators available from the original plan (though the relationship between these and the stated objectives of the plan were found to be difficult, if not impossible, to establish), issues to be dealt with tended to be thrown up not as a result of a divergence but rather as a problem arising independently of impact monitoring.

This brings us to our fourth point. We would like to suggest that when concerned with strategic planning in the context of uncertainty about economic, political and social changes, and where there is still a very imperfect understanding of the way these systems behave internally and interact with each other, we need to be not so much concerned with the intended consequences of our plans as with the unintended and unforeseen consequences. To take the example of housing in the 1960s, whether or not we were achieving our slum clearance and house building targets was of less interest than the discovery of the social consequences of breaking up traditional communities and of the problems caused by high rise flats. Similarly with the building of roads, monitoring our achievements in increasing road capacity revealed less useful information than the discovery of the increase in the total volume of traffic caused by greater road capacity. If we consider important changes of policy — the reversal of London's off-street parking policy, the switch to increased emphasis on public transport that is now taking place, the change from housing renewal to rehabilitation, the shift from regarding our forests as economic resources to seeing them as recreational assets — it is evident that failure to achieve our stated aims was secondary to our concern with reducing the unpleasant, unintended consequences or, as in the forestry example, with capitalising on the beneficial ones. The PEPR Unit should therefore be concerned with increasing the responsiveness of the region to these unintended consequences.

We would argue that to evaluate a current policy it is unhelpful to go back to the intention of the policy-makers. Rather one needs to evaluate the policy in terms of how it actually works, affecting the region in many more ways than the policy-makers were likely to take into account, and in terms of our current aims and understanding of needs.

When considering strategic issues we have found that:

(i) targets are often not available;
(ii) where targets do exist the formal comparison of these with monitored information is not very productive of issues to be considered;
(iii) relevant issues more often arise as problems concerned with the inintended consequences of our policies or problems unrelated to existing policies; and
(iv) aims, when a policy is reviewed, are likely to be different and may well bear little relationship with the targets originally set.

We therefore believe that collecting statistical data that are directly determined by the planned targets, should not be given undue emphasis. Instead we find that the monitoring function needs to be more concerned with the ability to perceive more quickly changes in factors relevant to the region, whether or not they had been considered during the planning stage.

Monitoring of planning assumptions

Planning can be seen as a process whereby aims, factual evidence and assumptions are translated by a process of logical argument into appropriate policies [7] which are intended to achieve the aims. The fact that time proves many assumptions to be false has important consequences for the planning process and for the nature of monitoring. When the outcomes of a plan deviate from expectations it is because some of these assumptions were incorrect. One class of assumptions relates to the accuracy of estimates of relevant factors (that is, independent variables; e.g. birth rates, industrial productivity, labour mobility), how they interact with each other, and in particular, the way they will change over time and affect the outcomes of the planned actions or policies. If these factors are monitored and projected into the future, whenever they are found to vary from the assumed levels, the plan or the implementing actions can be adjusted in response. It is desirable therefore not only to monitor outcomes but to reduce their likelihood of deviating by monitoring factual assumptions and making appropriate adjustments. We would like to take this further and, following the lead of Notts/Derbys, stress the need to monitor not only quantitative variables, as implied so far, but also qualitative variables; not only explicit assumptions, but also implicit ones; not only hard information but also soft information. We will develop these ideas in the following paragraphs.

First, a large number of assumptions relate to the occurrence, or non-occurrence, of certain events. Some examples of events that could be relevant to the *SPNW* are: (a) the adoption of a new formula for calculating rate support grant; (b) the possible liquidation of a major industrial firm in the NW; (c) a change in the EEC's regional fund policy; or (d) the proposed municipalisation of land.[8] The distinction between qualitative changes of this sort and quantitative changes, such as a sudden increase in the rate of inflation, is not always possible to maintain. The distinction is, more accurately, between individual items of information and a data stream. The words qualitative and quantitative, however, are a commonly used shorthand. The implications for monitoring of the existence of these more qualitative assumptions is plain. That is, it is necessary not only to be concerned with the collection of statistical data, but it is necessary also to monitor *events* that have an impact on the region, whether they occur within the region or outside, and whether they originate from public or private bodies.

Secondly, however well exposed are the assumptions on which the plan is based, the biggest assumption of all, and the one with the most far-reaching implications for the planning process, is that all factors not referred to in the plan are either irrelevant to the plan or that they will remain constant. This assumption is a catch-all for a multitude of implicit assumptions about factors which there was too little time, resources or knowledge to take into account when the plan was formulated, or which are essentially unpredictable.[9] By their nature, these assumptions cannot be monitored by collecting information specifically on each one. An assumption usually becomes of interest only when it is falsified or when an unexpected event occurs. These assumptions may be revealed as a result of diagnosing the cause of a deviation from an unexpected outcome — by which time the damage has already been done — or they may be discovered by a generalised scanning activity.

Finally, we want to stress the need for soft information. Many of the events that the PEPR Unit will have to monitor are the policies of local authorities and other public bodies, affecting the region. Riera and Jackson identify three ways in which policies became apparent:[10] (a) suddenly and spontaneously; (b) as the result of the cumulative effect of a number of actions; and (c) by a process of creeping 'commitment' during which analyses are done, negotiations entered into, alternatives considered and rejected and so on with increasing commitment until the policy is finally approved. Information about this process of creeping commitment and thus relevant to possible future events has been labelled 'soft' information.[11] Soft information about policies being considered is clearly very useful in speeding up the response that the Unit can make to emerging policies, and to enable its own analyses to be carried out in the knowledge of the directions in which other government bodies are moving.

The need for soft information implies not only the scanning of written material, but implies also the need to be in personal touch with key members of the principal bodies affecting the region. This makes the problem of access to information particularly critical, which in turn is a consideration affecting the organisational location of PEPR.

The relationship between planning and action

We have dealt in this section so far with issues concerned with the use of targets and the monitoring of planning assumptions. We are here concerned with the assumption in traditional monitoring models that planning leads to action and that monitoring is followed by corrective action. This bears little relationship to the conditions applicable to regional strategies. The function of the *SPNW* stated at the beginning of the report was:

(i) to guide decisions by central and local government on public expenditure and economic and social policies affecting the region; and

(ii) to provide a context for statutory planning by the local planning authorities under the Town and Country Planning Acts.

The plan is further described primarily as a framework:

a context for structure planning, and an aid to public expenditure decisions and the fashioning of social and economic policies. Those are the responsibilities of central and local government. The expression of the strategic plan — in policy recommendations, proposals, estimates and so on — is therefore directed in large part towards the next stage of statutory planning and the formulation of national and local policies pertinent to the North West.[12]

Two implications of the regional planning context seem important to us. First is the one referred to above, indicating that implementing the plan involves the adoption of plans and policies by central government departments and by local authorities, and we therefore need to be concerned with monitoring these plans and policies, as well as environmental variables. Secondly, as there is little formal executive authority and direct control at the regional level (though this will depend to some extent on the exact location of the Unit), it can only pass on information, either as such, or accompanied by advice and recommendations for action to bodies with authority to act. It will therefore be heavily dependent on the influence it can wield. This again points towards a consideration of the organisational arrangements for the Unit and of the personal characteristics of the leader and members of the Unit, both of which are considered later in this report.

It also leads us to believe that if the Unit is to make the best use of its limited resources, careful consideration needs to be given to the balance of effort that needs to be put into the three activities of information collection, analysis and the presentation of information and recommendations. Clearly there is little point in investing heavily in information collection systems if the information cannot be adequately analysed, and in particular if the chances of the Unit being able to influence action are slim. Great care is going to have to be taken to ensure that recommendations are well presented to the right people at the right time.

The role of the plan in defining information needs

To go back to the impact monitoring model, the information to be collected for that model is determined by the targets set and the assumptions built into the plan. However, in examining that model and relating it to the regional strategic context in the earlier parts of this section, we repeatedly had to widen the scope of the information with which the monitoring unit would have to be concerned. We have shown the need to collect information generally relevant to the regional policies, not limited to predetermined targets and assumptions but concerned also with possible contingencies, and unintended consequences.

This widening has to be taken a stage further if we take into account that no strategic plan is comprehensive. The *SPNW* report only claims to deal with six of the major issues affecting the Region. This is not a criticism; comprehensiveness is an unattainable goal. Continuous planning, as well as evaluating the performance of existing policies, must be concerned with developing new policies to deal with new problems and opportunities as they come to the forefront of our attention, or as they emerge. The information gathering function has to be concerned with all matters of possible regional concern, even though the scanning process will be most intense in relation to matters that are believed to have a high probability of providing regionally significant information.

Importance of future developments – the beginning of regional government?

We fel it necessary to concern ourselves with the future of the PEPR Unit as well as with its creation. It is entirely possible, but by no means certain, that some type of regional government may become a reality in the next 5-10 years. If in fact this does occur we believe that the Unit can continue to perform a valuable function in the North West. In some ways in fact its usefulness could actually be enhanced by such a reform.

Central Government is now in the process of actively considering a number of suggestions regarding devolution. Many of these suggestions were put forward by the Royal Commission on the Constitution (the Kilbrandon Commission) which presented its Report in 1973,[13] and which was also accompanied by a Memorandum of Dissent signed by two of its members.[14] The Majority Report suggests that eight English regional advisory councils – based on the present Economic Planning Council regions – be established.

More specifically, as the Green Paper, *Devolution Within the United Kingdom: Some Alternatives for Discussion*, indicates:

> The scheme is based on the view that it would not be right for the English regions to be given any legislative or executive powers now exercised by central government, and it would be illogical (following the reorganisation of local authorities) for them to take over powers from local government. Yet at the regional level it is believed that there is scope for more effective cooperation between local authorities and a need for more open discussion and democratic influence on those matters affecting the region which are decided by central government or by *ad hoc* bodies. To meet this need, and to give advice to the Central Government on regional problems, there would be regional councils primarily composed of local government councillors.[15]

It is also suggested that these regional advisory councils would replace the present Economic Planning Councils. The Minority Report suggests that directly elected regional assemblies be established which would have independent revenue raising powers and which would be executive in character.[16]

If either the Majority or the Minority Report were adopted we believe that our proposed PEPR would have a useful contribution to make in terms of providing information and serving as a technical back-up Unit. Any new regional body if it were to achieve its advisory or executive purposes would benefit from the kind of data, intelligence and analytical capability which PEPR would have established in the region. In addition the links which the Unit will have established with the local authorities in the North West would materially assist in facilitating the kind of more effective coordination and open discussion mentioned above and in the preceding sections.

Finally if either direct or indirect elections were introduced at the regional level it would help to meet the reservation regarding the need for political accountability. We feel that this would be a step in the right direction in the

189

attempt to strengthen democracy.

We have no real means of knowing what will occur in the near future with regard to the alteration of regional administrative machinery but just as we feel that PEPR is not solely and completely dependent on the *SPNW* so, by the same token, we do not feel that its usefulness is limited to serving the regional Economic Planning Council in its present form.

The importance of regional learning

Plans are falsified by events.[17] It is important to recognise that in spite of past and proposed reorganisation suggestions at both the regional and local levels the real point of such organisational alterations is to allow them to perform more effectively. Because of the experimental nature of the planning process the relationship between planning organisations and the implementation of a particular plan, however well thought out and researched initially, will always be imperfect. Equally clearly the extent to which the disparity between plan-making and plan implementation can be narrowed by simply structurally altering the regional level of government is limited. It could be argued in fact that something which could be termed the 'structural fallacy' exists in some quarters which asserts very roughly that if only a larger planning authority could be created regional planning would become a reality. In fact we believe that matters are a good deal more complex than this and that a more immediate consideration is to learn when components of a plan have lost their original meaning, or are simply unattainable.

If the regional planning process contained a learning component it would mean that at least in the near future the traditional concern with structural alterations would be replaced by an attempt to create a much less rigid 'plastic' type of control system. Plastic control would mean that continuous and systematic feedback would not be a regrettable interruption of the planning process but a central and integral component.[18] In this way future anticipation of events leading to commitment could be balanced by adaptation based on recent experience.

This type of plastic control process would mean uniting a number of factors. It would mean fusing the kinds of hard and soft information mentioned earlier. It would also mean combining two separate strands of the planning process. On the one hand the traditional physical or 'hard' planning approach which is concerned with demolition and construction such as the proposed Central Lancashire New Town (CLNT) for example. On the other hand it would also mean taking cognisance of the more recent 'soft' planning approach which is concerned primarily with various types of legislation and restriction rather than simply and directly with construction. Soft planning would include, for example, changing the Industrial Development Certificate limits in the North West, or altering the basic structure of Central Government grants as the *SPNW* suggests. Clearly both these hard and soft approaches will play an important part in planning the future of the region. Equally clearly neither approach can be pursued in isolation and one of the chief functions of a plastic control process will be to beneficially fuse these two components.

During the first few years of its life PEPR will have a good deal to learn. It must learn something in both quantitative and qualitative terms about the way in which the region works and about some of the factors, at least, which cause it to change. The Unit must also learn about what is occurring in other regions. As we noted earlier some regional monitoring units are already in existence and others are currently being discussed. In addition a variety of units in the larger local planning authorities which carry titles such as Corporate Planning or Research and Intelligence are already in operation. We believe that PEPR could both teach and learn from such units. Thirdly, the PEPR Unit must refine the procedures which it employs in collecting, analysing and presenting information. Data series and distribution networks must be established and altered as situations change, and s the Unit's capabilities are tested over time. A substantial degree of judgement and experience will therefore be required. In addition to learning about the North West and learning about other regions, the PEPR Unit must study its own operating procedures in order to learn about itself.

The purpose of regional planning

It would be easy but incorrect to adopt the view that PEPR possessed some type of intrinsic merit. It does not. Although the Unit will adopt a number of roles, sometimes simultaneously, during the mixed-scanning process it will fail in its purpose if it is seen as nothing more than a technical or organisational innovation. At various times the unit will act as a regional coordinator, sensor, catalyst and advocate but its purpose must remain that of trying to improve the lives of the people who live and work in the North West. We are conscious of the fact that strategic planning is primarily of interest to planners. When various components of the plan are translated into effect they become a matter of much wider concern. We feel that the PEPR Unit could help to make strategic planning not only more comprehensive but more comprehensible as well. One of the PEPR Unit's crucial and continuing tasks will be to help bridge the gap between the planners, the public organisations which are charged with implementing plans and most, importantly, the planned for, by means of the information which it will supply.[19]

The case for regional planning and monitoring is occasionally too easily assumed to have already been made. We do not believe that this is the case. A comprehensible regional strategy needs to be put before the people of the North West and its costs and benefits set out for the simple reason that any plan operating at this level is almost completely dependent on their willing cooperation if it is to have effect. As bitter experience has shown it is much easier to defeat a plan than it is to implement one. The SPNW Team in the closing days of their operation attempted to both argue the case for their plan and to publicise it. We believe that they achieved some measure of success in doing both but we also feel that the matter cannot be allowed to rest there. It should also be stated that they have succeeded in starting what could promise to be a very long term dialogue regarding the future of the North West. If this dialogue is to avoid being sterile and uninformed new information and indeed new strategies must be developed and publicly debated. We feel in many ways that regional planning is more threatened by lack of interest than it is by continuing controversy. PEPR would help to ensure that the regional planning process was not only comprehensible but credible as well. Considered discussion based on knowledge has long since replaced fiat as an effective means of securing public commitment. PEPR's stock in trade is the systematic development of such knowledge.

Suggestions for further work

Although PEPR will be initially based within the DOE we would expect that over time links will be forged with research and intelligence and corporate planning units within the major local authorities in the region. We feel that this activity should be systematically encouraged. In fact a technical panel could be drawn from senior officials in these authorities which could play an important part in advising the Economic Planning Council (or its potential successor) on joint areas of interest which would require further exploration. Over time the local authorities in the North West should play an extremely valuable role in helping to guide and contribute to the work of the Unit.

We have, on more than one occasion, stressed the experimental nature of a Unit like PEPR. We appreciate that consultation and discussion of the issues involved and their ramifications are called for. We do not believe that these can serve as a substitute for action however. There is widespread agreement on the need for some type of monitoring in the North West. The real question at issue is the form which such monitoring would take. As we indicated at the beginning of our report we believe that our mixed-scanning approach would serve as a useful point of departure for a newly created unit. We are aware that a good deal of work remains to be done since our broad brush sketch will need to be more finely drawn. We believe that the regional interest in this and a number of related spheres could best be served however by bringing PEPR into being as soon as possible.

Notes

[1] R. N. Anthony, *Planning and Control Systems: A Framework for Analysis*, Howard, 1965.
[2] A. Etzioni, 'Mixed-scanning: A "third" approach to decision-making', *Public Administration Review*, December 1967, and A. Etzioni, *The Active Society*, The Free Press, 1968.
[3] *Strategic Plan for the North West 1973*, HMSO, London, 1974, para 5.54.

[4] *SPNW*, para. 5.12.

[5] See: *An Examination of Issue Analysis in Monitoring.* Notts/Derbys Sub-Regional Monitoring and Advisory Unit, Internal paper, 1974.

[6] J. D. S. Gillis, S. Brazier, K. J. Chamberlain, R. J. P. Harris, D. J. Scott, *Monitoring and the Planning Process,* Institute of Local Government Studies, 1974, p. 23.

[7] Gillis, 1974, p. 69.

[8] See *Land,* HMSO, Cmnd 5730, 1974.

[9] *The SPNW Supplementary Report 1974* updates the original strategy in relation to a few such issues.

[10] B. Riera and M. R. Jackson, *The Design of a Monitoring and Advisory System for Sub-Regional Planning,* A study by ISCOL Ltd., Notts/Derbys Sub-Regional Monitoring and Advisory Unit, 1971, p. 65.

[11] See J. K. Friend and N. Jessop, *Local Government and Strategic Choice: An O. R. Approach to the Processes of Public Planning.* Tavistock, 1969, p. 130.

[12] *SPNW*, para 1.14.

[13] *Report of the Royal Commission on the Constitution,* Cmnd. 5460, HMSO, London, 1973.

[14] *Memorandum of Dissent,* Cmnd. 5460-1, HMSO, London, 1973.

[15] *Devolution Within the United Kingdom: Some Alternatives for Discussion,* HMSO, London, 1974, pp. 14-15.

[16] On this see *Devolution* (1974), pp. 9-11.

[17] See also on this section D. A. Hart, *Strategic Planning In London,* Pergamon, Oxford, 1976.

[18] On this see also Karl Popper 'Of clouds and clocks', in Karl Popper, *Objective Knowledge: An Evolutionary Approach,* p. 239.

[19] On this topic see Chapters 3 and 4 of the report.

Index